Precept One
FATHER, FORGIVE US,
We Haven't Been Listening

PRECEPT ONE

FATHER, FORGIVE US,
We Haven't Been Listening

DAVID JENKINS

Father, Forgive Us, We Haven't Been Listening

Copyright © 2023 by David Jenkins. All rights reserved.

No part of this publication may be reproduced, stored in a retrieval system or transmitted in any way by any means, electronic, mechanical, photocopy, recording or otherwise without the prior permission of the author except as provided by USA copyright law.

The opinions expressed by the author are not necessarily those of URLink Print and Media.

1603 Capitol Ave., Suite 310 Cheyenne, Wyoming USA 82001
1-888-980-6523 | admin@urlinkpublishing.com

URLink Print and Media is committed to excellence in the publishing industry.

Book design copyright © 2023 by URLink Print and Media. All rights reserved.

Published in the United States of America
Library of Congress Control Number: 2023919552
ISBN 978-1-68486-559-8 (Paperback)
ISBN 978-1-68486-560-4 (Hardback)
ISBN 978-1-68486-561-1 (Digital)

05.10.23

Contents

Precept One 7
Introduction 9
Fearing God 24
Prayer and Repentance 34
The Ten Commandments 40
It is Written 45
Obedience 50
Believing...58
The Old Covenant Verses the New Covenant 73
Who is Jesus?...109
Satan, the Mark of the Beast, and the Beast 174
God's Holy Days 183
A New Moon Begins the Year 190
The 1000 Year Reign with Christ 201
Reason for Animal Sacrifices 232
Let Us Make Man in Our Own Image........................235
Conclusion... 243
Works Cited 247

Precept One

This is the republication of the first book our Father had me write. Nothing of the contents of the first book has been changed. The only thing changed is the cover with the precept one, and my new website on the back cover. davidofpsalm89.com, is the name of the website and you can download all the manuscripts or any one if you cannot or do not want to pay for the books.

As I was finishing the sixth book, I felt the Father was telling me to republish the books. And have something referring to the six books that we have written as a series or something like that. And because our Father has been teaching me precept upon precept, line upon line, little bit here and a little bit there, I thought it would be a good idea to call each book a precept.

And Because each book is a continuation of the previous book. And at the same time, each book takes me and the reader deeper into the scriptures. With a better understanding of who our Father is and what He is doing, and why He is doing what He is doing. And hopefully you will come to agree with Him as I do.

Whom shall he teach knowledge? and whom shall he make to understand doctrine? them that are weaned from the milk, and drawn from the breasts. For precept must be upon precept, precept upon precept; line upon line, line upon line; here a little, and there a little: (Isaiah 28:9-10)

This book is the beginning of all of the teaching our Father has been teaching me. This book was originally published in April of 2015. I quit celebrating birthdays and man-made holidays shortly after our Father called me the Bible in 2011. Because I realized He never commanded us to celebrate these days, and because He is perfect, righteous, and justified, I knew that by celebrating these days, I would be seeking more than His perfection. And I put my trust into Him and all that He said and or did not say. Then about four years later on my 45th birthday, I woke up knowing what is in this book. A gift that came from above and not from man. A gift that keeps on giving that can never rust or taken away.

This is the milk that we need to desire if we are going to undertake the schooling that our Father is preparing us for.

Wherefore laying aside all malice, and all guile, and hypocrisies, and envies, and all evil speakings, As newborn babes, desire the sincere milk of the word, that ye may grow thereby: If so be ye have tasted that the Lord is gracious. To whom coming, as unto a living stone, disallowed indeed of men, but chosen of God, and precious, Ye also, as lively stones, are built up a spiritual house, an holy priesthood, to offer up spiritual sacrifices, acceptable to God by Jesus Christ. Wherefore also it is contained in the scripture, Behold, I lay in Sion a chief corner stone, elect, precious: and he that believeth on him shall not be confounded. (1 Peter 2:1-6)

If by any chance you have read any of the books, or precepts before this one, you most like found it more difficult to understand. However, if you are starting with precept one as I have, you will find it much easier to grasp all of this as you go. As explained in this book and others, we all are in schooling with our Father. I myself had to go through all the grades, metaphorically speaking, but with the knowledge our Father has taught me, I bring to you in a easy to understand form

You will be learning that I am the foolishness of the world that our Father is using to bring down the wise and prudent. I have only a 9th grade education and have been driving semi most of my adult life. I have been taught by our Father with hardcore, one on one, hands on training. He has physically and spiritually had me go through most of what you will be reading about in this book.

Introduction

Our Father has led me to place the greatest Commandment in the very front of this message so that all of us will open our hearts and TRULY realize how much He loves us. His love for us is so much greater than any of us have ever realized. We can hear how great our Father's love is if we just listen as we read about His love for us in the Greatest Commandment below.

> **(Matthew 22:37) Jesus said to unto them, THOU SHALT LOVE THE LORD THY GOD WITH ALL THY HEART, AND WITH ALL THY SOUL, AND WITH ALL THY MIND. 38 This is the first and greatest commandment. 39 And the second commandment is like unto it. THOU SHALT LOVE THY NEIGHBOR AS THYSELF. 40 On these two commandments, hang all the law and the prophets.**

Before we go any further we need to really break these verses down so we can keep this picture in our heads for the rest of the book.

These verses GIVE US A LOT of very valuable information. First, let us start by breaking them down. In Matthew 22:37, when we are told to love the Father with all of our heart, soul and minds, we are told to do so for what He has done, is doing, and will do for us. There is so much love shown here. We can see the love if we just listen to what the Father has done. We all know that Jesus died on the cross. This is the Father's only begotten Son. Jesus was born of God's seed and not mans'. God had so much love for us that He created His own Son from His own seed to die on the cross, just so we would have an example of what life would be like if we just obey and follow him. 1 Peter 2:21 says, "For even hereunto were ye called: because Christ also suffered for us, <u>leaving us an example</u>, that ye should follow his steps." 1 John 5:3 says, "For this is the love of God, that we keep his commandments: and his commandments are not grievous." We all know Jesus kept all of the commandments and they were not grievous to him.

Jesus demonstrated his love for the Father by being obedient even unto death. Philippians 2:8 tells us, "And being found in fashion as a man, he humbled himself, and became obedient unto death, even the death of the cross." Jesus knew his entire life that he was going to die to be an example for us, and knowing this, he was still obedient to the Father. He is also demonstrating his love for us by being obedient even unto death. His obedience to death was knowing he had to die for us, so we could see what would happen to us if we do as he did. Then, on top of that, Jesus himself asked the Father to forgive those that crucified him for they knew not what they were doing. We should ask ourselves how hard it is to forgive someone after an offense rather than torment ourselves with unforgiveness.

We now can better understand what he meant when he asked the Father to forgive them. The sin of the world was crucifying all that love, thereby sending a message to the Father that we do not want that kind of love here. This is how Jesus, too, demonstrated for us the second greatest command- ment. His love for his fellow man was so great that even though they were crucifying Him, he was asking our Father to forgive them so that they, too, could learn what we are beginning to learn. When we are done with this message you will be able to understand this so much better. Can we hear all the love and the obedience going on in these few verses? If we can hear the love going on here, we can surely see why Jesus tells us to hang all of the law on these two verses. To top that off, we can also hear that the Father has so much love for us that He even constructed this plan before it was done and then executed the plan without fail. All because He loves us and wants us to know how we can come spend eternity with Him. We can surely hear all the obedience going on in these verses. Jesus obeyed all of the law and obeyed his Father, even unto his own death, just so he could show us how to gain eternal life, with the Father, in heaven. Our Father, too, had to be obedient to His own plan. Just think how hard that would be for any one of us to do.

After actually listening to all that love, we have to ask ourselves, why would we not want that kind of love? We all strive all day every day for love. We want to be noticed. We want to be seen. We want people to like us. We want to feel welcome when we go somewhere. The truth is, we just want to be loved and we have ignored all of the love that our Father has been offering us since the beginning of creation. Remember it is our choice. Who reading this does not desire to receive our Father's love? We do not, at any time, have to accept our Father's love. We do not have to listen to what He has to say. This is where our free will comes into play. So if you're ready to listen to what our Father is saying and feel all that love, just keep reading this message our Father is giving us now.

This is a book that will explore the depths of the Bible and how we are living more for Satan than God. We will take a look at many ways the modern churches, which many of us go to on a regular basis, are not doing what God commands us to do. We will look at how we are told to pretty much do away with the Old Testament and to mainly focus on the New Testament. We will look at how we are to love our Father and not just focus on Him loving us. We will look at who Jesus really is by God's description and not mans'. We will look at when Jesus was born. We will look at the time of Jesus' resurrection. We will look at how man ignores the days that we are to keep Holy and how we follow traditions that we think are wor- shipping our Father, but are actually worshipping a false god. We will look at how we can please our Father with our worship and how we don't please Him. We will look at what really happens when Jesus comes back. We will actually see that there will still be people that will reject our Father's law, or His ways, during the 1000 year reign with Jesus. We will look at what it means to actually believe in Jesus and not just that he lived and was cru- cified for our sins. We will look at who is really the god of this world. We will learn what the mark of the beast is and who the beast will be. We will also have a much better understanding of how the truth shall set you free. These are just some of the things we will be going over in this book.

Our Father called me to write this message to all of His children and to all that want to become His children. This book is not targeted at any denomination or religion. Our Father's message is to everybody, every- where. It does not matter where you live, nor does it matter what race you are. All that matters is that you have been seeking the truth and are ready to be fully wrapped with the love that our Father has for us. He is calling us all back to His ways, as we have been blind to His ways for so long. This book is not, I repeat not, intended to prove that I am right nor is it intended to point a finger at anyone. It is not written by me to imply that I am any better than any other person that exists, or that has ever existed. It is nothing other than clarity coming from our Father.

At this time I would like all of us to try and remember what Jesus said when he said that he will go and prepare a mansion in his Father's house, in John 14 "Let not your heart be troubled: ye believe in God, believe also in me.2 In my Father's house are many mansions: if it were not so, I would have told you. I go to prepare a place for you.3 And if I go and prepare a place for you, I will come again, and receive you unto myself; that where I am, there ye may be also."

Through this message we will learn what we need to do in order to obtain one of those mansions in his Father's house.

I need to let all readers know right now that **I AM NOT GOD; I DO NOT KNOW WHEN JESUS IS RETURNING.** I have not been to heaven, nor have any angelic figures come to visit me. I am not a prophet. I am simply a man that loves our Father with all of his heart, soul, and mind. I want to mention at this time that all glory goes to the Father and NOT ME. The true author of this message is our Father. I am just an average 45-year-old man that is very thankful that our Father has chosen me to put this message on paper. I dropped out of school in the tenth grade and obtained my G.E.D a couple of years after that. I did, however, obtain that while I was in jail. I have just as many sins as everybody else. I, too, have been living in denial, not realizing that my life would have been completely different if I would have just listened to our Father. I have been married and divorced two times and lived with women in sin. I have been driving a semi since I was 21, with a year or two off here and there. I have tried college a couple of times but dropped out of that, as well. I am with my third wife now and am blessed with the woman I have always wanted. I now have a very good understanding of everything that has happened in my life and I am very grateful that our Father loves me, as He does all of us.

I mentioned that I am 45 and I need to mention that I recently had a birthday. I need to bring this to your attention because this is the first year that I have not desired to receive recognition of any kind from anybody for my birthday. I did receive something, but not from man. On my birthday I started understanding, in depth, our letter from our Father. I bring this up now, but will explain better later in the message. I know that a couple weeks before my birthday, I realized that the entire bible is all about obedience. I bring this to your attention early, in hopes that you, too, can hear what our Father has been telling us all along. Then you may start to understand that obedience is not a bad thing, but the steps we need to take before our Father can allow us to come into His house.

At this time I would like to warn all readers that this is not going to be a book that is going to tickle your ears. I am not going to write about easy stuff in this book. I am not going to make it sound like we might be going down the right path if the scripture clearly shows we are not. This book will make a lot of people angry, irritated, uneasy, troubled, and most of all confused on a lot of what they have been taught in the modern churches of today. My intention is to stir up souls and get people to dig into the scrip- tures (OLD TESTAMENT) and the NEW TESTAMENT and listen to our Father and not that pastor in the pulpit. Even though this might be tough to get through, please continue reading. When we finish this message, every- thing will make a lot more sense. Everyone should have a much better understanding of **Hebrews 4:12, "For the word of God is quick, and powerful, and sharper than any twoedged sword,**

piercing even to the dividing asunder of soul and spirit, and of the joints and marrow, and is a discerner of the thoughts and intents of the heart."

When we are finished with this message we will be able to understand that every problem that we have is simply our own fault and no one else's. Yes, I am saying things like 911, ISIS, and Ebola are our own fault. Yes these are big issues, but even the small issues that go wrong are our own fault. If we would have just listened to our Father from the beginning, we would be living in perfection now. As you read through our Father's mes- sage, your eyes and EARS will open just as mine have. You will start real- izing that we wouldn't get sick if we would only eat and drink what our Father has told us to eat and drink. There wouldn't be all this confusion on the Sabbath if we would have just listened to our Father. We wouldn't be honoring any other days other than what our Father has told us to honor, which causes a lot of us to actually be worshipping some other god than our Father. Once we start listening to our Father, everything makes so much sense.

We think that our Father will be lenient with us; we think we do not need to obey everything that was written in the Old Testament. We think our Father knows our hearts and will allow us into heaven just because we had good intentions. Our Father lets us know in His letter to us that our good heart is not enough. A good heart will not automatically get you into heaven. Jeremiah 17:9 says, "The heart is deceitful above all things, and desperately wicked: who can know it? 10 I the Lord search the heart; I try the reins, even to give every man according to his ways, and according to the fruit of his doings." If we think our Father will show slack in anything other than what He has commanded, we should really pay attention to how much detail went into the construction of the tabernacle.

> (Exodus 26) 1 Moreover thou shalt make the tabernacle with ten curtains of fine twined linen, and blue, and purple, and scarlet: with cherubims of cunning work shalt thou make them. 2 The length

of one curtain shall be eight and twenty cubits, and the breadth of one curtain four cubits: and every one of the curtains shall have one measure. 3 The five curtains shall be coupled together one to another; and other five curtains shall be coupled one to another. 4 And thou shalt make loops of blue upon the edge of the one curtain from the selvedge in the coupling; and likewise shalt thou make in the uttermost edge of another curtain, in the coupling of the second. 5 Fifty loops shalt thou make in the one curtain, and fifty loops shalt thou make in the edge of the curtain that is in the coupling of the second; that the loops may take hold one of another. 6 And thou shalt make fifty taches of gold, and couple the curtains together with the taches: and it shall be one tabernacle. 7 And thou shalt make curtains of goats' hair to be a covering upon the tabernacle: eleven curtains shalt thou make. 8 The length of one curtain shall be thirty cubits, and the breadth of one curtain four cubits: and the eleven curtains shall be all of one measure. 9 And thou shalt couple five curtains by themselves, and six curtains by themselves, and shalt double the sixth curtain in the forefront of the tabernacle. 10 And thou shalt make fifty loops on the edge of the one curtain that is outmost in the coupling, and fifty loops in the edge of the curtain which coupleth the second. 11 And thou shalt make fifty taches of brass, and put the taches into the loops, and couple the tent together, that it may be one. 12 And the remnant that remaineth of the curtains of the tent, the half curtain that remaineth, shall hang over the backside of the tabernacle. 13 And a cubit on the one side, and a cubit on the other side of that which remaineth in the length of the curtains of the tent, it shall hang over the sides of the tabernacle on this side and on that side, to cover it. 14 And thou shalt make a covering for the tent of rams' skins dyed red, and a covering above of badgers' skins. 15 And thou shalt make boards for the tabernacle of shittim wood standing up. 16 Ten cubits shall be the length of a board, and a cubit and a half shall be the breadth of one board. 17 Two tenons shall there be in one board, set in order one against another: thus shalt thou make for all the boards of the tabernacle. 18 And thou shalt make the boards for the tabernacle, twenty boards on the south side southward. 19 And thou shalt make forty sockets of silver under the twenty boards; two sockets under one board for his two tenons, and two sockets under another board for his two tenons. 20 And for the second side of the taber- nacle on the north side there shall be twenty boards: 21 And their forty sockets of silver; two sockets under one board, and two sockets under another board. 22 And for the sides of the tabernacle westward thou shalt make six boards. 23 And two boards shalt thou make for the cor- ners of the tabernacle in the two sides. 24 And they shall be coupled together beneath, and they shall be coupled together above the head of it unto one ring: thus shall it be for them both; they shall be for the two corners. 25 And they shall be eight boards, and their sockets of silver, sixteen sockets; two sockets under one board, and two sockets under another board. 26 And thou shalt make bars of shittim wood; five for the boards of the one side of the tabernacle, 27 And five bars for the boards of the other side of the tabernacle, and five bars for the boards of the side of the tabernacle, for the two sides westward. 28 And the middle bar in the midst of the boards shall reach from end to end. 29 And thou shalt overlay the boards with gold, and make their rings of gold for places for the bars: and thou shalt overlay the bars with gold. 30

> And thou shalt rear up the tabernacle according to the fashion thereof which was shewed thee in the mount. 31 And thou shalt make a vail of blue, and purple, and scarlet, and fine twined linen of cunning work: with cherubims shall it be made: 32 And thou shalt hang it upon four pillars of shittim wood over- laid with gold: their hooks shall be of gold, upon the four sockets of silver. 33 And thou shalt hang up the vail under the taches, that thou mayest bring in thither within the vail the ark of the testimony: and the vail shall divide unto you between the holy place and the most holy. 34 And thou shalt put the mercy seat upon the ark of the testimony in the most holy place. 35 And thou shalt set the table without the vail, and the candlestick over against the table on the side of the tabernacle toward the south: and thou shalt put the table on the north side. 36 And thou shalt make an hanging for the door of the tent, of blue, and purple, and scarlet, and fine twined linen, wrought with needle- work. 37 And thou shalt make for the hanging five pillars of shittim wood, and overlay them with gold, and their hooks shall be of gold: and thou shalt cast five sockets of brass for them.

Now after we listen to how detailed our Father commanded the tabernacle to be built, we would be silly to think that He will be slack in any of His laws.

We are told to teach boldly the word of God. Acts 4:29 says, "And now, Lord, behold their threatenings: and grant unto thy servants, that with all boldness they may speak thy word." We can see that Jesus taught boldly in John 7:26, "But, lo, he speaketh boldly, and they say nothing unto him. Do the rulers know indeed that this is the very Christ?" This does not mean to water it down. This does not mean to tell people what they want to hear so they can come to church once a week and give money, just so they can go home feeling like they did right by God. We are warned of this in 2 Timothy chapter 4, "I charge thee therefore before God, and the Lord Jesus Christ, who shall judge the quick and the dead at his appearing and his kingdom; 2 Preach the word; be instant in season, out of season; reprove, rebuke, exhort with all long suffering and doctrine. 3 For the time will come when they will not endure sound doctrine; but after their own lusts shall they heap to them- selves teachers, having itching ears; 4 And they shall turn away their ears from the truth, and shall be turned unto fables." Is this starting to sound like what we hear in the churches today? We today take things way too lightly. One thing that I think all of us need to be aware of is that this is nothing new. I am speaking of when Adam and Eve were created. They were being told that they did not have to obey God. They were told they would not die or perish if they disobeyed God.

> (Gen 3) 1 Now the serpent was more subtle than any beast of the field which the LORD God had made. And he said unto the woman, Yea, hath God said, Ye shall not eat of every tree of the garden? 2 And the woman said unto the serpent, We may eat of the fruit of the trees of the garden: 3 But of the fruit of the tree which is in the midst of the garden, God hath said, Ye shall not eat of it, neither shall ye touch it, lest ye die. 4 And the serpent said unto the woman, Ye shall not surely die: 5 For God doth know that in the day ye eat thereof, then your eyes shall be opened, and ye shall be as gods, knowing good and evil. 6 And when the woman saw that the tree was good for food, and that it was pleasant to the eyes, and a tree to be desired to make one wise, she took of the fruit thereof, and did eat, and gave also unto her husband with her; and he did eat. 7 And the eyes of them both were opened, and they knew that they were naked; and they sewed fig leaves together, and made themselves aprons.

As we can see, from the very beginning of it all, Satan told Eve that she would go unpunished for disobeying God. That is what is being taught in just about every church out here today. In one way or another, they say we are under grace and there is no reason to be obedient to **all** of God's laws. Something else we need to really listen to is how Adam and Eve reacted when the Father called upon them:

> (Genesis 3) 9 And the Lord God called unto Adam, and said unto him, Where art thou? 10 And he said, I heard thy voice in the garden, and I was afraid, because I was naked; and I hid myself. 11 And he said, Who told thee that thou wast naked? Hast thou eaten of the tree, whereof I com- manded thee that thou shouldest not eat? 12 And the man said, The woman whom thou gavest to be with me, she gave me of the tree, and I did eat. 13 And the Lord God said unto the woman, What is this that thou hast done? And the woman said, The serpent beguiled me, and I did eat.

Note how, in the very beginning, humans would not take the blame for their own actions. Adam blamed his fault on the woman and she, in turn, put the blame on the serpent.

Now all of us know that our Father is not the author of confusion. 1 Corinthians 14:33 says, "For God is not the author of confusion, but of peace, as in all churches of the saints." As we will hear as we listen to everything that our Father is telling us in His letter to us, we will learn that we are the authors of our own confusion. We can hear Him telling us that because of our being hard headed and stuck on doing things our own way, that we are the ones responsible for our own confusion. It is our own fault and we need to realize that. Satan is not the reason we decide to act on something. Satan does not force us to do anything. It's our own choice. We can hear our Father also telling us that because of us pushing our faults onto someone else, we can't even see our own sin or disobedience. We choose not to listen to our Father and, because of this, we have confused ourselves into thinking that our ways of living are better than the Father's. How many times within the scriptures are we told that man shall not live by bread alone, but by every word out of the mouth of God? We are told that we need nothing more and nothing less. Deuteronomy 4 says, "Now therefore hearken, O Israel, unto the statutes and unto the judgments, which I teach you, for to do them, that ye may live, and go in and possess the land which the Lord God of your fathers giveth you. 2 Ye <u>shall not add</u> unto the word which I command you, <u>neither shall ye diminish</u> ought from it, that ye may keep the commandments of the Lord your God which I command you." Also in Matthew 4, "Then was Jesus led up of the Spirit into the wil- derness to be tempted of the devil. 2 And when he had fasted forty days and forty nights, he was afterward an hungered. 3 And when the tempter came to him, he said, If thou be the Son of God, command that these stones be made bread. 4 But he answered and said, It is written, Man shall not live by bread alone, but by <u>every word that proceedeth out of the mouth of God."</u> Something that I want to point out before we really get started in this book is that everything I am going to talk about is talked about in our bibles; and because we do not take the time ourselves to listen to Him, our Father has warned us what will happen. The only things I will use outside of the bible are articles stating some facts around a few days that true believers have no business partaking in.

> (Hosea 4) 1 Hear the word of the Lord, ye children of Israel: for the Lord hath a controversy with the inhabitants of the land, **because there is no truth, nor mercy, nor knowledge of God in the land.** 2 By swearing, and lying, and killing, and stealing, and committing adultery, they break out, and blood toucheth blood. 3 Therefore shall the land mourn, and every one that dwelleth therein shall languish, with the beasts of the field, and with the fowls of heaven; yea, the fishes of the sea also shall be taken away. 4 Yet let no man strive, nor reprove another: for thy people are as they that strive with the priest. 5 Therefore shalt

thou fall in the day, and the prophet also shall fall with thee in the night, and I will destroy thy mother. 6 <u>My people are destroyed for lack of knowledge: because thou hast rejected knowledge, I will also reject thee, that thou shalt be no priest to me: seeing thou hast forgotten the law of thy God, I will also forget thy children.</u> 7 As they were increased, so they sinned against me: therefore will I change their glory into shame. 8 They eat up the sin of my people, and they set their heart on their iniquity. 9 And there shall be, like people, like priest: and I will punish them for their ways, and reward them their doings. 10 For they shall eat, and not have enough: they shall commit whoredom, and shall not increase: because they have left off to take heed to the Lord. 11 Whoredom and wine and new wine take away the heart. 12 My people ask counsel at their stocks, and their staff declareth unto them: for the spirit of whoredoms hath caused them to err, and they have gone a whoring from under their God. 13 They sacrifice upon the tops of the mountains, and burn incense upon the hills, under oaks and poplars and elms, because the shadow thereof is good: therefore your daughters shall commit whoredom, and your spouses shall commit adul- tery. 14 I will not punish your daughters when they commit whoredom, nor your spouses when they commit adultery: for themselves are separated with whores, and they sacri- fice with harlots: therefore the people that doth not under- stand shall fall. 15 Though thou, Israel, play the harlot, yet let not Judah offend; and come not ye unto Gilgal, neither go ye up to Bethaven, nor swear, The Lord liveth. 16 For Israel slideth back as a backsliding heifer: now the Lord will feed them as a lamb in a large place. 17 Ephraim is joined to idols: let him alone. 18 Their drink is sour: they have committed whoredom continually: her rulers with shame do love, Give ye. 19 The wind hath bound her up in her wings, and they shall be ashamed because of their sacrifices.

I included this entire chapter for us to really think about. This is the main problem with most churches today. We do not take the time ourselves to find out what our Father needs from us. For this very reason, our Father will allow us to continue to walk in our own ways, which will lead to our own destruction.

I also want to point out, at this time, that men are not to be shaving their beards unless they have leprosy or something of the sort. We see in Leviticus 14 that they were to shave after being pronounced clean from leprosy. Leviticus 14:8 says, "And he that is to be cleansed shall wash his clothes, and shave off all his hair, and wash himself in water, that he may be clean: and after that he shall come into the camp, and shall tarry abroad out of his tent seven days. 9 But it shall be on the seventh day, that he shall shave all his hair off his head and his beard and his eyebrows, even all his hair he shall shave off: and he shall wash his clothes, also he shall wash his flesh in water, and he shall be clean." We can find passages telling us not to trim or mar our beards. Leviticus 19:27 tells us, "Ye shall not round the corners of your heads, neither shalt thou mar the corners of thy beard." And again in Leviticus 21:5, "They shall not make baldness upon their head, neither shall they shave off the corner of their beard, nor make any cuttings in their flesh."

We will, however, find several passages that speak of men of God who had beards. Psalm 133:2 says, "It is like the precious ointment upon the head, that ran down upon the beard, even Aaron's beard: that went down to the skirts of his garments;" and 1 Samuel 12, "And David laid up these words in his heart, and was sore afraid of Achish the king of Gath.13 And he changed his behaviour before them, and feigned himself mad in their hands, and scrabbled on the doors of the gate, and let his spittle fall down upon his beard." As did Ezra, as we see in Ezra 9:3, "And when I heard this thing, I rent my garment and my mantle, and plucked off the hair of my head and of my beard, and sat down astonished." Then we need to look in Isaiah to see that even Jesus had a beard.

> (Isaiah 50) 4 The Lord God hath given me the tongue of the learned, that I should know how to speak a word in season to him that is weary: he wakeneth morning by morning, he wakeneth mine ear to hear as the learned. 5 The Lord God hath opened mine ear, and I was not rebel- lious, neither turned away back. 6 I gave my back to the smiters, and my cheeks to them that plucked off the hair: I hid not my face from shame and spitting. 7 For the Lord God will help me; therefore shall I not be confounded: therefore have I set my face like a flint, and I know that I shall not be ashamed.

I know that this does not say this is Jesus by name; but if we know any- thing at all about our bibles, then we know that this is actually talking about Jesus. Now that we know that Jesus had a beard, we also need to realize that Jesus was a living example for us, as told in 1 Peter 2:21, "For even hereunto were ye called: because Christ also suffered for us, <u>leaving us an example</u>, that ye should follow his steps."

We can also know that Jesus did not have long hair. We should know that all scripture was inspired by God. 2 Timothy 3:16 says, "All scripture is given by inspiration of God, and is profitable for doctrine, for reproof, for correction, for instruction in righteousness." So we can now understand that Jesus didn't have long hair when we listen to what our Father said through Paul in 1 Corinthians 11: 14, "Doth not even nature itself teach you, that, **if a man have long hair, it is a shame unto him?"**

So yes, we can safely say that all these pictures that we have of this character with long hair and well-trimmed beard are not pictures of the actual Jesus.

Fearing God

We are told throughout the Scriptures to fear God. I hear pastors and preachers telling us to fear God but, with what our pastors teach us, what is there to fear? Our sins are forgiven. Jesus, the Son of God, is only about love. When he died on the cross, he took the place of our sins, so what do we really have to fear? They make it sound as if there is no such thing as sin anymore. How could there be if Jesus died and all sins are now forgiven? Why are we told to fear God if Jesus is about love and our sins are forgiven? Why would God tell us to fear Him if we had nothing to worry about? I guess we need to look into what fearing God is all about.

Let us take a look at a time when a well-known figure of the bible feared God.

Beginning in Genesis 22:11, "And the angel of the Lord called unto him out of heaven, and said, Abraham, Abraham: and he said, Here am I. 12 And he said, Lay not thine hand upon the lad, neither do thou anything unto him: for now I know that **thou fearest God,** seeing thou hast not withheld thy son, thine only son from me. 13 And Abraham lifted up his eyes, and looked, and behold behind him a ram caught in a thicket by his horns: and Abraham went and took the ram, and offered him up for a burnt offering in the stead of his son."

We see very early in the bible that God will test us to see if we fear him or not. This should tell us all that fearing God is a VERY important part of our eternal life. Just think about how hard this type of test would impact your life. This is obviously not a joking matter or something we should be taking too lightly. Let us move on to some more times that persons of the bible feared God.

Exodus 1:20 says, "Therefore God dealt well with the midwives: and the people multiplied, and waxed very mighty. 21 And it came to pass, **because the midwives feared God**, that he made them houses. 22 And Pharaoh charged all his people, saying, Every son that is born ye shall cast into the river, and every daughter ye shall save alive." Here we see that the midwives feared God and God dealt well with them. We can look over the scriptures all we want, but we will not find any verse that tells us that God rewarded anyone for not fearing him.

> (Exodus 18) 20 And thou shalt teach them ordinances and laws, and shalt shew them the way wherein they must walk, and the work that they must do. <u>21 Moreover thou shalt provide out of all the people able men, such as fear</u> God, men of truth, hating covetousness; and place such over them, to be rulers of thousands, and rulers of hun- dreds, rulers of fifties, and rulers of tens: 22 And let them judge the people at all seasons: and it shall be, that every great matter they shall bring unto thee, but every small matter they shall judge: so shall it be easier for thyself, and they shall bear the burden with thee.

As we see here, **men of truth fear God**. The men that fear God shall be rulers of thousands, and hundreds, etc.

> (Leviticus 25) 16 According to the multitude of years thou shalt increase the price thereof, and according to the fewness of years thou shalt diminish the price of it: for according to the number of the years of the fruits doth he sell unto thee. 17 Ye shall not therefore oppress one another; **but thou shalt fear thy God:** for I am the Lord your God. 18 Wherefore ye shall do my statutes, and keep my judgments, and do them; and ye shall dwell in the land in safety.

Here we start to see that the fear of God will encourage us to do God's statutes, keep His judgments.

> (Deuteronomy 4) 9 Only take heed to thyself, and keep thy soul diligently, lest thou forget the things which thine eyes have seen, and lest they depart from thy heart all the days of thy life: but teach them thy sons, and thy sons' sons; 10 Specially the day that thou stoodest before the Lord thy God in Horeb, when the Lord said unto me, Gather me the people together, and I will make them hear my words, **that they may learn to fear me all the days** that they shall live upon the earth, and that they may teach their children. 11 And ye came near and stood under the mountain; and the mountain burned with fire unto the midst of heaven, with darkness, clouds, and thick darkness.

Here we see God telling Israel to fear Him and to teach their children and their grandchildren to do the same. Are you starting to see a pattern yet?

> (Deuteronomy 6) 2 **That thou mightest fear the Lord thy God, to keep all his statutes and his commandments**, which I command thee, thou, and thy son, and thy son's son, all the days of thy life; and that thy days may be prolonged.

> (Deuteronomy 6) 12 Then beware lest thou forget the Lord, which brought thee forth out of the land of Egypt, from the house of bondage. 13 **Thou shalt fear the Lord thy God, and serve him, and shalt swear by his name.** 14 Ye shall not go after other gods, of the gods of the people which are round about you.

> (Deuteronomy 8) 6 Therefore thou shalt keep the com- mandments of the Lord thy God, to walk in his ways, **and to fear him.**

(Deuteronomy 10) 12 And now, Israel, what doth the Lord thy God require of thee, **but to fear the Lord thy God, to walk in <u>all</u> his ways, and to love him, and to serve the Lord thy God with all thy heart and with all thy soul.**

(Deuteronomy 13) 4 Ye shall walk after the Lord your God, **and fear him,** and keep his commandments, and obey his voice, and ye shall serve him, and cleave unto him.

(Deuteronomy 17) 19 And it shall be with him, and he shall read therein all the days of his life: **that he may learn to** fear the Lord his God, <u>to keep all the words of this law</u> <u>and these statutes, to do them.</u>

Now we need to listen to what our Father is telling us can, and will, happen to us if we choose not to fear God:

(Deuteronomy 28) 57 And toward her young one that cometh out from between her feet, and toward her chil- dren which she shall bear: for she shall eat them for want of all things secretly in the siege and straitness, wherewith thine enemy shall distress thee in thy gates. **58 If thou wilt not observe to do all the words of this law that are written in this book, that thou mayest fear this glorious and fearful name, The Lord Thy God;** 59 Then the Lord will make thy plagues wonderful, and the plagues of thy seed, even great plagues, and of long continuance, and sore sicknesses, and of long continuance.

(1 Samuel 12) 13 Now therefore behold the king whom ye have chosen, and whom ye have desired! And, behold, the Lord hath set a king over you. 14

> If ye will fear the Lord, and serve him, and obey his voice, and not rebel against the commandment of the Lord, then shall both ye and also the king that reigneth over you continue following the Lord your God: 15 **But if ye will not obey the voice of the Lord, but rebel against the commandment of the Lord, then shall the hand of the Lord be against you, as it was against your fathers.**

We see that not fearing God will put God against us. To put it bluntly, if we think that our sins are paid for and that we have nothing to fear, **THEN WE SHOULD BE TREMBLING WITH FEAR.**

Now that we have heard what our Father is telling us in the Old Testament, let us listen to what He is telling us in the New Testament. Acts 10:22 says, "And they said, Cornelius the centurion, a just man, **and one that feareth God,** and of good report among all the nation of the Jews, was warned from God by an holy angel to send for thee into his house, and to hear words of thee." We see here that Cornelius was a just man in God's eyes because he feared God.

> (Acts 13) 25 And as John fulfilled his course, he said, Whom think ye that I am? I am not he. But, behold, there cometh one after me, whose shoes of his feet I am not worthy to loose. 26 Men and brethren, children of the stock of Abraham, **and whosoever among you feareth God**, to you is the word of this salvation sent. 27 For they that dwell at Jerusalem, and their rulers, because they knew him not, nor yet the voices of the prophets which are read every Sabbath day, they have fulfilled them in condemning him.

We see here that only to those who fear God will the word of salvation be given.

2 Corinthians 7:1 says, "Having therefore these promises, dearly beloved, let us cleanse ourselves from all filthiness of the flesh and

spirit, perfecting holiness in the fear of God." Here we see that we can perfect ourselves in the fear of God. This doesn't mean that we can actually be perfect, but this is the road to perfection.

> (Romans 3) 1 What advantage then hath the Jew? or what profit is there of circumcision? 2 Much every way: chiefly, because that unto them were committed the oracles of God. 3 For what if some did not believe? shall their unbelief make the faith of God without effect? 4 God forbid: yea, let God be true, but every man a liar; as it is written, That thou mightest be justified in thy sayings, and mightest overcome when thou art judged. 5 But if our unrighteous- ness commend the righteousness of God, what shall we say? Is God unrighteous who taketh vengeance? (I speak as a man) 6 God forbid: for then how shall God judge the world? 7 For if the truth of God hath more abounded through my lie unto his glory; why yet am I also judged as a sinner? 8 And not rather, (as we be slanderously reported, and as some affirm that we say,) Let us do evil, that good may come? whose damnation is just? 9 What then? are we better than they? No, in no wise: for we have before proved both Jews and Gentiles, that they are all under sin; 10 As it is written, There is none righteous, no, not one: 11 There is none that understandeth, there is none that seeketh after God. 12 They are all gone out of the way, they are together become unprofitable; there is none that doeth good, no, not one. 13 Their throat is an open sepulchre; with their tongues they have used deceit; the poison of asps is under their lips: 14 Whose mouth is full of cursing and bitterness: 15 Their feet are swift to shed blood: 16 Destruction and misery are in their ways: 17 And the way of peace have they not known: 18 <u>There is no fear of God before their</u>

eyes. 19 Now we know that what things soever the law saith, it saith to them who are under the law: that every mouth may be stopped, and all the world may become guilty before God. 20 Therefore by the deeds of the law there shall no flesh be justified in his sight: for by the law is the knowledge of sin. 21 But now the righteousness of God without the law is manifested, being witnessed by the law and the prophets; 22 Even the righteousness of God which is by faith of Jesus Christ unto all and upon all them that believe: for there is no difference: 23 For all have sinned, and come short of the glory of God; 24 Being justified freely by his grace through the redemption that is in Christ Jesus: 25 Whom God hath set forth to be a propitiation through faith in his blood, to declare his righteousness for the remission of sins that are past, through the forbearance of God; 26 To declare, I say, at this time his righteousness: that he might be just, and the justifier of him which believeth in Jesus. 27 Where is boasting then? It is excluded. By what law? of works? Nay: but by the law of faith. 28 Therefore we conclude that a man is justified by faith without the deeds of the law. 29 Is he the God of the Jews only? is he not also of the Gentiles? Yes, of the Gentiles also: 30 Seeing it is one God, which shall justify the circumcision by faith, and uncircumcision through faith. 31 Do we then make void the law through faith? God forbid: yea, we estab- lish the law.

I know some, after reading this chapter, will say this proves that we do not need to follow the law. But as you can see in verse 31, we establish the law because of our faith, not get rid of it. We are being told that our faith, once we understand better, will allow us to show others how they, too, can be set free from the law. Once we start listening to our Father, and when we acknowledge all of our own sins, then repent and open our hearts and let our Father in, we then become obedient to everything He has commanded and then we will be set free. This will be easier to understand once we are finished with this message.

This message shows us that the lack of the fear of God is what destroys us. Revelation 14:7 says, "Saying with a loud voice, Fear God, and give glory to him; for the hour of his judgment is come: and worship him that made heaven, and earth, and the sea, and the fountains of waters." After reading and thinking about all that has been written, we now see that this is the main reason for fearing God. God's judgment is going to happen whether we like it or not. Even if you do not believe in God, judgment will come upon you also. If we have no fear of God, then we have no desire to find out what God wants from us. We have no desire to read the scriptures and listen to our Father himself speak through the prophets. We then have no way of knowing if we did what we needed to do when the judgement comes. This is why Jesus himself said these very words:

> (Matthew 7) 21 Not every one that saith unto me, Lord, Lord, shall enter into the kingdom of heaven; but he that doeth the will of my Father which is in heaven. 22 Many will say to me in that day, Lord, Lord, have we not proph- esied in thy name? and in thy name have cast out devils? and in thy name done many wonderful works? 23 And then will I profess unto them, I never knew you: depart from me, ye that work iniquity.

How will we explain ourselves? Will we say we were too busy? Will we say that the pastor said we didn't need to know? Will we say that we didn't think He would mind if we just tweaked His law a bit? Will we say that we thought His love for us was so great that we didn't need to love Him back? Will we say it was inconvenient for us? Will we do as we always do and try and push our faults on to someone else? Either way, fearing God is the beginning of all wisdom. Psalm 111:10 tells us, "The fear of the Lord is the beginning of wisdom: a good understanding have all they that do his commandments: his praise endureth forever." If we have no fear of God, then we have no desire to please him! How can we expect him to please us if we do not please him or even have the desire to please Him? In Matthew 7:12 Jesus says, "Therefore all things whatsoever ye would that men should do to you, do ye even so to them: for this is the law and the prophets." Notice how we are the ones that will need to explain our own actions. It is not your neighbor, or even the pastor, that will be explaining your actions. It is not Satan that will have to explain why you did what you did. **EVERYTHING YOU HAVE DONE WAS YOUR OWN CHOICE AND NOT ANYONE ELSES.**

Before we get too far into this message, there a few things that our Father wants us to be aware of. Most of us have heard of the lost books of the bible. These books have no value when it comes to the truth of our Father. We all know that the Father is in control of everything. Our Father would not allow these books to be within our letter from Him. Everything we need to know about the Father, and what he desires from us, is within the 66 books in the bible. And as we know, our Father is not the author of confusion. If He would have allowed these books to stay within our bibles, then he would have had something to do with confusing us. We can verify this if we just listen to our Father and what He is saying through Paul, in Galatians 1:8, "But though we, or an angel from heaven, preach any other gospel unto you than that which we have preached unto you, let him be accursed." If we just listen to this, it does not give a lot of information, but let's listen to what He is saying in 1 Corinthians 6:2, "Do ye not know that the saints shall judge the world? and if the world shall be judged by you, are ye unworthy to judge the smallest matters? 3 Know ye not that we shall judge angels? how much more things that pertain to this life?" We can hear Him telling us that even the angels that reside with Him now will be judged, as we will be judged, for all sin that we have committed against our Father after we have become aware of our sin. Hebrews 10:26 says, "For if we sin wilfully after that we have received the knowledge of the truth, there remaineth no more sacrifice for sins, 27 But a certain fearful looking for of judgment and fiery indignation, which shall devour the adversaries." Once we become aware and understand everything our Father is telling us, and let Him do His work within us, we worry that we will not please Him with our own actions. This is what we are being told when we hear our Father speaking through Paul in Philippians 2:12, "Wherefore, my beloved, as ye have always obeyed, not as in my presence only, but now much more in my absence, work out your own salvation with **fear and trembling**.13 For it is God which worketh in you both to will and to do of his good pleasure."

Prayer and Repentance

Another topic we need to cover is the issue of praying. While I am driving, I tend to listen to the radio a lot. I am constantly hearing about asking others to pray for us. I keep hearing about this prayer app for our phones. Our Father at no time instructs us to ask people to pray for us. He at no time tells us to make our prayers public. In fact, He actually tells us to do just the opposite.

> (Matthew 6) 5 And when thou prayest, thou shalt not be as the hypocrites are: for they love to pray standing in the synagogues and in the corners of the streets, that they may be seen of men. Verily I say unto you, They have their reward. 6 But thou, when thou prayest, enter into thy closet, and when thou hast shut thy door, pray to thy **Father which is in secret;** and thy Father which seeth in secret shall reward thee openly. 7 But when ye pray, use not vain repetitions, as the heathen do: for they think that they shall be heard for their much speaking. 8 Be not ye therefore like unto them: for your Father knoweth what things ye have need of, before ye ask him.

Now when we start listening to what Jesus is telling us, we can hear that the hypocrites stand in the synagogues and on the corners of the street so they can be seen by men. No we don't use synagogues today, but we use churches. Who are we putting our trust in when we ask others to pray for us? Are we putting our trust in our Father or are we putting our trust in someone else's faith? These synagogues are for learning and not for anyone to share their problems with everyone else. We can hear Jesus telling us to take our prayer into the closet. Now why would we be told to do this if we are to share our prayers with anybody else? Jesus himself demonstrates this several times, but I will only show a couple of times.

> (Matthew 26) 36 Then cometh Jesus with them unto a place called Gethsemane, and saith unto the disciples, Sit ye here, <u>while I go and pray yonder</u>. 37 And he took with him Peter and the two sons of Zebedee, and began to be sorrowful and very heavy. 38 Then saith he unto them, My soul is exceeding sorrowful, even unto death: tarry ye here, and watch with me. 39 <u>And he went a little farther, and fell on his face, and prayed, saying, O my Father, if it be possible, let this cup pass from me: nevertheless not as I will, but as thou wilt.</u>

We can see that Luke tells us the same thing in Luke 6:11, "And they were filled with madness; and communed one with another what they might do to Jesus. 12 And it came to pass in those days, <u>that he went out into a mountain to pray, and continued all night in prayer to God.</u> 13 And when it was day, he called unto him his disciples: and of them he chose twelve, whom also he named apostles."

We hear Jesus himself instructing us to pray to the Father, which is in secret. When we listen to what Jesus said as a whole, we can hear that the preacher up in front of the church shouldn't be praying (not out loud, anyway). The church or synagogue is for learning and understanding what the Father is saying in His letter to us. We are not to ask someone else to pray for us. We are not to tell others that we will pray for them. All of our prayers are to be kept between ourselves and our Father. He knows what we need at all times. At no time whatsoever are we to make our prayers known by others. Our Father wants to work on each one of us individu- ally. This will be better understood by the time we are done with this mes- sage. We are not even supposed to be praying before our meals. This is a man-made tradition. We are specifically told to pray after our bellies are full. Deuteronomy 8:10 says, "When thou hast eaten and art full, then thou shalt bless the Lord thy God for the good land which he hath given thee." We can further illustrate this when we listen to Matthew at the last supper.

> (Matthew 26) 17 Now the first day of the feast of unleav- ened bread the disciples came to Jesus, saying unto him, Where wilt thou that we prepare for thee to eat the pass- over? 18 And he said, Go into the city to such a man, and say unto him, The Master saith, My time is at hand; I will keep the passover at thy house with my disciples. 19 And the disciples did as Jesus had appointed them; and they made ready the passover. 20 Now when the even was come, he sat down with the twelve. 21 And as they did eat, he said, Verily I say unto you, that one of you shall betray me. 22 And they were exceeding sorrowful, and began every one of them to say unto him, Lord, is it I? 23 And he answered and said, He that dippeth his hand with me in the dish, the same shall betray me. 24 The Son of man goeth as it is written of him: but woe unto that man by whom the Son of man is betrayed! it had been good for that man if he had not been born. 25 Then Judas, which betrayed him, answered and said, Master, is it I? He said unto him, Thou hast said. 26 **And as they were eating, Jesus took bread, and blessed it,** and brake it, and gave it to the disciples, and said, Take, eat; this is my body. **27 And he took the cup, and gave thanks,** and gave it to them, saying, Drink ye all of it; 28 For this is my blood of the new testament, which is shed for many for the remission of sins.

To verify that Jesus didn't eat after he gave thanks, we need to look in Luke.

> (Luke 22) 8 And he sent Peter and John, saying, Go and prepare us the passover, that we may eat.9 And they said unto him, Where wilt thou that we prepare? 10 And he said unto them, Behold, when ye are entered into the city, there shall a man meet you, bearing a pitcher of water; follow him into the house where he entereth in.11 And ye shall say unto the goodman of the house, The Master saith unto thee, Where is the guestchamber, where I shall eat the passover with my disciples? 12 And he shall shew you a large upper room furnished: there make ready. 13 And they went, and found as he had said unto them: and they made ready the passover.14 And when the hour was come, he sat down, and the twelve apostles with him.15 And he said unto them, With desire I have desired to eat this passover with you before I suffer: 16 For I say unto you, I will not any more eat thereof, until it be fulfilled in the kingdom of God. 17 And he took the cup, and gave thanks, and said, Take this, and divide it among yourselves: 18 For I say unto you, I will not drink of the fruit of the vine, until the kingdom of God shall come.

Now when we listen to all that we are being told here, we can hear that Jesus did not give thanks until after they had already been eating. Now after what we just read in Deuteronomy 8:10, and then in Matthew 26:17-28, we can know without a doubt that we are not to give thanks before we eat.

1 Thessalonians 5:16 says, "Rejoice evermore. 17 Pray without ceasing. 18 In every thing give thanks: for this is the will of God in Christ Jesus concerning you." I have heard pastors saying that it is not possible for us to continually give thanks and pray always. Let us just

think of a few things to be thankful for. To do this I will list a few minor issues and a few bigger issues to show how we can give thanks in EVERYTHING. Can we give thanks for waking up this morning? Can we give thanks that our car started? Can we give thanks that our car got us to where we were going? Can we give thanks that the radio works? Can we give thanks that our windshield wipers or headlights are working? Now I know these are smaller issues so let me ask you this: if you fall down and break your arm, would you give our Father thanks? If you say no, then I would have to ask why you aren't thankful you didn't break both arms. If you get a speeding ticket, would you thank our Father? If you say no, then I would have to ask why you are not thankful that you didn't go to jail. If you get into a car accident and your arms and legs are broken, and all of your teeth got knocked out and you also are now blind, would you give thanks to our Father? If not then I would have to ask why not, as you are still alive and have all the opportunity to learn what our Father is telling us. You can still learn that all you need to do is start listening to our Father. Remember we will be made new once we get to heaven. We can give thanks for the opportunity to teach others what we have misunderstood for so long. We all know that some things can happen that really seem hard to give thanks for but when we truly think about it, the only time we can't give thanks is once our hearts stop beating. Once we start thanking our Father for everything, no matter how small or large of an issue, we soon realize that we are constantly praying to our Father.

 Something else we need to think about as we listen to what our Father is telling us in this message is repenting. This is something we hear church leaders telling us to do. If we don't realize that we sin, or that our sins have not been forgiven yet, then what are we to repent of? We can hear our Father say several times throughout the entire letter that He has written for us, repent and turn back to His ways. Ezekiel 18:30 says, "Therefore I will judge you, O house of Israel, every one according to his ways, saith the Lord God. Repent, and turn yourselves from all your transgressions; so iniquity shall not be your ruin." Matthew 9:13 tells us, "But go ye and learn what that meaneth, I will have mercy, and not sacrifice: for I am not come to call the righteous, but sinners to repentance." Also Mark 1:15, "And saying, The time is fulfilled, and the kingdom of God is at hand: repent ye, and believe the gospel." Luke 13:3 says, "I tell you, Nay: but, except ye repent, ye shall all likewise perish." Acts 3:19 tells us, "Repent ye there- fore, and be converted, that your sins may be blotted out, when the times of refreshing shall come from the presence of the Lord." This verse should send shivers down our spines.

We are clearly told if we do not repent, our sins will not be blotted out. Acts 17:30 says, "And the times of this ignorance God winked at; but now commandeth all men every where to repent." Also in Acts 26:20, "But shewed first unto them of Damascus, and at Jerusalem, and throughout all the coasts of Judaea, and then to the Gentiles, that they should repent and turn to God, and do works meet for repentance." We could go on forever, it seems, with all the times we are told to repent, but I really think by now we are all starting to get the picture. If we listen to the Father and ask Him what it is that we need to be doing to please Him, He will let us know.

Now I want to touch on a subject that boggles me. I constantly hear pastors tell us to surrender to God. Not only that, I hear people say that they have surrendered to God. How can we think we have surrendered to God if we don't listen to Him and obey everything He has commanded? When we realize that we are the ones at fault with all of this mess, and start listening and doing everything that He has commanded, then we can say we surrender. We don't even realize what we are supposed to surrender to yet. We all need to look in our letters, or our bibles, and instead of looking for what we have to do or what we don't have to do, we should be asking our Father, what is it you need me to do? That is when we will actually repent and turn back to His ways. We are, and have been, very confused for a very long time. Now that the Father is revealing His message to us, and we are now starting to realize that it has been right under our noses the whole time, we can actually start listening to our Father and truly look forward to spending eternity with Him. AMEN!!!

The Ten Commandments

Our Father has led me to list the Ten Commandments here so we can break them down and understand how we are breaking some of these also.

(Exodus 20) 1 And God spake all these words, saying, 2 I am the Lord thy God, which have brought thee out of the land of Egypt, out of the house of bondage. 3 Thou shalt have no other gods before me. 4 Thou shalt not make unto thee any graven image, or any likeness of any thing that is in heaven above, or that is in the earth beneath, or that is in the water under the earth. 5 Thou shalt not bow down thyself to them, nor serve them: for I the Lord thy God am a jealous God, visiting the iniquity of the fathers upon the children unto the third and fourth generation of them that hate me; 6 And shewing mercy unto thousands of them that love me, and keep my commandments. 7 Thou shalt not take the name of the Lord thy God in vain; for the Lord will not hold him guiltless that taketh his name in vain. 8 Remember the sabbath day, to keep it holy. 9 Six days shalt thou labour, and do all thy work: 10 But the seventh day is the sabbath of the Lord thy God: in it thou shalt not do any work, thou, nor thy son, nor thy daughter, thy manservant, nor thy maidservant, nor thy cattle, nor thy stranger that is within thy gates: 11 For in six days the Lord made heaven and earth, the sea, and all that in them is, and rested the seventh day: wherefore the Lord blessed the sabbath day, and hallowed it. 12 Honour thy father and thy mother: that thy days may be long upon the land which the Lord thy God giveth thee. 13 Thou shalt not kill. 14 Thou shalt not commit adultery. 15 Thou shalt not steal. 16 Thou shalt not bear false witness against thy neighbour. 17 Thou shalt not covet thy neighbour's house, thou shalt not covet thy neighbour's wife, nor his manservant, nor his maidservant, nor his ox, nor his ass, nor any thing that is thy neighbour's.

We will start from the first commandment: "thou shalt have no other gods before me." When we listen to this we can hear that we put God first, before anything and everything. Our entertainment that we seek is not putting God first. When we seek drugs to make ourselves feel different for a while, we are not putting God first. When, and if, we do anything without checking to see if this is what God wants us to do, then we are putting whatever we are doing in front of God. This means we are replacing God Almighty with another god.

Then we need to look at the second commandment: "Thou shalt not make unto thee any graven image, or any likeness of any thing that is in heaven above, or that is in the earth beneath, or that is in the water under the earth. 5 Thou shalt not bow down thyself to them, nor serve them: for I the Lord thy God am a jealous God, visiting the iniquity of the fathers upon the children unto the third and fourth generation of them that hate me." Now we should be listening to God when He tells us not to make any graven image or any likeness of anything that is in heaven, or in the earth, or in the waters of the earth. This means don't make or keep pictures of what is in heaven, earth, and the waters of the earth. Then He goes on to say not to bow down to the things in heaven, earth, and the waters. He is specifically telling us not to make any image; so do not make ourselves any- thing whatsoever that resembles anything that was made by God. He is not saying do not bow down to those things He just instructed us not to make. Now let us look at the third commandment: "Thou shalt not take the name of the Lord thy God in vain; for the Lord will not hold him guiltless that taketh his name in vain." Now I know a lot of people think that this is when someone uses the GD words. That is included with the cursing tongue that our Father hates. We hear this in Ephesians 4:29, "Let no corrupt com- munication proceed out of your mouth, but that which is good to the use of edifying, that it may minister grace unto the hearers." Also in 1 Peter 3:10, "For he that will love life, and see good days, let him refrain his tongue from evil, and his lips that they speak no guile." There are many other verses that talk against cursing, but that is not what this section is about so we need to move on. We need to look in e-sword, or a concordance, to see what the definition of vain is. H7723 שׁוא וּ שׁא o shâv' shav shawv, shav From the same as H7722 in the sense of desolating; evil (as destructive), literally (ruin) or morally (especially guile); figuratively idolatry (as false, subjectively), **uselessness (as deceptive, objectively; also adverbially in vain): - false (-ly), lie, lying, vain, vanity**. We are not to think that God is not going to do what He has said He will do. Don't think that His words are useless. Don't think He will do something other than what He has told us He will do within His letter of 66 books to us.

Now we need to look at the fourth commandment: "Remember the sab- bath day, to keep it holy. 9 Six days shalt thou labour, and do all thy work: 10 But the seventh day is the sabbath of the Lord thy God: in it thou shalt not do any work, thou, nor thy son, nor thy daughter, thy manservant, nor thy maidservant, nor thy cattle, nor thy stranger that is within thy gates: 11 For in six days the Lord made heaven and earth, the sea, and all that in them is, and rested the seventh day: wherefore the Lord blessed the sab- bath day, and hallowed it." This is a big one; we break this commandment in so many ways. First of all, we try and say that any seventh day can be a Sabbath. We say that Sunday is the new Sabbath. We say that Jesus finished the law so we don't have to obey the Sabbath anymore. This is just how we start to break the Sabbath. Then we work overtime on the true Sabbath, we go shopping on the Sabbath, we go out to eat on the Sabbath. But when we listen to our Father, we can hear Him say that we are not to do any work nor our son, daughter, manservant, maidservant, cattle, nor thy stranger that is <u>within thy gates.</u> Now we can hear that we are to stay within our own gates. How can we drive somewhere and put gas in our vehicle? How can we buy groceries if we have someone ring up the sale? How can we have someone serve us food? I could go on forever with the ways we break this commandment, but we should be getting the picture by now.

So let us look at the fifth commandment: "Honour thy father and thymother: that thy days may be long upon the land which the Lord thy God giveth thee." This one should not be too hard to break down. This does not mean once you turn of age to leave and never talk to your father and mother again. This does not mean to always rely on them for everything once you become of age. This simply means to give your father and mother the respect they deserve. Obviously, if you have parents that abuse you this does not mean that you should honor that abuse, but that you respect them as your parents. Even after we are of age and move out, we are to respect them for the rest of their days with us. God did use them to bring us into this world, so they deserve to be honored for that if nothing else. We all have to talk with the Father and let Him help us know how to honor our parents.

Now let us look at the sixth commandment: "Thou shalt not kill." We all know that this is telling us that we are not to kill anyone, so this one does not need any more explanation.

The seventh commandment: "Thou shalt not commit adultery." Now instead of looking into the spiritual adultery covered in another place of this book, we will only look at adultery against the spouse. We all know that once we are married we are not to cheat with another. This also means we are not to even think of such a thing. Matthew 5:27 says, "Ye have heard that it was said by them of old time, Thou shalt not commit adultery: 28 But I say unto you, That whosoever looketh on a woman to lust after her hath committed adultery with her already in his heart." We will learn that there is to be no iniquity within our hearts, so this is something that we have to get rid of if we want to go to heaven.

So now we need to look at the eighth commandment: "Thou shalt not steal." We think this is pretty simple, but we really should be thinking about what stealing consists of. This simply means that we are not to take some- thing that is not ours, right? Now let us think about this for a minute. How many of us take breaks at work when we are not supposed to be taking a break? How many of us slack at the work we do and expect others to cover the slack for us? Are we not stealing from our boss if we agreed to do a certain amount of work for a certain wage and then slack in any way of performing our work and expecting to get paid the amount agreed on? Are we not stealing if a vending machine gives our money back and the product that we purchased and we keep both? There are a lot of ways we steal that we do not think of as a form of stealing, but if we are taking anything at all that is not ours then we are stealing.

So now we move onto the ninth commandment: "Thou shalt not bear false witness against thy neighbour." This is pretty simple to explain. This simply means that we are to tell it as we see it. We do not say something other than exactly what we saw. If we see our neighbor steal a candy bar and the store owner asks us to be a witness, then we are obligated to tell the truth. If we know that this person (accused of stealing the candy bar) didn't steal the candy bar, then we are not to say that he or she did. Do not speak anything but the truth.

Then we move to the tenth commandment: "Thou shalt not covet thy neighbour's house; thou shalt not covet thy neighbour's wife, nor his man- servant, nor his maidservant, nor his ox, nor his ass, nor any thing that is thy neighbour's." Now this does not only mean our next-door neighbor, but all people. We are not to want anything that belongs to someone else. Yes we can want a house like our neighbor's, but we are not to want his or her house itself. If we do not covet anything that our neighbor has, then it will be much simpler not to break the other Commandments.

It is Written

Let us start out looking at how many times within the New Testament that it must be done as it is written and how many times we are referred to the scriptures. We need to keep in mind at all times that the only scripture that existed in the time the New Testament was written was the Old Testament. Let us look at a few verses and then we will refer back to the Old Testament to get the entire picture of whatever it is that we should know. This is just one of the ways that we are not doing as God has told us to do. I want to note here that most, if not all, references will be shown from the King James Version of the bible on Bible Gateway. Matt 26:24 says, "The Son of man goeth as it is written of him: but woe unto that man by whom the Son of man is betrayed! It had been good for that man if he had not been born."

Now let us look in the Old Testament to see what Jesus is referring to.

> (Isaiah 53) 1 Who hath believed our report? and to whom is the arm of the Lord revealed? 2 For he shall grow up before him as a tender plant, and as a root out of a dry ground: he hath no form nor comeliness; and when we shall see him, there is no beauty that we should desire him. 3 He is despised and rejected of men; a man of sor- rows, and acquainted with grief: and we hid as it were our faces from him; he was despised, and we esteemed him not. 4 Surely he hath borne our griefs, and carried our sor- rows: yet we did esteem him stricken, smitten of God, and afflicted. 5 But he was wounded for our transgressions, he

was bruised for our iniquities: the chastisement of our peace was upon him; and with his stripes we are healed. 6 All we like sheep have gone astray; we have turned every one to his own way; and the Lord hath laid on him the iniquity of us all. 7 He was oppressed, and he was afflicted, yet he opened not his mouth: he is brought as a lamb to the slaughter, and as a sheep before her shearers is dumb, so he openeth not his mouth 8 He was taken from prison and from judgment: and who shall declare his generation? for he was cut off out of the land of the living: for the trans- gression of my people was he stricken. 9 And he made his grave with the wicked and with the rich in his death; because he had done no violence, neither was any deceit in his mouth. 10 Yet it pleased the Lord to bruise him; he hath put him to grief: when thou shalt make his soul an offering for sin, he shall see his seed, he shall prolong his days, and the pleasure of the Lord shall prosper in his hand. 11 He shall see of the travail of his soul, and shall be satis- fied: by his knowledge shall my righteous servant justify many; for he shall bear their iniquities. 12 Therefore will I divide him a portion with the great, and he shall divide the spoil with the strong; because he hath poured out his soul unto death: and he was numbered with the transgres- sors; and he bare the sin of many, and made intercession for the transgressors.

As we can see, we are told of our king coming and the purpose of his life, death, and resurrection. Let us look at other times we are told to refer back to the Old Testament. Mark 1:2 tells us, "As it is written in the prophets, Behold, I send my messenger before thy face, which shall prepare thy way before thee." This passage is referring to Malachi 3, which says, "Behold, I will send my messenger, and he shall prepare the way before me: and the Lord, whom ye seek, shall suddenly come to his temple, even the mes- senger of the covenant, whom ye delight in: behold, he shall come, saith the Lord of hosts."

In John 6:31 we read, "Our fathers did eat manna in the desert; as it is written, He gave them bread from heaven to eat." As we can see here we are being told to refer back in Exodus, to the time in which the Father in heaven sent manna to the children of Israel.

> (Exodus 16) 12 I have heard the murmurings of the chil- dren of Israel: speak unto them, saying, At even ye shall eat flesh, and in the morning ye shall be filled with bread; and ye shall know that I am the Lord your God.13 And it came to pass, that at even the quails came up, and covered the camp: and in the morning the dew lay round about the host.14 And when the dew that lay was gone up, behold, upon the face of the wilderness there lay a small round thing, as small as the hoar frost on the ground.15 And when the children of Israel saw it, they said one to another, It is manna: for they wist not what it was. And Moses said unto them, This is the bread which the Lord hath given you to eat.

We see another example in John 12:14, "And Jesus, when he had found a young ass, sat thereon; as it is written." This is written in Zech 9:9, "Rejoice greatly, O daughter of Zion; shout, O daughter of Jerusalem: behold, thy King cometh unto thee: he is just, and having salvation; lowly, and riding upon an ass, and upon a colt the foal of an ass." As we see, here we are told about our Messiah riding in to Jerusalem on an ass. This, of course, is when he was riding just before he was to be crucified.

In Matthew 21:42 Jesus said to them, "Have you never read in the Scriptures: 'The stone the builders rejected has become the cornerstone; the Lord has done this, and it is marvelous in our eyes'?" He is referring to Psalm 118:22, which says, "The stone which the builders refused is become the head stone of the corner. 23 This is the

Lord's doing; it is mar- velous in our eyes." We can see here that the priests are talking about the Messiah that would be rejected. Jesus himself continually refers back to the Old Testament.

Mark 7:6 tells us, "He answered and said unto them, Well hath Esaias prophesied of you hypocrites, as it is written, This people honoureth me with their lips, but their heart is far from me." This is written in Isaiah 29:13, "Wherefore the Lord said, Forasmuch as this people draw near me with their mouth, and with their lips do honour me, but have removed their heart far from me, and their fear toward me is taught by the precept of men."

Also, in Matthew 22:29 Jesus replied, "You are in error because you do not know the Scriptures or the power of God." We can go back through the scriptures all over and see all kinds of power from our Father. Matthew 26:54 says, "But how then would the Scriptures be fulfilled that say it must happen in this way?"

> (Isaiah 53) 1 Who hath believed our report? and to whom is the arm of the Lord revealed?2 For he shall grow up before him as a tender plant, and as a root out of a dry ground: he hath no form nor comeliness; and when we shall see him, there is no beauty that we should desire him.3 He is despised and rejected of men; a man of sor- rows, and acquainted with grief: and we hid as it were our faces from him; he was despised, and we esteemed him not.4 Surely he hath borne our griefs, and carried our sorrows: yet we did esteem him stricken, smitten of God, and afflicted.5 But he was wounded for our transgressions, he was bruised for our iniquities: the chastisement of our peace was upon him; and with his stripes we are healed.6 All we like sheep have gone astray; we have turned every one to his own way; and the Lord hath laid on him the iniquity of us all.7 He was oppressed, and he was afflicted, yet he opened not his mouth: he is brought as a lamb to the slaughter, and as a

sheep before her shearers is dumb, so he openeth not his mouth.8 He was taken from prison and from judgment: and who shall declare his generation? for he was cut off out of the land of the living: for the trans- gression of my people was he stricken.9 And he made his grave with the wicked, and with the rich in his death; because he had done no violence, neither was any deceit in his mouth.10 Yet it pleased the Lord to bruise him; he hath put him to grief: when thou shalt make his soul an offering for sin, he shall see his seed, he shall prolong his days, and the pleasure of the Lord shall prosper in his hand.11 He shall see of the travail of his soul, and shall be satis- fied: by his knowledge shall my righteous servant justify many; for he shall bear their iniquities.12 Therefore will I divide him a portion with the great, and he shall divide the spoil with the strong; because he hath poured out his soul unto death: and he was numbered with the transgres- sors; and he bare the sin of many, and made intercession for the transgressors.

These last examples that I included here are not the last, or even close to being the last, of the times that we are told to refer to the scriptures. I wanted the last few to emphasize the importance of the scriptures. In Mark, Jesus himself said that we would honor him with our lips but our hearts would be far from him. He told us in Matthew that we error because we do not know the scriptures. And, as you can see above, he also stated in Matthew that it MUST happen as the scriptures told that it would happen. These are just a few of the times that we are clearly told we must refer back to the scriptures. If we want to follow Jesus, then we MUST do as he tells us. There is no other way around it. A lot of churches today tell us to only focus on the New Testament and, as you can see here, they are telling us to specifically go against what Jesus told us to do.

Obedience

I have just shown a small part of how we are actually told that we must refer to the Old Testament. Now I want to show that we are also told to be obedient, just as Jesus was obedient and, because of his obedience, he was exalted above all. In Philippians 2:7 we are told, "But made himself of no reputation, and took upon him the form of a servant, and was made in the likeness of men: 8 And being found in fashion as a man, he humbled himself, and became obedient unto death, even the death of the cross. 9 Wherefore God also hath highly exalted him, and given him a name which is above every name." What was Jesus obedient to? Was it man's laws or God's laws? Acts 5:29 says, "Then Peter and the other apos- tles answered and said, We ought to obey God rather than men." Romans 5:19 tells us, "For as by one man's disobedience many were made sinners, so by the obedience of one shall many be made righteous." Here we see that disobedience is all about sin. Do we think this means being obedient to anything other than what God commands us to do is considered obedience?

I have also heard of some asking what it means that Jesus had to learn to be obedient. Let us take a moment and look at the verses that state such matters. As noted above, we see in Philippians 2:8 that it reads "being found in fashion as a man, he humbled himself and became obedient." Then we see in Hebrews 5:8, "Though he were a Son, yet learned he obedience by the things which he suffered."

First let us break down the Philippians verse, where we see that he humbled himself. What does it mean to humble oneself? I will use e-sword to show the definition in the Greek language.--- ταπεινόω tapeinoō tap- i-no'-o From G5011; to depress; figuratively to humiliate (in condition or heart): - abase, bring low, humble (self). I underline bring low to bring this to our attention. This tells us that Jesus realized that he was **nothing** without God the Father. He illustrates this several times throughout the Bible. Realizing that he is nothing without the Father, he read the scrip- tures (OLD TESTAMENT) and became obedient to all that his Father had inspired the prophets to write. Then we look at Hebrews 5:8 and we see that he learned obedience by the things which he suffered. Now at first glance we can easily think that Jesus suffered a lot, but if we look up the definition of suffered in the concordance we can notice something different. G3958 πάσχω, πάθω, πένθω paschō pathō penthō pas'-kho, path'-o, pen'-tho Apparently a primary verb (the third form used only in certain tenses for it); to experience a sensation or impression (usually painful): - **feel, passion,** suffer, vex.

Once again I bring attention to the underlined word passion. Jesus had a sincere passion to do all that his Father commanded. Just because we know the word suffering to mean that something bad had to happen to him, we need to seek what the Greek meaning of words have. There are usually several different definitions to one word, so we need to find the definition that best fits into the context of what is being said. He had passion to be obedient to His Father. We are to follow Jesus, so we should also have that same passion to become obedient.

Now I want to look at Matthew 22 when the lawyer, who was tempting him, asked which the great commandment was in the law. I will just put the verses here to illustrate my point.

> (Matthew 22) 34 But when the Pharisees had heard that he had put the Sadducees to silence, they were gathered together. 35 Then one of them, which was a lawyer, asked him a question, tempting him, and saying, 36 Master, which is the great commandment in the law? 37 Jesus said unto him, Thou shalt love the Lord thy God with all thy heart, and with all thy soul, and with all thy mind. 38 This is the first and great commandment. 39 And the second is like unto it, Thou shalt love thy neighbour as thyself. 40 On

these two commandments hang all the law and the prophets.

Now I ask that we take a long hard look at verse 40. What does Jesus mean by hang <u>all</u> the law and prophets? I think we can rule out hang them in a tree. I think this clearly states that we need to make sure that we realize that every bit of the law comes with these two commandments. It also means that everything that the prophets wrote comes with these two command- ments. This does not mean that we can move the Sabbath around. This does not mean we can do anything other than what God commands us on the Sabbath. This does not mean that we can steal as long as we do not get caught. Nor does it mean we can commit adultery. We MUST do as God commanded. This means also that we must believe everything the prophets have written. Every word that the prophets wrote was inspired by God. Hebrews 1 says, "<u>God, who at sundry times and in divers manners spake in time past unto the fathers by the prophets.</u>" Why in the world would any of us think that anything they said would be false in any manner? This is God the Almighty we are talking about.

We, today, think of ourselves more than anything else. We think we need not obey all that God commanded. In fact, we call people that try to be obedient to God's law legalist and quickly say that our works will not get us into heaven. Well, we need to seek the truth more instead of listening to what others tell us. We need to seek for ourselves and not let the influ- ence of others lead us to anything other than what the bible actually tells us. Colossians 2:16 tells us, "Let no man therefore judge you in meat, or in drink, or in respect of an holyday, or of the new moon, or of the sabbath days: 17 Which are a shadow of things to come; but the body is of Christ." Notice how we are being told that these are a shadow of things to come. That will be very clear by the time we get done reading this book.

Before I dive into the topic of obedience further, I want to ask everyone to take note of the beginning of your bible and see why man fell. He fell due to his disobedience. Then look at the end of your bible and look at why God destroys the world. It is because of man's disobedience. So the next time someone tells you that you can interpret the bible many dif- ferent ways, tell them there is only one way to interpret the bible: **FROM THE BEGINNING TO THE END, THE ENTIRE BIBLE IS ABOUT OBEDIENCE.**

In James 2:14-16 we read, "What doth it profit, my brethren, though a man say he hath faith, and have not works? can faith save him? If a brother or sister be naked, and destitute of daily food, And one of you say unto them, Depart in peace, be ye warmed and filled; notwithstanding ye give them not those things which are needful to the body; what doth it profit?" My understanding of the bible is that we must have faith in God and His Son. Faith is not just believing that Jesus was born, lived, and then was cru- cified for all of our sins. If this was the case, then there would be no need for the bible and everyone would be going to heaven. We can all agree that the bible does not indicate any such thing. Faith is believing that God's ways are the best way to live. If we have faith that God's ways are the best ways to live, then our works of obeying everything that God commanded will come naturally. We all live the way we think is best for us, at least to best of our abilities. If we live life thinking that the <u>ALL</u> of God's laws, ways, statutes, and commandments have been done away with, or that Jesus finished the Law, then how can we have faith that our Father's way will lead us to heaven? Why would we think that the law would change in any way? We are told the law is perfect in Psalm 19:7, "The law of the Lord is perfect, converting the soul: the testimony of the Lord is sure, making wise the simple." Why would God change his own law if it is already perfect? Is there such a thing as better than perfect? Do we think God is anything but perfect? Is God going to say well they can't obey so I will change my perfect ways? Once again, if we think any way of living other than how God told us to live is better than his ways, then we should be questioning our faith. Then we are told in Malachi that God does not change. Malachi 3:6 says, "For I am the Lord, <u>I change not</u>; therefore ye sons of Jacob are not consumed." Why do we think that God gave us his Son so we do not have to obey the laws that He already put in place? Wouldn't that mean He would be changing?

Now I want to take a few minutes to show that Jesus said we must obey him and that everything he said came from the Father. Let us look at how many times we are told that everything that Jesus did was because it was what the Father willed. Matthew 28:18 states, "And Jesus came and spake unto them, saying, All power is given unto me in heaven and in earth." Luke 10:22 says, "All things are delivered to me of my Father: and no man knoweth who the Son is, but the Father; and who the Father is, but the Son, and he to whom the Son will reveal him." Also in John 5:30, "I can of mine own self do nothing: as I hear, I judge: and my judgment is just; because I seek not mine own will, but the will of the Father which hath sent me." Again in John 6:39, "And this is the Father's will which hath sent me, that of all which he hath given me I should lose nothing, but should raise it up again at the last day." As we can see here, Jesus did nothing that was not the Fathers will. Even Jesus is showing us his obedience.

We tell ourselves that we walk like Jesus did, but do we really? We say the law is now gone, but what did Jesus say? In Matthew 5:17 he says, "Think not that I am come to destroy the law, or the prophets: I am not come to destroy, but to fulfil. 18 For verily I say unto you, Till heaven and earth pass, one jot or one tittle shall in no wise pass from the law, till all be fulfilled."

Now I know a lot of us think that this is where Jesus ended the law. A lot of us think that Jesus put an end to the law with these verses. We need to break these verses down to see what they really mean. First we notice he said that he did not come to destroy the law, so we need to look at what destroy means in Greek. G2647 καταλύω kataluō kat-al-oo'-o From G2596 and G3089; to loosen down (disintegrate), that is, (by implication) to demolish (literally or figuratively); specifically (compare G2646) to halt for the night: - destroy, dissolve, be guest, lodge, come to nought, over- throw, throw down. I think that all of us could agree with these definitions and that to destroy would mean to end.

Then we notice that he said that he came to fulfill the law. This is where a lot think he ended the law, so let us look at the definition of fulfill in Greek. G4137 πληρόω plēroō play-ro'-o From G4134; to make replete, that is, (literally) to cram (a net), level up (a hollow), or (figuratively) to furnish (or imbue, diffuse, influence), satisfy, execute (an office), finish (a period or task), verify (or coincide with a prediction), etc.: - accomplish, X after, (be) complete, end, expire, fill (up), fulfil, (be, make) full (come), **fully preach**, perfect, supply. If we take each of these definitions, place each one in place of fulfill, the only one that makes any sense with the fol- lowing verse of 19 is fully preach.

Let us just make this verse in our own words, as if Jesus meant that ful- fill was to end the law. Think not that I came to end the law or the prophets; I come not to end, but to end. NOW HOW WOULD THAT MAKE ANY SENSE at all? We should also note that he said in verse 18 that not one jot nor tittle will pass from the law until heaven and earth pass. Well, you're reading this book on earth still and you can look to the heavens, so I guess that means Jesus himself said that ALL the law is still here.

We claim we love Jesus, but do we really? We say we want to do as Jesus would do. Well, let us think about that for a minute. We all know that Jesus was without sin. We know that he followed the law perfectly, or at least had the passion to. We can also know that he wasn't perfect. We know this because He, too, had to learn obedience. We know this from looking at Hebrews 5:8 again, which states, "Though he were a Son, yet **learned he obedience** by the things which he suffered; 9 **And being made** perfect, he became the author of eternal salvation unto all them that obey him; 10 Called of God an high priest after the order of Melchisedec." We all know he gave all thanks to the Father in heaven." Why is it, the first thing we do when we open our bibles is look for a reason not to have to follow God's laws? We try to say Jesus put an end to the law, but why would he have strived to walk the law perfectly, and still gave thanks to the Father, if he knew that he was going to put an end to the law?

The truth is we do not love, nor want to be, like Jesus. Sure, we will obey some laws if it is convenient for us. How can we say we love him when we refuse to put him first? How can we say we want to be like him, yet not want to obey God's laws? Jesus said it himself, in

Matthew 15:8, "This people draweth nigh unto me with their mouth, and honoureth me with their lips; but their heart is far from me." We say we want to be like him, but do we really?

We see in John 14:15, "If ye love me, keep my commandments." We also see him saying the same in verse 21, "He that hath my commandments, and keepeth them, he it is that loveth me: and he that loveth me shall be loved of my Father, and I will love him, and will manifest myself to him." This continues below:

> (John 14) 23 Jesus answered and said unto him, If a man love me, he will keep my words: and my Father will love him, and we will come unto him, and make our abode with him. 24 He that loveth me not keepeth not my sayings: and the word which ye hear is not mine, but the Father's which sent me. 25 These things have I spoken unto you, being yet present with you. 26 But the Comforter, which is the Holy Ghost, whom the Father will send in my name, he shall teach you all things, and bring all things to your remembrance, whatsoever I have said unto you. 27 Peace I leave with you, my peace I give unto you: not as the world giveth, give I unto you. Let not your heart be troubled, neither let it be afraid. 28 Ye have heard how I said unto you, I go away, and come again unto you. If ye loved me, ye would rejoice, because I said, I go unto the Father: for my Father is greater than I. 29 And now I have told you before it come to pass, that, when it is come to pass, ye might believe. 30 Hereafter I will not talk much with you: for the prince of this world cometh, and hath nothing in me. 31 But that the world may know that I love the Father; and as the Father gave me commandment, even so I do. Arise, let us go hence.

Now that we see that Jesus has definitely proclaimed his love for the Father, and that all that he does is the will of the Father, we need to see what loving the Father is about.

> (1 John 5) 1 Whosoever believeth that Jesus is the Christ is born of God: and every one that loveth him that begat loveth him also that is begotten of him. 2 By this we know that we love the children of God, when we love God, <u>and keep his commandments</u>. 3 <u>For this is the love of God, that we keep his commandments: and his commandments are not grievous.</u> 4 For whatsoever is born of God over- cometh the world: and this is the victory that overcometh the world, even our faith.5 Who is he that overcometh the world, but he that believeth that Jesus is the Son of God?

Believing

A lot of churches teach that Jesus is God. This is something people need to stop and think about. I am going to show, within our bibles, that Jesus is not God. If you believe that he is God, then you actually do **not** believe in the Son of God. Let us look in Matthew 1 starting with verse 19.

> (Matthew 1) 19 Then Joseph her husband, being a just man, and not willing to make her a public example, was minded to put her away privily. 20 But while he thought on these things, behold, the angel of the Lord appeared unto him in a dream, saying, Joseph, thou son of David, fear not to take unto thee Mary thy wife: for that which is conceived in her is of the Holy Ghost. 21 And she shall bring forth a son, and thou shalt call his name Jesus: for he shall save his people from their sins. 22 Now all this was done, that it might be fulfilled which was spoken of the Lord by the prophet, saying, 23 Behold, a virgin shall be with child, and shall bring forth a son, and they shall call his name Emmanuel, which being interpreted is, God with us.

I show this because we need to realize that it is the Holy Ghost, or Holy Spirit, which brought about the seed that caused the child to grow in the womb. This is not the seed of man, but the seed of the Holy Ghost which comes from God.

I think a lot of us can't wrap our minds around the fact that a child could actually be born without the seed of a man. This is why we tend to believe it must be God himself that was in Mary's womb. We need to start looking at it differently and realize that this is what makes Jesus the Son of God and not God himself.

We claim to believe in Jesus. I will show now that believing in Jesus is not only believing that he was born, grew up knowing the scriptures, performed miracles, ministered, was crucified, rose from the dead, and conquered death.

Let us look at what believing in Jesus means. We begin by looking at John 1, beginning in verse 14, "And the Word was made flesh, and dwelt among us, (and we beheld his glory, the glory as of the only begotten of the Father,) full of grace and truth."

Have we ever really wondered what the word is? If we look back into the Old Testament, we can see that the word is actually all of God's law. Here are a few examples. Deuteronomy 31:12 says, "Gather the people together, men and women, and children, and thy stranger that is within thy gates, that they may hear, and that they may learn, and fear the Lord your God, <u>and observe to do all the words of this law</u>." Joshua 8:34 tells us, "And afterward he read <u>all the words of the law,</u> the blessings and cursings, according to all that is written in the book of the law." Also in Nehemiah 8:9, "And Nehemiah, which is the Tirshatha, and Ezra the priest the scribe, and the Levites that taught the people, said unto all the people, This day is holy unto the Lord your God; mourn not, nor weep. For all the people wept<u>, when they heard the words of the law</u>." Continuing on to Isaiah 5:24, "Therefore as the fire devoureth the stubble, and the flame consumeth the chaff, so their root shall be as rottenness, and their blossom shall go up as dust: <u>because they have cast away the law of the Lord of hosts, and despised the word of the Holy One of Israel</u>." And Isaiah 8:20, "<u>To the law and to the testimony: if they speak not according to this word, it is because there is no light in them</u>." As we can see, the word is actually all of God's laws. Now we need to think about that when we read that the word became flesh in John.

Now let us look at what God actually said about the coming of Jesus. Deuteronomy 18:18 says, "I will raise them up a Prophet from among their brethren, like unto thee, <u>and will put my words in his</u>

mouth; and he shall <u>speak unto them all that I shall command him</u>." As you can see here, God is actually saying that he will put his words (his law) in his mouth. I know it does not say law in the verse but if we really think about it, all of God's words are his laws. He created everything by his own laws.

Now let us look at what Jesus himself said he is in John 14:6, "Jesus saith unto him, I am the way, the truth, and the life: no man cometh unto the Father, but by me."

First he said he is the way, so we need to find out what the way is. Let's refer to Joshua 1:8, "This book of the law shall not depart out of thy mouth; but thou shalt meditate therein day and night, that thou <u>mayest observe to do according to all that is written therein: for then thou shalt make thy way prosperous,</u> and then thou shalt have good success." 1 Kings 2:3 says, "And keep the charge of the Lord thy God, <u>to walk in his ways</u>, to keep his statutes, and his commandments, and his judgments, and his testimo- nies, as it is written in the law of Moses, that thou mayest prosper in all that thou doest, and whithersoever thou turnest thyself." Also, in 2 Kings 17:13, "Yet the Lord testified against Israel, and against Judah, by all the prophets, and by all the seers, saying, <u>Turn ye from your evil ways, and keep my commandments and my statutes, according to all the law which I commanded your fathers, and which I sent to you by my servants the prophets</u>." Proverbs 6:23 tells us, "For the commandment is a lamp; and the law is light; and reproofs of instruction are the <u>way of life</u>." Now we can see that doing anything other than what God said is not the way to a prosperous life. We can also see that doing anything other than what God commanded is our evil ways.

Next we notice that Jesus said he is the truth. So what is the truth? Psalm 119:142 explains, "Thy righteousness is an everlasting righteous- ness, <u>and thy law is the truth</u>." Daniel 9:13 says, "As it is written in the law of Moses, all this evil is come upon us: yet made we not our prayer before the Lord our God, <u>that we might turn from our iniquities, and understand thy truth</u>." We can see here that the truth is actually all of God's law, again. Then Jesus said he is the life, so we look in Proverbs 6:23, "For the commandment is a lamp; and the law is light; and reproofs <u>of instruction</u> <u>are the way of life</u>." As we can see here, the law is the light which is the way of life. If we really believe in Jesus, then should we not listen to what he said he is? He did not say that he was the end of the law, but actually said that he is the law in the flesh.

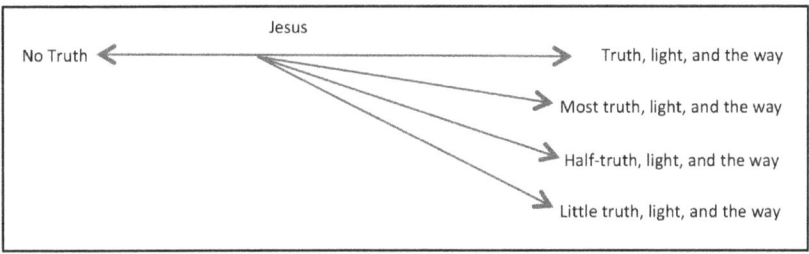

We are to take up our cross daily and follow him, as stated in Luke 9:23, "And he said to them all, If any man will come after me, let him deny him- self, and take up his cross daily, and follow me." How can we follow Jesus if we constantly try to find ways to not obey our Father's law?

As we can see in this illustration if Jesus walks in a straight line and we go any other direction than which he is, we are not following him. How can we say that we believe in Jesus when we refuse to do as he did? If we believe in Jesus, then **we do as he did.**

I heard someone use an analogy once that really caught my attention. I will add some more to it for a deeper understanding of how it relates to what we need to see. If we walk into our house and smell gas, we believe there is a gas leak, right? We then either look for the source or we call the utility company or whoever to fix the problem, right? We act on our belief. Now let us picture ourselves sleeping in our home with a family of four. We wake up in the middle of the night and smell smoke. We first wake up our spouse and make them aware of the situation. Our spouse is going to get out of bed and help look for the source because they believe you. Once you find the source you will act accordingly, either eliminating the source or getting the children up and out of the house.

Now let us just think for a minute and say that your spouse did not believe you when you woke them up. They just laid their head back down and went back to sleep. A few minutes after continuing to try and wake him, or her, the entire house is filling with smoke. Seconds later the entire house is engulfed in flames. This is because your spouse did **not actually believe you.** Now what?

What happens when we do not believe in Jesus? As I showed in the earlier illustration, when we walk any way other than the way Jesus did we are going a different direction. The longer we go in disbelief, the fur- ther away we get from the solution to the problem. Let us say that because of your spouse's disbelief in you smelling the smoke, the house got to be fully engulfed in flames. You woke your spouse up again and now both of you get the children. When you all move toward an exit you can't get there because of the flames being too large. Now all of you are having trouble breathing and within just a few minutes, everyone falls asleep from smoke inhalation. The next morning it is broadcasted on the news that a family of four died in a house fire last night.

This could have been prevented if only the spouse would have truly listened and believed his or her spouse. If the spouse would have believed in their heart, then they could have reacted to the first problem and acted accordingly. But because of his (or her) not listening and not believing, the entire family perished. Just as it is with Jesus, if we would just listen to what he has to say and TRULY believe in him then we can, and will, act accordingly.

I use this example because it shows us how easy it is to get away from what we need to know if we do not listen to God and Jesus. If we let someone else tell us how the fire will develop, we are not putting our trust in God himself. It does not take long for a big problem to evolve if we do not act accordingly and quickly. The longer we stay away from the truth of the bible, the harder it will be to get back to the truth. If only the spouse would have believed more quickly, they would have just had smoke damage. The longer we don't seek out the truth through the bible the longer we will stay confused, which will lead us to our own destruction.

Now let us look at the famous verse that a lot of people are very familiar with. This would be John 3:15, which states, "That whosoever believeth in him should not perish, but have eternal life. 16 <u>For God so loved the</u> <u>world, that he gave his only begotten Son, that whosoever</u> <u>believeth in him</u> <u>should not perish, but have everlasting</u> <u>life</u>. 17 For God sent not his Son into the world to condemn the world; but that the world through him <u>might</u> <u>be saved</u>." Please notice in verse 17 that we are told the world, through him, might be saved. As I have shown you within your own bibles, Jesus is actually the living law in the flesh. After studying this, we can actually read this verse something like this: For God sent not his law into the world to condemn the world; but that the world, through the law, might be saved. Another point that I want to bring up is the Word. We all know that, as stated in John 1, the word became flesh.

> (John 1) 1 In the beginning was the Word, and the Word was with God, and the Word was God. 2 The same was in the beginning with God. 3 All things were made by him; and without him was not anything made that was made. 4 In him was life; and the life was the light of men. 5 And the light shineth in darkness; and the darkness comprehended it not. 6 There was a man sent from God, whose name was John. 7 The same came for a witness, to bear witness of the Light, that all men through him might believe. 8 He was not that Light, but was sent to bear witness of that Light. 9 That was the true Light, which lighteth every man that cometh into the world. 10 He was in the world, and the world was made by him, and the world knew him not. 11 He came unto his own, and his own received him not. 12 But as many as received him, to them gave he power to become the sons of God, even to them that believe on his name: 13 Which were born, not of blood, nor of the will of the flesh, nor of the will of man, but of God. 14 And the Word was

made flesh, and dwelt among us, (and we beheld his glory, the glory as of the only begotten of the Father,) full of grace and truth.

Now I realize a lot of churches use this to show that Jesus is actually God himself, which is totally wrong. We must refer back to the Old Testament again to really get a feeling for what the Word is. I am going to pull up sev- eral different verses that will show a better understanding of what the Word is. Beginning with Deuteronomy 4:2, which says, "Ye shall not add unto the word which I command you, neither shall ye diminish ought from it, that ye may keep the commandments of the Lord your God which I command you." Deuteronomy 9:10 tells us, "And the Lord delivered unto me two tables of stone written with the finger of God; and on them was written according to <u>all the words</u>, which the Lord spake with you in the mount out of the midst of the fire in the day of the assembly." Continuing in Deuteronomy 12:28, <u>*"Observe and hear* all these words which I command thee</u>, that it may go well with thee, and with thy children after thee forever, when thou doest that which is good and right in the sight of the Lord thy God."

Here we are starting to see that all the words from God are good and right. Deuteronomy 17:19 says, "And it shall be with him, and he shall read therein all the days of his life: that he may learn to fear the Lord his God<u>, to</u> <u>keep all the words of this law and these statutes, to do them.</u>" Deuteronomy 28:14 tells us, "<u>And thou shalt not go aside from any of the words which</u> <u>I command thee this day</u>, to the right hand, or to the left, to go after other gods to serve them." Also Deuteronomy 28 below:

> (Deuteronomy 28) 58, "<u>If thou wilt not observe to do all</u> <u>the words of this law that are written in this book</u>, that thou mayest fear this glorious and fearful name, The Lord Thy God; 59 Then the Lord will make thy plagues wonderful, and the plagues of thy seed, even great plagues, and of long continuance, and sore

sicknesses, and of long con- tinuance. 60 Moreover he will bring upon thee all the dis- eases of Egypt, which thou wast afraid of; and they shall cleave unto thee. 61 Also every sickness, and every plague, which is not written in the book of this law, them will the Lord bring upon thee, until thou be destroyed. 62 And ye shall be left few in number, whereas ye were as the stars of heaven for multitude; because thou wouldest not obey the voice of the Lord thy God. 63 And it shall come to pass, that as the Lord rejoiced over you to do you good, and to multiply you; so the Lord will rejoice over you to destroy you, and to bring you to nought; and ye shall be plucked from off the land whither thou goest to possess it. 64 And the Lord shall scatter thee among all people, from the one end of the earth even unto the other; and there thou shalt serve other gods, which neither thou nor thy fathers have known, even wood and stone. 65 And among these nations shalt thou find no ease, neither shall the sole of thy foot have rest: but the Lord shall give thee there a trembling heart, and failing of eyes, and sorrow of mind: 66 And thy life shall hang in doubt before thee; and thou shalt fear day and night, and shalt have none assurance of thy life: 67 In the morning thou shalt say, Would God it were even! and at even thou shalt say, Would God it were morning! for the fear of thine heart wherewith thou shalt fear, and for the sight of thine eyes which thou shalt see

As we can see here, God said there will be many problems for us if we do not obey all of what God has commanded. This is not just the Ten Commandments; it is all of his law, judgments, statutes, and right ways.

Deuteronomy 29:29 states, "The secret things belong unto the Lord our God: but those things which are revealed belong unto us and to our chil- dren forever, that we may do all the words of this law." Deuteronomy 31:12 says, "Gather the people together, men and women, and children, and thy stranger that is within thy gates, that they may hear, and that they may learn, and fear the Lord your God, and observe to do all the words of this law."

This continues in 1 Kings 13:26, "And when the prophet that brought him back from the way heard thereof, he said, It is the man of God, who was disobedient unto the word of the Lord: therefore the Lord hath deliv- ered him unto the lion, which hath torn him, and slain him, according to the word of the Lord, which he spake unto him." Also in 1 Kings 17:24, "And the woman said to Elijah, Now by this I know that thou art a man of God, and that the word of the Lord in thy mouth is truth." Nehemiah 8:9 tells us, "And Nehemiah, which is the Tirshatha, and Ezra the priest the scribe, and the Levites that taught the people, said unto all the people, This day is holy unto the Lord your God; mourn not, nor weep. For all the people wept, when they heard the words of the law." Another example in found in Psalm 18:30, "As for God, his way is perfect: the word of the Lord is tried: he is a buckler to all those that trust in him."

This should speak to all of us when we know God's way is perfect. How can anyone think that doing anything other than what God spoke is right or better than God's ways? Psalm 107:11 says, "Because they rebelled against the words of God, and contemned the counsel of the most High."

What about Proverbs 30:5, which says, "Every word of God is pure: he is a shield unto them that put their trust in him." Once again, here we see that his word is pure. If we do anything other than every word of God, it would now become impure. Isaiah 2:3 tells us, "And many people shall go and say, Come ye, and let us go up to the mountain of the Lord, to the house of the God of Jacob; and he will teach us of his ways, and we will walk in his paths: for out of Zion shall go forth the law, and the word of the Lord from Jerusalem." And Isaiah 40:8, "The grass withereth, the flower fadeth: but the word of our God shall stand forever."

Unless you have a different timeline than God, I think forever means until the end of time. Not the end of this week, month, year, decade, cen- tury, or even this millennium. Forever is forever.

> (Jeremiah 13) 10 This evil people, <u>which refuse to hear my words</u>, which walk in the imagination of their heart, and walk after other gods, to serve them, and to worship them, shall even be as this girdle, <u>which is good for nothing</u>. (Jeremiah 19) 15 Thus saith the Lord of hosts, the God of Israel; Behold, I will bring upon this city and upon all her towns all the evil that I have pronounced against it, because they have hardened their necks<u>, that they might not hear my words</u>. (Jeremiah 23) 36 And the burden of the Lord shall ye mention no more: for every man's word shall be his burden; for ye have perverted the words of the living God, of the Lord of hosts our God.

Here we see that, at the least, it will be a burden if we choose to change the words of God. Matthew 4:4 says, "But he answered and said, It is written, Man shall not live by bread alone, but by every word that proceedeth out of the mouth of God." We see here that every word that proceeds out of God's mouth is what will give us eternal life.

> (Mark 7) 13 Making the word of God of none effect through your tradition, which ye have delivered: and many such like things do ye.

> (Luke 11) 28 But he said, Yea rather, blessed are they that hear the word of God, and keep it.

> (Acts 13:46)<u> Then Paul and Barnabas waxed bold, and said, It was necessary that the word of God should first</u> <u>have been spoken to you: but seeing ye put it from</u>

you, and judge yourselves unworthy of everlasting life, lo, we turn to the Gentiles.

(Ephesians 6) 17 And take the helmet of salvation, and the sword of the Spirit, which is the word of God:

(1 Thessalonians 2) 13 **For this cause also thank we God without ceasing, because, when ye received the word of God which ye heard of us, ye received it not as the word of men, but as it is in truth, the word of God,** which effectually worketh also in you that believe.

(1 Peter 1) 23 Being born again, not of corruptible seed, but of incorruptible, by the word of God, which liveth and abideth forever.

(1 John 2) 5 But whoso keepeth his word, in him verily is the love of God perfected: hereby know we that we are in him.

(1 John 2) 14 I have written unto you, fathers, because ye have known him that is from the beginning. I have written unto you, young men, because ye are strong, and the word of God abideth in you, and ye have overcome the wicked one.

As we can see, the word of God should always abide within us. This is not just part, or some of his word, but every word. His word is what allows us to overcome the wickedness of this world.

Everybody seems to think that Jesus came here just so our sins would be forgiven, but we need to look into this a little deeper. Let us look at John 1

(John 1) 1 In the beginning was the Word, and the Word was with God, and the Word was God. 2 The same was in the beginning with God. 3 All things were made by him; and without him was not any thing made that was made. 4 In him was life; and the life was the light of men. 5 And the light shineth in darkness; and the darkness comprehended it not. 6 There was a man sent from God, whose name was John. 7 The same came for a witness, to bear witness of the Light, that all men through him might believe. 8 He was not that Light, but was sent to bear witness of that Light. 9 That was the true Light, which lighteth every man that cometh into the world. 10 He was in the world, and the world was made by him, and the world knew him not. 11 He came unto his own, and his own received him not. 12 But as many as received him, to them gave he power to become the sons of God, even to them that believe on his name: 13 Which were born, not of blood, nor of the will of the flesh, nor of the will of man, but of God. 14 And the Word was made flesh, and dwelt among us, (and we beheld his glory, the glory as of the only begotten of the Father,) full of grace and truth.

As I have mentioned before, we all know that the word became flesh, which is showing us that the word became Jesus. No brainer, right? Well, have any of us even given consideration to the following verses? Jeremiah 23:29 says, "Is not my word like as a fire? saith the Lord; and like a hammer that breaketh the rock in pieces? Hebrews 4:12 tells us, "For the word of God is quick, and powerful, and sharper than any two-edged sword, piercing even to the dividing asunder of soul and spirit, and of the joints and marrow, and is a discerner of the thoughts and intents of the heart." And Revelation 1:16, "And he had in his right hand seven stars: and out of his mouth went a sharp two-edged sword: and his countenance was as the sun shineth in his strength."

As we can see, when we take the time to actually find out what God, and Jesus, have been saying to us all along, Jesus brings all of

God's word into the world, but in the flesh. This two-edged sword, that is Jesus, is going to pierce us. It is going to make us do things differently than most everyone else. It is going to hurt. We will always be chasing ourselves in our own minds wondering what God really wants from us. Once the word enters into our minds, we will constantly be chasing negative thoughts out of our minds. These negative thoughts are anything that goes against God's word.

Now let us look at what Jesus said in John 12:

> (John 12) 44 Jesus cried and said, He that believeth on me, believeth not on me, but on him that sent me. 45 And he that seeth me seeth him that sent me. 46 I am come a light into the world, that whosoever believeth on me should not abide in darkness. 47 And if any man hear my words, and believe not, I judge him not: for I came not to judge the world, but to save the world. 48 He that rejecteth me, and receiveth not my words, hath one that judgeth him: the word that I have spoken, the same shall judge him in the last day. 49 For I have not spoken of myself; but the Father which sent me, he gave me a commandment, what I should say, and what I should speak. 50 And I know that his commandment is life everlasting: whatsoever I speak therefore, even as the Father said unto me, so I speak.

Jesus clearly said here that everything that he spoke came from the Father. He only spoke what his Father had said to him. He, at no time, changed any of God's laws nor did away with any of them. He was, and is, God's living word: God's commandments, judgments, statutes, and way of living. If we think any way of living, other than the way God instructed us, is better than God's way, then we need to be asking ourselves where our trust is.

To bring this into a better perspective, we need to hear what Jesus himself said about it. In Matthew 7:21-23, he says, "21 Not every one that saith unto me, Lord, Lord, shall enter into the kingdom of heaven; but he that doeth the will of my Father which is in heaven. 22 Many will say to me in that day, Lord, Lord, have we not prophesied in thy name? and in thy name have cast out devils? and in thy name done many wonderful works? 23 And then will I profess unto them, I never knew you: depart from me, ye that work iniquity."

For those that think that Jesus fulfilled the law when he died on the cross, those that actually think we need not worry about following the law anymore, what is Jesus talking about when he tells the workers of iniq- uity to depart from him? Let us look at what iniquity means in Greek on e-sword. G458 ἀνομία anomia an-om-ee'-ah From G459; illegality, that is, violation of law or (generally) wickedness: - iniquity, X transgress (-ion of) the law, unrighteousness.

If we look at the English Standard Version (ESV) Bible, we see it put into plain simple words. 21 "Not everyone who says to me, 'Lord, Lord,' will enter the kingdom of heaven, but the one who does the will of my Father who is in heaven. 22 On that day many will say to me, 'Lord, Lord, did we not prophesy in your name, and cast out demons in your name, and do many mighty works in your name?' 23 And then will I declare to them, 'I never knew you; depart from me, you workers of lawlessness.'"

As we see here, Jesus is telling the workers of lawlessness to depart from him. Now why in the world would he tell the people that do not follow the law to depart from him, if the law had been put to an end? We need to pay attention to what God and His Son, Jesus, said and not anyone else.

In Mark 7:6, "He answered and said unto them, Well hath Esaias proph- esied of you hypocrites, as it is written, This people honoureth me with their lips, but their heart is far from me."

Do we really think that making our own rules and saying God's laws have changed or been abolished, is honoring Jesus or God's laws with our hearts? NO, we are honoring something other than Jesus or God's laws, which is putting our trust in something other than God.

When Jesus said he will send many away, he did not mean anything other than many. When I hear this it tends to disappoint me, because all I ever hear is pastors teaching something other than what God spoke. Are we honoring God with our lips, or our hearts? Our lips will say we will obey everything of God, but our hearts don't want to obey every word of God. Yes, if we truly want to obey the Father then that means no cutting corners, nor thinking the laws have changed, but actually taking the time to find out what God spoke and LISTEN TO EVERY WORD AND DO EVERY WORD. **NOTHING MORE AND NOTHING LESS.**

One more word on the matter of Jesus being the Word, which is actually all of God's law: John 12:48 states, "He that rejecteth me, and receiveth not my words, hath one that judgeth him: the word that I have spoken, the same shall judge him in the last day." If Jesus' words are going to be what judges us on the last day, and I have shown that the words that come from Jesus are actually the words that come from God, don't you think that maybe we should obey the very thing that is going to judge us? There will be more information about who Jesus really is later.

The Old Covenant Verses the New Covenant

I realize that there are a lot of people out here that say we are under the new covenant. As we look through the entire bible we will not find any passage that says that we are presently under a new covenant. I know a lot of us just look at the basic rules of the old and new covenants and just listen to what others say, instead of listening to our Father. So, at this time, we need to look a little deeper into the matter. This is a topic that is greatly misunderstood. Before we look into the old covenant, we need to pay attention to something else. There is a lot of hype out here in the world that believe God divorced Israel. But if we listen to everything that our Father is saying, we will notice that the divorce did **NOT BECOME FINAL.**

> 8 And I saw, when for all the causes whereby backsliding Israel committed adultery I had put her away, <u>and given her a bill of divorce</u>; yet her treacherous sister Judah feared not, but went and played the harlot also. 9 And it came to pass through the lightness of her whoredom, that she defiled the land, and committed adultery with stones and with stocks. 10 And yet for all this her treacherous sister Judah hath not turned unto me with her <u>whole heart</u>, but feignedly, saith the Lord. 11 And the Lord said unto me, The backsliding Israel hath justified herself more than treacherous Judah. 12 Go and proclaim these words toward the north, and say, **Return, thou backsliding Israel**, saith the Lord; and I will not

> cause mine anger to fall upon you: for I am merciful, saith the Lord, and I will not keep anger for ever. 13 Only acknowledge thine iniquity, that thou hast transgressed against the Lord thy God, and hast scattered thy ways to the strangers under every green tree, and ye have not obeyed my voice, saith the Lord. 14 Turn, O backsliding children, saith the Lord; **for I am married unto you:** and I will take you one of a city, and two of a family, and I will bring you to Zion.

Now when we look at this we have to wonder how can God divorce Israel, yet say He is married unto Israel a few verses later? It is because He has not divorced us yet. If a married couple have problems and one decides to give his/her spouse a bill of divorcement (file for divorce), does that mean the divorce is final? Of course not! They can always make up and throw the divorce paper away, just like our Father is doing with us. He filed for divorce with us but also told us that if we return to Him, acknowledge our iniquity and start obeying His voice, He will still be our husband. He is telling us that this is exactly what is going on when we look at Jeremiah 3:

> (Jeremiah 3) 20, "Surely as a wife treacherously departeth from her husband, so have ye dealt treacherously with me, O house of Israel, saith the Lord." Then, again, in the very next two verses, He tells us that when we finally give up and realize we can't do it our own way, and turn back to Him, that He will heal our backslidings. 21 "A voice was heard upon the high places, weeping and supplications of the children of Israel: for they have perverted their way, and they have forgotten the Lord their God. 22 Return, ye backsliding children, and I will heal your backslidings. Behold, we come unto thee; for thou art the Lord our God."

So let us look at the old covenant that was given to Moses in Exodus.

> (Exodus 20) And God spake all these words, saying, 2 I am the Lord thy God, which have brought thee out of the land of Egypt, out of the house of bondage. 3 Thou shalt have no other gods before me. 4 Thou shalt not make unto thee any graven image, or any likeness of any thing that is in heaven above, or that is in the earth beneath, or that is in the water under the earth. 5 Thou shalt not bow down thyself to them, nor serve them: for I the Lord thy God am a jealous God, visiting the iniquity of the fathers upon the children unto the third and fourth generation of them that hate me; 6 And shewing mercy unto thousands of them that love me, and keep my commandments. 7 Thou shalt not take the name of the Lord thy God in vain; for the Lord will not hold him guiltless that taketh his name in vain. 8 Remember the sabbath day, to keep it holy. 9 Six days shalt thou labour, and do all thy work: 10 But the seventh day is the sabbath of the Lord thy God: in it thou shalt not do any work, thou, nor thy son, nor thy daughter, thy manservant, nor thy maidservant, nor thy cattle, nor thy stranger that is within thy gates: 11 For in six days the Lord made heaven and earth, the sea, and all that in them is, and rested the seventh day: wherefore the Lord blessed the sabbath day, and hallowed it. 12 Honour thy father and thy mother: that thy days may be long upon the land which the Lord thy God giveth thee. 13 Thou shalt not kill. 14 Thou shalt not commit adultery. 15 Thou shalt not steal. 16 Thou shalt not bear false witness against thy neighbor. 17 Thou shalt not covet thy neighbour's house, thou shalt not covet thy neighbour's wife, nor his manservant, nor his maidservant, nor his ox, nor his ass, nor any thing

that is thy neighbour's. 18 And all the people saw the thun- derings, and the lightnings, and the noise of the trumpet, and the mountain smoking: and when the people saw it, they removed, and stood afar off. 19 And they said unto Moses, Speak thou with us, and we will hear: but let not God speak with us, lest we die. 20 And Moses said unto the people, Fear not: for God is come to prove you, and that his fear may be before your faces, that ye sin not. 21 And the people stood afar off, and Moses drew near unto the thick darkness where God was. 22 And the Lord said unto Moses, Thus thou shalt say unto the children of Israel, Ye have seen that I have talked with you from heaven. 23 Ye shall not make with me gods of silver, neither shall ye make unto you gods of gold. 24 An altar of earth thou shalt make unto me, and shalt sacrifice thereon thy burnt offerings, and thy peace offerings, thy sheep, and thine oxen: in all places where I record my name I will come unto thee, and I will bless thee. 25 And if thou wilt make me an altar of stone, thou shalt not build it of hewn stone: for if thou lift up thy tool upon it, thou hast polluted it. 26 Neither shalt thou go up by steps unto mine altar, that thy nakedness be not discovered thereon.

(Exodus 21) Now these are the judgments which thou shalt set before them. 2 If thou buy an Hebrew servant, six years he shall serve: and in the seventh he shall go out free for nothing. 3 If he came in by himself, he shall go out by him- self: if he were married, then his wife shall go out with him. 4 If his master have given him a wife, and she have born him sons or daughters; the wife and her children shall be her master's, and he shall go out by himself. 5 And if the servant shall plainly say, I love my master, my wife, and my children; I will not go out free: 6 Then his master shall bring him unto the judges; he shall also bring him to the door, or unto the door post; and his master shall bore his ear through with an aul; and he shall serve him for ever. 7 And if a man sell his daughter to be a maidservant, she shall not go out as the menservants do. 8 If she please not her master, who hath betrothed her to himself, then shall he let her be redeemed: to sell her unto a strange nation he shall have no power, seeing he hath dealt deceitfully with her. 9 And if he have betrothed her unto his son, he shall deal with her after the manner of daughters. 10 If he take him another wife; her food, her raiment, and her duty of marriage, shall he not diminish. 11 And if he do not these three unto her, then shall she go out free without money. 12 He that smiteth a man, so that he die, shall be surely put to death. 13 And if a man lie not in wait, but God deliver him into his hand; then I will appoint thee a place whither he shall flee. 14 But if a man come presumptuously upon his neighbour, to slay him with guile; thou shalt take him from mine altar, that he may die. 15 And he that smiteth his father, or his mother, shall be surely put to death. 16 And he that stealeth a man, and selleth him, or if he be found in his hand, he shall surely be put to death. 17 And he that curseth his father, or his mother, shall surely be put to death. 18 And if men strive together, and one smite another with a stone, or with his fist, and he die not, but keepeth his bed: 19 If he rise again, and walk abroad upon his staff, then shall he that smote him be quit: only he shall pay for the loss of his time, and shall cause him to be thoroughly healed. 20 And if a man smite his servant, or his maid, with a rod, and he die under his hand; he shall be surely punished. 21 Notwithstanding, if he continue a day or two, he shall not be punished: for he is his money. 22 If men strive, and hurt a woman with child, so that her fruit depart from her, and yet no mischief follow: he shall be surely punished, according as the woman's husband will lay upon him; and he shall pay as the judges determine. 23 And if any mischief follow, then thou shalt give life for life, 24 Eye for eye, tooth for tooth, hand for hand, foot for foot, 25 Burning for burning, wound for wound, stripe for stripe. 26 And if a man smite the eye of his servant, or the eye of his maid, that it perish; he shall let him go free for his eye's sake. 27 And if he smite out his manservant's tooth, or his maidservant's tooth; he shall let him go free for his tooth's sake. 28 If an ox gore a man or a woman, that they die: then the ox shall be surely stoned, and his flesh shall not be eaten; but the owner of the ox shall be quit. 29 But if the ox were wont to push with his horn in time past, and it hath been testified to his owner, and he hath not kept him in, but that he hath killed a man or a woman; the ox shall be stoned, and his owner also shall be put to death. 30 If there be laid on him a sum of money, then he shall give for the ransom of his life whatsoever is laid upon him. 31 Whether he have gored a son, or have gored a daughter, according to this judgment shall it be done unto him. 32 If the ox shall push a manservant or a maidservant; he shall give unto their master thirty shekels of silver, and the ox shall be stoned. 33 And if a man shall open a pit, or if a man shall dig a pit, and not cover it, and an ox or an ass fall therein; 34 The owner of the pit shall make it good, and give money unto the owner of them; and the dead beast shall be his. 35 And if one man's ox hurt another's, that he die; then they shall sell the live ox, and divide the money of it; and the dead ox also they shall divide. 36 Or if it be known that the ox hath used to push in time past, and his owner hath not kept him in; he shall surely pay ox for ox; and the dead shall be his own.

(Exodus 22) If a man shall steal an ox, or a sheep, and kill it, or sell it; he shall restore five oxen for an ox, and four sheep for a sheep. 2 If a thief be found breaking up, and be smitten that he die, there shall no blood be shed for him. 3 If the sun be risen upon him, there shall be blood shed for him; for he should make full restitution; if he have nothing, then he shall be sold for his theft. 4 If the theft be certainly found in his hand alive, whether it be ox, or ass, or sheep; he shall restore double. 5 If a man shall cause a field or vineyard to be eaten, and shall put in his beast, and shall feed in another man's field; of the best of his own field, and of the best of his own vineyard, shall he make restitution. 6 If fire break out, and catch in thorns, so that the stacks of corn, or the standing corn, or the field, be consumed therewith; he that kindled the fire shall surely make restitution. 7 If a man shall deliver unto his neighbour money or stuff to keep, and it be stolen out of the man's house; if the thief be found, let him pay double. 8 If the thief be not found, then the master of the house shall be brought unto the judges, to see whether he have put his hand unto his neighbour's goods. 9 For all manner of trespass, whether it be for ox, for ass, for sheep, for raiment, or for any manner of lost thing which another challengeth to be his, the cause of both parties shall come before the judges; and whom the judges shall condemn, he shall pay double unto his neigh- bour. 10 If a man deliver unto his neighbour an ass, or an ox, or a sheep, or any beast, to keep; and it die, or be hurt, or driven away, no man seeing it: 11 Then shall an oath of the Lord be between them both, that he hath not put his hand unto his neighbour's goods; and the owner of it shall accept thereof, and he shall not make it good. 12 And if it be stolen from him, he shall make restitution unto the owner thereof. 13 If it be torn in pieces, then let him bring it for witness, and he shall not make good that which was torn. 14 And if a man borrow ought of his neighbour, and it be hurt, or die, the owner thereof being not with it, he shall surely make it good. 15 But if the owner thereof be with it, he shall not make it good: if it be an hired thing, it came for his hire. 16 And if a man entice a maid that is not betrothed, and lie with her, he shall surely endow her to be his wife. 17 If her father utterly refuse to give her unto him, he shall pay money according to the dowry of virgins. 18 Thou shalt not suffer a witch to live. 19 Whosoever lieth with a beast shall surely be put to death. 20 He that sacri- ficeth unto any god, save unto the Lord only, he shall be utterly destroyed. 21 Thou shalt neither vex a stranger, nor oppress him: for ye were strangers in the land of Egypt. 22 Ye shall not afflict any widow, or fatherless child. 23 If thou afflict them in any wise, and they cry at all unto me, I will surely hear their cry; 24 And my wrath shall wax hot, and I will kill you with the sword; and your wives shall be widows, and your children fatherless. 25 If thou lend money to any of my people that is poor by thee, thou shalt not be to him as an usurer, neither shalt thou lay upon him usury. 26 If thou at all take thy neighbour's raiment to pledge, thou shalt deliver it unto him by that the sun goeth down: 27 For that is his covering only, it is his raiment for his skin: wherein shall he sleep? and it shall come to pass, when he crieth unto me, that I will hear; for I am gracious.

28 Thou shalt not revile the gods, nor curse the ruler of thy people. 29 Thou shalt not delay to offer the first of thy ripe fruits, and of thy liquors: the firstborn of thy sons shalt thou give unto me. 30 Likewise shalt thou do with thine oxen, and with thy sheep: seven days it shall be with his dam; on the eighth day thou shalt give it me. 31 And ye shall be holy men unto me: neither shall ye eat any flesh that is torn of beasts in the field; ye shall cast it to the dogs.

(Exodus 23) Thou shalt not raise a false report: put not thine hand with the wicked to be an unrighteous witness. 2 Thou shalt not follow a multitude to do evil; neither shalt thou speak in a cause to decline after many to wrest judgment: 3 Neither shalt thou countenance a poor man in his cause. 4 If thou meet thine enemy's ox or his ass going astray, thou shalt surely bring it back to him again. 5 If thou see the ass of him that hateth thee lying under his burden, and wouldest forbear to help him, thou shalt surely help with him. 6 Thou shalt not wrest the judg- ment of thy poor in his cause. 7 Keep thee far from a false matter; and the innocent and righteous slay thou not: for I will not justify the wicked. 8 And thou shalt take no gift: for the gift blindeth the wise, and perverteth the words of the righteous. 9 Also thou shalt not oppress a stranger: for ye know the heart of a stranger, seeing ye were strangers in the land of Egypt. 10 And six years thou shalt sow thy land, and shalt gather in the fruits thereof: 11 But the sev- enth year thou shalt let it rest and lie still; that the poor of thy people may eat: and what they leave the beasts of the field shall eat. In like manner thou shalt deal with thy vine- yard, and with thy oliveyard. 12 Six days thou shalt do thy work, and on the seventh day thou shalt rest: that thine ox and thine ass may rest, and the son of thy handmaid, and the stranger, may be refreshed. 13 And in all things that I have said unto you be circumspect: and make no men- tion of the name of other gods, neither let it be heard out of thy mouth. 14 Three times thou shalt keep a feast unto me in the year. 15 Thou shalt keep the feast of unleav- ened bread: (thou shalt eat unleavened bread seven days, as I commanded thee, in the time appointed of the month Abib; for in it thou camest out from Egypt: and none shall appear before me empty:) 16 And the feast of harvest, the firstfruits of thy labours, which thou hast sown in the field: and the feast of ingathering, which is in the end of the year, when thou hast gathered in thy labours out of the field. 17 Three times in the year all thy males shall appear before the Lord God. 18 Thou shalt not offer the blood of my sacrifice with leavened bread; neither shall the fat of my sacrifice remain until the morning. 19 The first of the firstfruits of thy land thou shalt bring into the house of the Lord thy God. Thou shalt not seethe a kid in his mother's milk. 20 Behold, I send an Angel before thee, to keep thee in the way, and to bring thee into the place which I have prepared. 21 Beware of him, and obey his voice, provoke him not; for he will not pardon your transgressions: for my name is in him. 22 But if thou shalt indeed obey his voice, and do all that I speak; then I will be an enemy unto thine enemies, and an adversary unto thine adversaries. 23 For mine Angel shall go before thee, and bring thee in unto the Amorites, and the Hittites, and the Perizzites, and the Canaanites, the Hivites, and the Jebusites: and I will cut them off. 24 Thou shalt not bow down to their gods, nor serve them, nor do after their works: but thou shalt utterly overthrow them, and quite break down their images. 25 And ye shall serve the Lord your God, and he shall bless thy bread, and thy water; and I will take sickness away from the midst of thee. 26 There shall nothing cast their young, nor be barren, in thy land: the number of thy days I will fulfil. 27 I will send my fear before thee, and will destroy all the people to whom thou shalt come, and I will make all thine enemies turn their backs unto thee. 28 And I will send hornets before thee, which shall drive out the Hivite, the Canaanite, and the Hittite, from before thee. 29 I will not drive them out from before thee in one year; lest the land become desolate, and the beast of the field mul- tiply against thee. 30 By little and little I will drive them out from before thee, until thou be increased, and inherit the land. 31 And I will set thy bounds from the Red sea even unto the sea of the Philistines, and from the desert unto the river: for I will deliver the inhabitants of the land into your hand; and thou shalt drive them out before thee. 32 Thou shalt make no covenant with them, nor with their gods. 33 They shall not dwell in thy land, lest they make thee sin against me: for if thou serve their gods, it will surely be a snare unto thee.

These are not all of the laws covered in the Covenant. There are many more covered in Leviticus and Deuteronomy, and other places in the Old Testament. I think we all are very well aware of that. Now we know God promises to make a New Covenant with His people and we find this in Jeremiah.

> (Jeremiah31) 31 Behold, the days come, saith the Lord, that I will make a new covenant with the house of Israel, and with the house of Judah: 32 Not according to the cov- enant that I made with their fathers in the day that I took them by the hand to bring them

out of the land of Egypt; which my covenant they brake, although I was an husband unto them, saith the Lord: 33 But this shall be the covenant that I will make with the house of Israel; After those days, saith the Lord, I will put my law in their inward parts, and write it in their hearts; and will be their God, and they shall be my people. 34 And they shall teach no more every man his neighbour, and every man his brother, saying, Know the Lord: for they shall all know me, from the least of them unto the greatest of them, saith the Lord: for I will forgive their iniquity, and I will remember their sin no more.

Now let us think for a minute how much better things would be if only we would listen to our Father. There would be no stealing, fraud, false witnessing, adultery, killing, and confusion on the Sabbath. I know a lot are thinking that these are the Ten Commandments and, yes, they are; but all the laws are also commandments. We can hear this when we look at Leviticus:

(Leviticus 22) And the Lord spake unto Moses, saying, 2 Speak unto Aaron and to his sons, that they separate them- selves from the holy things of the children of Israel, and that they profane not my holy name in those things which they hallow unto me: I am the Lord. 3 Say unto them, Whosoever he be of all your seed among your generations, that goeth unto the holy things, which the children of Israel hallow unto the Lord, having his uncleanness upon him, that soul shall be cut off from my presence: I am the Lord. 4 What man soever of the seed of Aaron is a leper, or hath a running issue; he shall not eat of the holy things, until he be clean. And whoso toucheth any thing that is unclean by the dead, or a man whose seed goeth from him; 5 Or who- soever toucheth any creeping thing, whereby he may be made unclean, or a man of whom he may take uncleanness, whatsoever uncleanness he hath; 6 The soul which hath touched any such shall be unclean until even, and shall not eat of the holy things, unless he wash his flesh with water. 7 And when the sun is down, he shall be clean, and shall afterward eat of the holy things; because it is his food. 8 That which dieth of itself, or is torn with beasts, he shall not eat to defile himself therewith; I am the Lord. 9 They shall therefore keep mine ordinance, lest they bear sin for it, and die therefore, if they profane it: I the Lord do sanc- tify them. 10 There shall no stranger eat of the holy thing: a sojourner of the priest, or an hired servant, shall not eat of the holy thing. 11 But if the priest buy any soul with his money, he shall eat of it, and he that is born in his house: they shall eat of his meat. 12 If the priest's daughter also be married unto a stranger, she may not eat of an offering of the holy things. 13 But if the priest's daughter be a widow, or divorced, and have no child, and is returned unto her father's house, as in her youth, she shall eat of her father's meat: but there shall be no stranger eat thereof. 14 And if a man eat of the holy thing unwittingly, then he shall put the fifth part thereof unto it, and shall give it unto the priest with the holy thing. 15 And they shall not profane the holy things of the children of Israel, which they offer unto the Lord; 16 Or suffer them to bear the iniquity of trespass, when they eat their holy things: for I the Lord do sanctify them. 17 And the Lord spake unto Moses, saying, 18 Speak unto Aaron, and to his sons, and unto all the children of Israel, and say unto them, Whatsoever he be of the house of Israel, or of the strangers in Israel, that will offer his oblation for all his vows, and for all his freewill offerings, which they will offer unto the Lord for a burnt offering; 19 Ye shall offer at your own will a male without blemish, of the beeves, of the sheep, or of the goats. 20 But whatsoever hath a blemish, that shall ye not offer: for it shall not be acceptable for you. 21 And whosoever offereth a sacrifice of peace offerings unto the Lord to accomplish his vow, or a freewill offering in beeves or sheep, it shall be perfect to be accepted; there shall be no blemish therein. 22 Blind, or broken, or maimed, or having a wen, or scurvy, or scabbed, ye shall not offer these unto the Lord, nor make an offering by fire of them upon the altar unto the Lord. 23 Either a bullock or a lamb that hath any thing superfluous or lacking in his parts, that mayest thou offer for a freewill offering; but for a vow it shall not be accepted. 24 Ye shall not offer unto the Lord that which is bruised, or crushed, or broken, or cut; neither shall ye make any offering thereof in your land. 25 Neither from a stranger's hand shall ye offer the bread of your God of any of these; because their corruption is in them, and blemishes be in them: they shall not be accepted for you.

26 And the Lord spake unto Moses, saying, 27 When a bullock, or a sheep, or a goat, is brought forth, then it shall be seven days under the dam; and from the eighth day and thenceforth it shall be accepted for an offering made by fire unto the Lord. 28 And whether it be cow, or ewe, ye shall not kill it and her young both in one day. 29 And when ye will offer a sacrifice of thanksgiving unto the Lord, offer it at your own will. 30 On the same day it shall be eaten up; ye shall leave none of it until the morrow: I am the Lord. 31 **Therefore shall ye keep my command- ments, and do them: I am the Lord.** 32 Neither shall ye profane

my holy name; but I will be hallowed among the children of Israel: I am the Lord which hallow you, 33 That brought you out of the land of Egypt, to be your God: I am the Lord.

Now we know that this is not all of the laws, but we can know, just by this one chapter, that everything that our Father has said is a commandment, not just the Ten Commandments. Now let us also realize how things would be different if we would just listen to our Father when he is instructing us of what to eat and drink.

> (Leviticus 11) And the Lord spake unto Moses and to Aaron, saying unto them, 2 Speak unto the children of Israel, saying, These are the beasts which ye shall eat among all the beasts that are on the earth. 3 Whatsoever parteth the hoof, and is clovenfooted, and cheweth the cud, among the beasts, that shall ye eat. 4 Nevertheless these shall ye not eat of them that chew the cud, or of them that divide the hoof: as the camel, because he cheweth the cud, but divideth not the hoof; he is unclean unto you. 5 And the coney, because he cheweth the cud, but divideth not the hoof; he is unclean unto you. 6 And the hare, because he cheweth the cud, but divideth not the hoof; he is unclean unto you. 7 And the swine, though he divide the hoof, and be clovenfooted, yet he cheweth not the cud; he is unclean to you. 8 Of their flesh shall ye not eat, and their carcase shall ye not touch; they are unclean to you. 9 These shall ye eat of all that are in the waters: whatsoever hath fins and scales in the waters, in the seas, and in the rivers, them shall ye eat. 10 And all that have not fins and scales in the seas, and in the rivers, of all that move in the waters, and of any living thing which is in the waters, they shall be an abomination unto you: 11 They shall be even

an abomi- nation unto you; ye shall not eat of their flesh, but ye shall have their carcases in abomination. 12 Whatsoever hath no fins nor scales in the waters, that shall be an abomina- tion unto you. 13 And these are they which ye shall have in abomination among the fowls; they shall not be eaten, they are an abomination: the eagle, and the ossifrage, and the ospray, 14 And the vulture, and the kite after his kind; 15 Every raven after his kind; 16 And the owl, and the night hawk, and the cuckow, and the hawk after his kind, 17 And the little owl, and the cormorant, and the great owl, 18 And the swan, and the pelican, and the gier eagle, 19 And the stork, the heron after her kind, and the lap- wing, and the bat. 20 All fowls that creep, going upon all four, shall be an abomination unto you. 21 Yet these may ye eat of every flying creeping thing that goeth upon all four, which have legs above their feet, to leap withal upon the earth; 22 Even these of them ye may eat; the locust after his kind, and the bald locust after his kind, and the beetle after his kind, and the grasshopper after his kind. 23 But all other flying creeping things, which have four feet, shall be an abomination unto you. 24 And for these ye shall be unclean: whosoever toucheth the carcase of them shall be unclean until the even. 25 And whosoever beareth ought of the carcase of them shall wash his clothes, and be unclean until the even. 26 The carcases of every beast which divideth the hoof, and is not clovenfooted, nor cheweth the cud, are unclean unto you: every one that toucheth them shall be unclean. 27 And whatsoever goeth upon his paws, among all manner of beasts that go on all four, those are unclean unto you: whoso toucheth their car- case shall be unclean until the even. 28 And he that beareth the carcase of them shall wash his clothes, and be unclean until the even: they are unclean unto you. 29 These also shall be unclean unto you among the creeping things that creep upon the earth; the weasel, and the mouse, and the tortoise after his kind, 30 And the ferret, and the chame- leon, and the lizard, and the snail, and the mole. 31 These are unclean to you among all that creep: whosoever doth touch them, when they be dead, shall be unclean until the even. 32 And upon whatsoever any of them, when they are dead, doth fall, it shall be unclean; whether it be any vessel of wood, or raiment, or skin, or sack, whatsoever vessel it be, wherein any work is done, it must be put into water, and it shall be unclean until the even; so it shall be cleansed. 33 And every earthen vessel, whereinto any of them falleth, whatsoever is in it shall be unclean; and ye shall break it. 34 Of all meat which may be eaten, that on which such water cometh shall be unclean: and all drink that may be drunk in every such vessel shall be unclean. 35 And every thing whereupon any part of their carcase falleth shall be unclean; whether it be oven, or ranges for pots, they shall be broken down: for they are unclean and shall be unclean unto you. 36 Nevertheless a fountain or pit, wherein there is plenty of water, shall be clean: but that which toucheth their carcase shall be unclean. 37 And if any part of their carcase fall upon any sowing seed which is to be sown, it shall be clean. 38 But if any water be put upon the seed, and any part of their carcase fall thereon, it shall be unclean unto you. 39 And if any beast, of which ye may eat, die; he that toucheth the carcase thereof shall be unclean until the even. 40 And he that eateth of the carcase of it shall wash his clothes, and be unclean until the even: he also that beareth the carcase of it shall wash his clothes, and be unclean until the even. 41 And every

> creeping thing that creepeth upon the earth shall be an abomination; it shall not be eaten. 42 Whatsoever goeth upon the belly, and whatsoever goeth upon all four, or whatsoever hath more feet among all creeping things that creep upon the earth, them ye shall not eat; for they are an abomination. 43 Ye shall not make yourselves abomi- nable with any creeping thing that creepeth, neither shall ye make yourselves unclean with them, that ye should be defiled thereby. 44 For I am the Lord your God: ye shall therefore sanctify yourselves, and ye shall be holy; for I am holy: neither shall ye defile yourselves with any manner of creeping thing that creepeth upon the earth. 45 For I am the Lord that bringeth you up out of the land of Egypt, to be your God: ye shall therefore be holy, for I am holy. 46 This is the law of the beasts, and of the fowl, and of every living creature that moveth in the waters, and of every creature that creepeth upon the earth: 47 To make a difference between the unclean and the clean, and between the beast that may be eaten and the beast that may not be eaten.

There would be no obesity, diabetes, heart complications, etc. Now I know we are thinking these health problems just come naturally, but we need to listen to our Father. Because we haven't been listening to our Father, He has promised that these health problems would exist. We are going to look at Deuteronomy 28 to show how our Father has cursed us because of our disobedience. He starts out letting us know of the blessing that He will give us if we listen to Him then goes on to tell us what will happen to us when we don't.

> (Deuteronomy 28) And it shall come to pass, if thou shalt hearken diligently unto the voice of the Lord thy God, to observe and to do all his commandments which I com- mand thee this day, that the Lord thy

God will set thee on high above all nations of the earth: 2 And all these bless- ings shall come on thee, and overtake thee, if thou shalt hearken unto the voice of the Lord thy God. 3 Blessed shalt thou be in the city, and blessed shalt thou be in the field. 4 Blessed shall be the fruit of thy body, and the fruit of thy ground, and the fruit of thy cattle, the increase of thy kine, and the flocks of thy sheep. 5 Blessed shall be thy basket and thy store. 6 Blessed shalt thou be when thou comest in, and blessed shalt thou be when thou goest out. 7 The Lord shall cause thine enemies that rise up against thee to be smitten before thy face: they shall come out against thee one way, and flee before thee seven ways. 8 The Lord shall command the blessing upon thee in thy storehouses, and in all that thou settest thine hand unto; and he shall bless thee in the land which the Lord thy God giveth thee. 9 The Lord shall establish thee an holy people unto himself, as he hath sworn unto thee, if thou shalt keep the commandments of the Lord thy God, and walk in his ways. 10 And all people of the earth shall see that thou art called by the name of the Lord; and they shall be afraid of thee. 11 And the Lord shall make thee plenteous in goods, in the fruit of thy body, and in the fruit of thy cattle, and in the fruit of thy ground, in the land which the Lord sware unto thy fathers to give thee. 12 The Lord shall open unto thee his good treasure, the heaven to give the rain unto thy land in his season, and to bless all the work of thine hand: and thou shalt lend unto many nations, and thou shalt not borrow. 13 And the Lord shall make thee the head, and not the tail; and thou shalt be above only, and thou shalt not be beneath; if that thou hearken unto the commandments of the Lord thy God, which I command thee this day, to observe and to do them:

14 And thou shalt not go aside from any of the words which I command thee this day, to the right hand, or to the left, to go after other gods to serve them. 15 But it shall come to pass, if thou wilt not hearken unto the voice of the Lord thy God, to observe to do all his commandments and his statutes which I command thee this day; that all <u>these curses</u> shall come upon thee, and overtake thee: 16 <u>Cursed shalt thou be in the city, and</u> <u>cursed shalt thou be in the field</u>. 17 Cursed shall be thy basket and thy store. 18 <u>Cursed shall be the fruit of thy body,</u> and the fruit of thy land, the increase of thy kine, and the flocks of thy sheep. 19 Cursed shalt thou be when thou comest in, and cursed shalt thou be when thou goest out. 20 The Lord shall send upon thee cursing, vexation, and rebuke, in all that thou settest thine hand unto for to do, until thou be destroyed, <u>and until thou perish quickly</u>; because of the wickedness of thy doings, whereby thou hast forsaken me. 21 The Lord shall make the pestilence cleave unto thee, until he have consumed thee from off the land, whither thou goest to possess it. 22 The Lord shall smite thee with a consumption, <u>and with a fever, and with an inflammation,</u> and with an extreme burning, and with the sword, and with blasting, and with mildew; and they shall pursue thee until thou perish. 23 And thy heaven that is over thy head shall be brass, and the earth that is under thee shall be iron. 24 The Lord shall make the rain of thy land powder and dust: from heaven shall it come down upon thee, until thou be destroyed. 25 The Lord shall cause thee to be smitten before thine enemies: thou shalt go out one way against them, and flee seven ways before them: and shalt be removed into all the kingdoms of the earth. 26 And thy carcase shall be meat unto all fowls of the

air, and unto the beasts of the earth, and no man shall fray them away. 27 The Lord will smite thee with the botch of Egypt, and with the emerods, and <u>with the scab, and with the itch,</u> whereof thou canst not be healed. 28 The Lord shall smite thee with madness, and blindness<u>, and aston- ishment of heart:</u> 29 And thou shalt grope at noonday, as the blind gropeth in darkness, and thou shalt not prosper in thy ways: and thou shalt be only oppressed and spoiled evermore, and no man shall save thee. 30 Thou shalt betroth a wife, <u>and another man shall lie with her</u>: <u>thou shalt build an house, and thou shalt not dwell therein</u>: thou shalt plant a vineyard, and shalt not gather the grapes thereof. 31 Thine ox shall be slain before thine eyes, and thou shalt not eat thereof: thine ass shall be violently taken away from before thy face, and shall not be restored to thee: thy sheep shall be given unto thine enemies, and thou shalt have none to rescue them. 32 Thy <u>sons and thy</u> <u>daughters shall be given unto another people</u>, and thine eyes shall look, and fail with longing for them all the day long; and there shall be no might in thine hand. 33 The fruit of thy land, and all thy labours, shall a nation which thou knowest not eat up; and thou shalt be only oppressed and crushed alway: 34 So that thou shalt be mad for the sight of thine eyes which thou shalt see. 35 <u>The Lord shall</u> <u>smite thee in the knees, and in the legs, with a sore botch</u> <u>that cannot be healed, from the sole of thy foot unto the</u> <u>top of thy head.</u> 36 The Lord shall bring thee, and thy king which thou shalt set over thee, unto a nation which neither thou nor thy fathers have known; and there shalt thou serve other gods, wood and stone. 37 And thou shalt become an astonishment, a proverb, and a byword, among all nations whither the Lord shall lead thee. 38 <u>Thou</u>

shalt carry much seed out into the field, and shalt gather but little in; for the locust shall consume it. 39 Thou shalt plant vineyards, and dress them, but shalt neither drink of the wine, nor gather the grapes; for the worms shall eat them. 40 Thou shalt have olive trees throughout all thy coasts, but thou shalt not anoint thyself with the oil; for thine olive shall cast his fruit. 41 Thou shalt beget sons and daughters, but thou shalt not enjoy them; for they shall go into captivity. 42 All thy trees and fruit of thy land shall the locust consume. 43 The stranger that is within thee shall get up above thee very high; and thou shalt come down very low. 44 He shall lend to thee, and thou shalt not lend to him: he shall be the head, and thou shalt be the tail. 45 **Moreover all these curses shall come upon thee, and shall pursue thee, and overtake thee, till thou be destroyed; because thou hearkenedst not unto the voice of the Lord thy God, to keep his commandments and his statutes which he commanded thee:** 46 And they shall be upon thee for a sign and for a wonder, and upon thy seed for ever. 47 Because thou servedst not the Lord thy God with joyful- ness, and with gladness of heart, for the abundance of all things; 48 Therefore shalt thou serve thine enemies which the Lord shall send against thee, in hunger, and in thirst, and in nakedness, and in want of all things: and he shall put a yoke of iron upon thy neck, until he have destroyed thee. 49 The Lord shall bring a nation against thee from far, from the end of the earth, as swift as the eagle flieth; a nation whose tongue thou shalt not understand; 50 A nation of fierce countenance, which shall not regard the person of the old, nor shew favour to the young: 51 And he shall eat the fruit of thy cattle, and the fruit of thy land, until thou be destroyed: which also shall not leave thee either corn, wine, or oil, or the increase of thy kine, or flocks of thy sheep, until he have destroyed thee. 52 And he shall besiege thee in all thy gates, until thy high and fenced walls come down, wherein thou trustedst, throughout all thy land: and he shall besiege thee in all thy gates throughout all thy land, which the Lord thy God hath given thee. 53 And thou shalt eat the fruit of thine own body, the flesh of thy sons and of thy daughters, which the Lord thy God hath given thee, in the siege, and in the strait- ness, wherewith thine enemies shall distress thee: 54 So that the man that is tender among you, and very delicate, his eye shall be evil toward his brother, and toward the wife of his bosom, and toward the remnant of his children which he shall leave: 55 So that he will not give to any of them of the flesh of his children whom he shall eat: because he hath nothing left him in the siege, and in the straitness, wherewith thine enemies shall distress thee in all thy gates. 56 The tender and delicate woman among you, which would not adventure to set the sole of her foot upon the ground for delicateness and tenderness, her eye shall be evil toward the husband of her bosom, and toward her son, and toward her daughter, 57 And toward her young one that cometh out from between her feet, and toward her children which she shall bear: for she shall eat them for want of all things secretly in the siege and straitness, wherewith thine enemy shall distress thee in thy gates.58 If thou wilt not observe to do all the words of this law that are written in this book, that thou mayest fear this glorious and fearful name, The Lord Thy God; 59 Then the Lord will make <u>thy plagues wonderful, and the plagues of thy seed, even great plagues, and of long continuance, and sore sicknesses, and of long continuance.</u> 60 <u>Moreover</u>

he will bring upon thee all the diseases of Egypt, which thou wast afraid of; and they shall cleave unto thee. 61 Also every sickness, and every plague, which is not written in the book of this law, them will the Lord bring upon thee, until thou be destroyed. 62 And ye shall be left few in number, whereas ye were as the stars of heaven for multi- tude; **because thou wouldest not obey the voice of the Lord thy God.** 63 And it shall come to pass, that as the Lord rejoiced over you to do you good, and to multiply you; so the Lord will rejoice over you to destroy you, and to bring you to nought; and ye shall be plucked from off the land whither thou goest to possess it. 64 And the Lord shall scatter thee among all people, from the one end of the earth even unto the other; and there thou shalt serve other gods, which neither thou nor thy fathers have known, even wood and stone. 65 And among these nations shalt thou find no ease, neither shall the sole of thy foot have rest: but the Lord shall give thee there a trembling heart, and failing of eyes, and sorrow of mind: 66 And thy life shall hang in doubt before thee; and thou shalt fear day and night, and shalt have none assurance of thy life: 67 In the morning thou shalt say, Would God it were even! and at even thou shalt say, Would God it were morning! for the fear of thine heart wherewith thou shalt fear, and for the sight of thine eyes which thou shalt see. 68 And the Lord shall bring thee into Egypt again with ships, by the way whereof I spake unto thee, Thou shalt see it no more again: and there ye shall be sold unto your enemies for bondmen and bondwomen, and no man shall buy you.

We should notice how our Father is talking about our cursing and vexa- tion in verse 20. We all hear all the cursing going on all day, every day. And how many of us worry about what tomorrow might bring or the next week for that matter? Do we ever feel totally comfortable for a very long time? Then move on to our health problems that we will endure. These health problems are because we choose to eat what we think is better than what He has told us to eat. Because of our thinking that we don't need His guidelines is why we get bloated or overweight, we get sick, we catch a cold, we have diabetes, we have heart problems and the list just goes on forever. We just keep finding different medications and such to make us live longer, as we see it. All we are doing is fighting our Father's curse that He has put on us because of our disobedience. We are going to lose any fight with our Father. Have you ever wondered how could the figures of the Old Testament live for hundreds of years? Well, I have no doubt whatsoever that if we would have listened to our Father from the time of our births, that we too would live that long. They only ate what the Father told them. They did not eat pork. They did not eat lobster. They didn't drink all the beer people consume nowadays. They didn't smoke cigarettes. They did not find ways to make things sweet, like we do, with candy and such. They did not add chemicals to their food. They obeyed all the laws of what we can and cannot eat. Just think of how long our teeth would last if we would only eat what our Father commanded. And what is all the hype about fluoride in our toothpaste? Do you really think we would even need toothpaste if we only ate what our Father has instructed? Think of how many less health problems we would have.

Then He lets us know that we will fight amongst ourselves. He lets us know that we will have adultery within our homes. He lets us know that we will lose our children to other men. Then He even goes on to lets us know that nations will go to war against other nations. Then He will allow plaques to fall upon us. We know of the rate of divorce. We know of the fatherless children because of the divorce rate and fornication. Just think of how actual families would be now. He lets us know that nations will go to war against each other. How many wars have there been? What is going on with ISIS? What is all this tension going on with Russia? He then lets us know of plaques wonderful; no, He is not saying that will be joyful wonderful, rather that they will greatly spread throughout the nations. We have Stone man syndrome, bone diseases, CJD-Human mad cow disease, LNS also known as Nyhams syndrome, HIV/aids, Ebola, etc. There is a list so long of complications that I don't need to list them all, I think we are starting to get the picture. We have all of this because we choose not to listen to our Father. Now imagine for a minute if you will: Health problems would be gone. Anger and rage would completely go away. We wouldn't have all these wars going. We wouldn't have all these non-curable diseases floating around all over the world. We would be living in perfection if we obey everything that our Father has commanded.

Now I am sure there are many that are saying that we can't stone people or destroy them. We can't do most of those laws. We know that if we obey those laws, we will be breaking the laws of today. Yes we would, but we haven't been listening to our Father. We think just because laws are placed in different areas of our bibles that not all of it is part of the covenant. We should listen to what our Father has been telling us. The entire Torah, or First Five Books of the Bible, is the Old Covenant, as we like to call it. And we need to realize that is what our problem is: We don't listen to every word that proceeded out of our Father's mouth.

> (Deuteronomy 17) 14 When thou art come unto the land which the Lord thy God giveth thee, and shalt possess it, and shalt dwell therein, and shalt say, I will set a king over me, like as all the nations that are about me; 15 Thou shalt in any wise set him king over thee, whom the Lord thy God shall choose: one from among thy brethren shalt thou set king over thee: thou mayest not set a stranger over thee, which is not thy brother. 16 But he shall not multiply horses to himself, nor cause the people to return to Egypt, to the end that he should multiply horses: forasmuch as the Lord hath said unto you, Ye shall henceforth return no

> more that way. 17 Neither shall he multiply wives to him- self, that his heart turn not away: neither shall he greatly multiply to himself silver and gold. 18 And it shall be, when he sitteth upon the throne of his kingdom, that he shall write him a copy of this law in a book out of that which is before the priests the Levites: 19 And it shall be with him, and he shall read therein all the days of his life: that he may learn to fear the Lord his God, to keep all the words of this law and these statutes, to do them: 20 That his heart be not lifted up above his brethren, and that he turn not aside from the commandment, to the right hand, or to the left: to the end that he may prolong his days in his kingdom, he, and his children, in the midst of Israel.

We can hear that we are to listen to our governments. To further illustrate this we need to also look into the New Testament so we are clear that this has been instructed for us at all times.

This is where we are to listen to what our Father has spoken through Paul in Romans.

> (Romans 13) Let every soul be subject unto the higher powers. For there is no power but of God: the powers that be are ordained of God. 2 Whosoever therefore resisteth the power, resisteth the ordinance of God: and they that resist shall receive to themselves damnation. 3 For rulers are not a terror to good works, but to the evil. Wilt thou then not be afraid of the power? do that which is good, and thou shalt have praise of the same: 4 For he is the minister of God to thee for good. But if thou do that which is evil, be afraid; for he beareth not the sword in vain: for he is the minister of God, a revenger to execute wrath upon him that doeth evil. 5 Wherefore ye must needs be subject, not only for wrath, but also for conscience

sake. 6 For for this cause pay ye tribute also: for they are God's ministers, attending continually upon this very thing. 7 Render therefore to all their dues: tribute to whom tribute is due; custom to whom custom; fear to whom fear; honour to whom honour. 8 Owe no man any thing, but to love one another: for he that loveth another hath fulfilled the law. 9 For this, Thou shalt not commit adultery, Thou shalt not kill, Thou shalt not steal, Thou shalt not bear false witness, Thou shalt not covet; <u>and if there be any other commandment</u>, it is briefly comprehended in this saying, namely, Thou shalt love thy neighbour as thyself. 10 Love worketh no ill to his neighbour: therefore love is the <u>fulfilling of the law.</u> 11 And that, knowing the time, that now it is high time to awake out of sleep: for now is our salvation nearer than when we believed. 12 The night is far spent, the day is at hand: let us therefore cast off the works of darkness, and let us put on the armour of light. 13 Let us walk honestly, as in the day; not in rioting and drunkenness, not in cham- bering and wantonness, not in strife and envying. 14 But put ye on the Lord Jesus Christ, and make not provision for the flesh, to fulfil the lusts thereof.

Then we go to 1 Peter 2, which says "13 Submit yourselves to every ordi- nance of man for the Lord's sake: whether it be to the king, as supreme; 14 Or unto governors, as unto them that are sent by him for the punish- ment of evildoers, and for the praise of them that do well. 15 For so is the will of God, that with well doing ye may put to silence the ignorance of foolish men."

Now when we listen to what our Father is telling us, we soon realize that we are to obey our governments. We are to obey all city, county, state, and federal laws. Notice how Paul also lists some of the Ten Commandments and then states "and if there be any other commandment". He is letting us know that this, too, is part of the covenant. Remember they only had the Old Testament to go by. This can help us understand why we don't stone people and why we do not marry more than one woman anymore. We are to obey the current laws of our governments or we would **not** be listening to every word that proceeded out of God's mouth. Yes that means all city, county, state, and federal laws. I know a lot of you are thinking that it was never biblical to marry more than one woman. But when we truly listen to what our Father has been telling us all along, we can hear something totally different.

To show you this we need to look back in 1 Samuel.

> (1 Samuel 15) 10 Then came the word of the Lord unto Samuel, saying,11 It repenteth me that I have set up Saul to be king: for he is turned back from following me, and hath not performed my commandments. And it grieved Samuel; and he cried unto the Lord all night.

Now we see that God repenteth that He chose Saul but let us find out what happens when we continue;

> 12 And when Samuel rose early to meet Saul in the morning, it was told Samuel, saying, Saul came to Carmel, and, behold, he set him up a place, and is gone about, and passed on, and gone down to Gilgal.13 And Samuel came to Saul: and Saul said unto him, Blessed be thou of the Lord: I have performed the commandment of the Lord.14 And Samuel said, What meaneth then this bleating of the sheep in mine ears, and the lowing of the oxen which I hear?15 And Saul said, They have brought them from the Amalekites: for the people spared the best of the sheep and of the oxen, to sacrifice unto the Lord thy God; and the rest we have utterly destroyed.16 Then Samuel said unto Saul, Stay, and I will tell thee what

> the Lord hath said to me this night. And he said unto him, Say on.17 And Samuel said, When thou wast little in thine own sight, wast thou not made the head of the tribes of Israel, and the Lord anointed thee king over Israel?18 And the Lord sent thee on a journey, and said, Go and utterly destroy the sinners the Amalekites, and fight against them until they be consumed. 19 **Wherefore then didst thou not obey the voice of the Lord, but didst fly upon the spoil, and didst evil in the sight of the Lord?**20 And Saul said unto Samuel, Yea, I have obeyed the voice of the Lord, and have gone the way which the Lord sent me, and have brought Agag the king of Amalek, and have utterly destroyed the Amalekites.21 But the people took of the spoil, sheep and oxen, the chief of the things which should have been utterly destroyed, to sacrifice unto the Lord thy God in Gilgal.22 And Samuel said, Hath the Lord as great delight in burnt offerings and sacrifices, as in obeying the voice of the Lord? Behold, to obey is better than sacrifice, and to hearken than the fat of rams. 23 For rebellion is as the sin of witchcraft, and stubbornness is as iniquity and idolatry. Because thou hast rejected the word of the Lord, he hath also rejected thee from being king.

Now when we listen here, we can tell that Saul went against what our Father was telling him to do. He therefore broke the commandment of God. Now we to go further in 1 Samuel:

> (1 Samuel 25) 39 And when David heard that Nabal was dead, he said, Blessed be the Lord, that hath pleaded the cause of my reproach from the hand of Nabal, and hath kept his servant from evil: for the Lord hath returned the wickedness of Nabal upon his own head. And David sent and communed with

> Abigail, to take her to him to wife.40 And when the servants of David were come to Abigail to Carmel, they spake unto her, saying, David sent us unto thee, to take thee to him to wife.41 And she arose, and bowed herself on her face to the earth, and said, Behold, let thine handmaid be a servant to wash the feet of the servants of my lord.42 <u>And Abigail hasted, and arose and rode upon an ass, with five damsels of hers that went after her; and she went after the messengers of David, and became his wife.43 David also took Ahinoam of Jezreel</u>; and they were also both of them his wives.44 But Saul had given Michal his daughter, David's wife, to Phalti the son of Laish, which was of Gallim.

Now I know by just looking at the man-made commentary at the bottom of the KJV bible, that the commentators said it was not scriptural for David to marry more than one. But we need to also keep reading what our Father is telling us. Let us go to 1 Samuel 30:8, "And David enquired at the Lord, saying, Shall I pursue after this troop? shall I overtake them? **And he answered him, Pursue: for thou shalt surely overtake them, and without fail recover all.**" Now we can hear that God was still working with David even when he had two wives. But just in case that does not convince us yet, we read on:

> (2 Samuel 5)12 And David perceived that the Lord had established him king over Israel, and that he had exalted his kingdom for his people Israel's sake.13 <u>And David took him more concubines and wives out of Jerusalem, after he was come from Hebron: and there were yet sons and daughters born to David</u>.14 And these be the names of those that were born unto him in Jerusalem; Shammuah, and Shobab, and Nathan, and Solomon,15 Ibhar also, and Elishua, and

Nepheg, and Japhia,16 And Elishama, and Eliada, and Eliphalet.

Now we hear that David took on several wives, yet our Father is not mad at him. We just need the rest of the chapter to see this.

> (2 Samuel 5) 17 But when the Philistines heard that they had anointed David king over Israel, all the Philistines came up to seek David; and David heard of it, and went down to the hold.18 The Philistines also came and spread them- selves in the valley of Rephaim.19 <u>And David enquired of the Lord, saying, Shall I go up to the Philistines? wilt thou deliver them into mine hand?</u> **And the Lord said unto David, Go up: for I will doubtless deliver the Philistines into thine hand.**20 <u>And David came to Baalperazim, and David smote them there, and said, The Lord hath broken forth upon mine enemies before me, as the breach of waters. Therefore he called the name of that place Baalperazim.</u>21 And there they left their images, and David and his men burned them.22 And the Philistines came up yet again, and spread themselves in the valley of Rephaim.23 And when David enquired of the Lord, he said, Thou shalt not go up; but fetch a compass behind them, and come upon them over against the mulberry trees. 24 And let it be, when thou hearest the sound of a going in the tops of the mulberry trees, that then thou shalt bestir thyself: for then shall the Lord go out before thee, to smite the host of the Philistines.25 And David did so, as the Lord had commanded him; and smote the Philistines from Geba until thou come to Gazer.

Okay, we have just read that David took on many wives and yet our Father did not remove him from being king over Israel, as He did with

Saul. This can only mean one thing; this was not against God's laws. Deuteronomy 17:17 says, "Neither shall he multiply wives to himself, that his heart turn not away." They were allowed to have more than one wife as long as they didn't have too many that their hearts would fall away from our Father, as we hear that Solomon did in 1 Kings below:

> (1 Kings 11) But king Solomon loved many strange women, together with the daughter of Pharaoh, women of the Moabites, Ammonites, Edomites, Zidonians, and Hittites: 2 Of the nations concerning which the Lord said unto the children of Israel, Ye shall not go in to them, nei- ther shall they come in unto you: for surely they will turn away your heart after their gods: Solomon clave unto these in love. 3 And he had seven hundred wives, princesses, and three hundred concubines: and his wives turned away his heart. 4 For it came to pass, when Solomon was old, that his wives turned away his heart after other gods: and his heart was not perfect with the Lord his God, as was the heart of David his father.

We think because it is against the law now that it must have been then, also. No, they did not have the laws of governments as we do now. God allowed it back then. He must have or He would have dethroned David the same way He did Saul. Now the government tells us that it is illegal, so we do not marry more than one woman. We today can't imagine how women could even think of sharing a husband with another wife. We need to listen and realize that they didn't have ceremonies for weddings; they did marriages different than we do today. Remember, we are to obey the governments so if we marry more than one woman, we are not obeying every word that proceeds out of God's mouth. We just haven't been listening.

If we would be listening to what our Father has commanded, then none of us would ever leave our driveways with an unsafe vehicle. We would always be checking our mirrors correctly; we would be having both hands on the steering wheel instead of eating, drinking, talking on the phone, and texting. We would be coming to a complete stop at all lights and stop signs. We would be obeying the speed limit. We would be leaving proper following distance. This is just some of the laws that would improve our driving habits. Just think of how smoothly things would go if only we would just start listening to our Father on everything. Just think about it; if we would have listened to our Father we wouldn't have health problems. We would not be fighting amongst each other. Families would stay together. There would be no coveting of everyone else's belongings, which would lead to no theft. There would be no adultery, so most families would stay together. Prisons would be gone. The world would just seem to work in unity. We could call it a perfect world. But we choose to do things our own way instead of our Father's way. He is perfect, which means that all the instructions, laws, statutes, judgments, and ordinances are perfect, as well. We just haven't been listening.

Now after listening to what we have just read, we should start seeing that the new covenant is not yet established. We need to remember that our Father said that he **will** establish a new covenant. He did not say that He did or that He has established a new Covenant. He said He **will** establish a new covenant. We can further understand that we are not there yet because we all are still learning about our Father. Remember He did say that all will know who He is. Let us look at it again in Jeremiah 31:33, "But this shall be the covenant that I **will** make with the house of Israel; <u>After those days</u>, saith the Lord, I will put my law in their inward parts, and write it in their hearts; and will be their God, and they shall be my people.34 **<u>And they shall teach no more every man his neighbour, and every man his brother, saying, Know the Lord: for they shall all know me, from the least of them unto the greatest of them,</u>** saith the Lord: for I will forgive their iniquity, and I will remember their sin no more." Now we can hear our Father letting us know that the New Covenant is not set up yet.

This is a good time to show within the scriptures that we are actually living in Satan's world right now. Why would God set up his

New Covenant in Satan's world? When Jesus sets up God's Kingdom, Satan will be locked up for a thousand years. Revelation 20 shows this, "And I saw an angel come down from heaven, having the key of the bottomless pit and a great chain in his hand. 2 And he laid hold on the dragon, that old serpent, which is the Devil, and Satan, and bound him a thousand years, 3 And cast him into the bottomless pit, and shut him up, and set a seal upon him, that he should deceive the nations no more, till the thousand years should be ful- filled: and after that he must be loosed a little season."

Now that we see that Satan will be locked up for a thousand years when God's kingdom is set up, we can know that Satan has domination over the very world in which we now live. We just need to listen what we are being told.

> (2 Corinthians 4) Therefore seeing we have this ministry, as we have received mercy, we faint not; 2 But have renounced the hidden things of dishonesty, not walking in craftiness, nor handling the word of God deceitfully; but by manifestation of the truth commending ourselves to every man's conscience in the sight of God. 3 But if our gospel be hid, it is hid to them that are lost: <u>4 In whom the god of this world hath blinded the minds of them which believe not, lest the light of the glorious gospel of Christ</u>, who is the image of God, should shine unto them.

Then, if we look in Ephesians, we can see that once we are truly saved we will see the truth of the matter.

> (Ephesians 2) And you hath he quickened, who were dead in trespasses and sins; 2 Wherein in time past ye walked according to the course of this world, **<u>according to the prince of the power of the air</u>, the spirit that now wor- keth in the children of disobedience:** 3 Among whom also we all had our

conversation in times past in the lusts of our flesh, fulfilling the desires of the flesh and of the mind; and were by nature the children of wrath, even as others.

We can hear that once we are truly saved that we will no longer have the spirit of disobedience. As we continue reading this message, I ask that you keep in mind the prince of the power of the air.

Matthew12:25 says, **"And Jesus knew their thoughts,** and said unto them, Every kingdom divided against itself is brought to desolation; and every city or house divided against itself shall not stand: 26 And if Satan cast out Satan, he is divided against himself; how shall then his kingdom stand?"** We have been told (more than just a couple of times) that we are living in Satan's kingdom now, so why do some of us think that God has already established this new covenant? I wanted to put these verses in to show that we are actually living in Satan's kingdom right now and will be living in his kingdom until Jesus returns and our Father locks him up for a thousand years.

Who is Jesus?

Let us first look at John 3:16, "For God so loved the world, that he gave his only begotten Son, that whosoever believeth in him should not perish, but have everlasting life." This verse is very well known but very much misunderstood.

Now I know this will be a very big issue with many, but this is some- thing that is being taught wrong. There are many that will perish for believing in Jesus in the wrong way; or should I say that there are a lot of people that believe Jesus is someone he is not. There are many who think that Jesus is God. There are those who think he is a god. There are those who think he is the second Adam. There are those who think he existed in the Old Testament. There are those who think he is someone else other than the **ONLY BEGOTTEN SON OF THE FATHER.**

I know that very many now are putting up their defenses and saying I already know who Jesus is and why he died on the cross. I ask that you be patient with me and truly try to see the picture our Father is going to paint for us. You will have a much deeper understanding of who Jesus really is and why he had to die on the cross.

Please keep in mind what the Father is saying to us as you read this chapter. Hosea 4:6 tells us, "**My people are destroyed for lack of knowl- edge: because thou hast rejected knowledge, I will also reject thee, that** thou shalt be no priest to me: seeing thou hast forgotten the law of thy God, I will also forget thy children."

First, I want to dive into the topic of people thinking Jesus is God. I want to use Jesus' baptism first to show that there were actually three sep- arate things, or persons, at work here. In Matthew 3:16, "And Jesus, when he was baptized, went up straightway out of the water: and, lo, the heavens were opened unto him, and he saw the Spirit of God descending like a dove, and lighting upon him: 17 And lo a voice from heaven, saying, This is my beloved Son, in whom I am well pleased."

Now, before anyone robs God from having His only begotten Son, we need to pay close attention to this verse. Just after Jesus was baptized, the heavens opened up and God sent His Spirit descending like a dove to fall upon His Son. As this was happening, God Himself declared that this was his beloved Son in whom He was well pleased. This was an actual voice that sounded from the heavens. This was not Jesus thinking out loud and saying weird things about himself. This was his actual Father announcing that this was His Son and that He was proud of him.

Picture this if you will. You have a 15-year-old son and he plays on the school football team. You are attending the championship game at the end of the season. Your son's team has won every game of the season and now is battling for biggest game of the season. Your son is the quarterback, with just a few seconds left on the clock and the score is tied. He throws a great throw to one of his teammates, who has already made it to the end zone. Your son's throw is near perfect and the touchdown is made, as you stand up yelling from the top of your lungs that is my son and I am proud of him. Everyone around you tells you immediately that your son had nothing to do with winning the game and that you shouldn't be proud of that. Imagine the disappointment you will feel. That is what we are doing to God when we do not acknowledge His only begotten Son. I wanted to bring this occurrence in the beginning of this chapter because I need to draw attention to what we are doing by putting Jesus in the place of God, or even placing Jesus on that same plane as God. We are taking God's only begotten Son away from Him. Please keep this in mind as we go through this chapter.

First thing I need to do here is go through most of the verses that people think shows that Jesus is actually God. Let us start with John 1:

(John 1) In the beginning was the Word, and the Word was with God, and the Word was God. 2 The same was in the beginning with God. 3 All things were made by him; and without him was not any thing made that was made. 4 In him was life; and the life was the light of men. 5 And the light shineth in darkness; and the darkness comprehended it not. 6 There was a man sent from God, whose name was John. 7 The same came for a witness, to bear witness of the **Light,** that all men through him might believe. 8 He was not that **Light,** but was sent to bear witness of that **Light.** 9 That was the true **Light,** which lighteth every man that cometh into the world. 10 He was in the world, and the world was made by him, and the world knew him not. 11 He came unto his own, and his own received him not. 12 But as many as received him, to them gave he power to become the sons of God, even to them that believe on his name: 13 Which were born, not of blood, nor of the will of the flesh, nor of the will of man, but of God. 14 And the Word was made flesh, and dwelt among us, (and we beheld his glory, the glory as of the only begotten of the Father,) full of grace and truth.

The first thing we should be listening to is how our Father is drawing our attention to the true light by capitalizing light at the end of the sentence. Now after reading how the word became flesh, let us see what the word is.

> (Deuteronomy 4:2) Ye shall not add unto the <u>word which I command you</u>, neither shall ye diminish ought from it, that ye may keep the commandments of the Lord your God which I command

(Deuteronomy 9:10) And the Lord delivered unto me two tables of stone written with the finger of God; and on them was written according to <u>all the words</u>, which the Lord spake with you in the mount out of the midst of the fire in the day of the assembly

(Deuteronomy 12:28) <u>Observe and hear all these words which I command thee,</u> that it may go well with thee, and with thy children after thee for ever, when thou doest that which is good and right in the sight of the Lord thy God. (Deuteronomy 27:3) <u>And thou shalt write upon them all</u> <u>the words of this law,</u> when thou art passed over, that thou mayest go in unto the land which the Lord thy God giveth thee, a land that floweth with milk and honey; as the Lord God of thy fathers hath promised thee.

(Deuteronomy 28:14) <u>And thou shalt not go aside from any of the words which I command thee this day,</u> to the right hand, or to the left, to go after other gods to serve them. (Deuteronomy 28:58) <u>If thou wilt not observe to do all</u> <u>the words of this law that are written in this book,</u> that thou mayest fear this glorious and fearful name, The Lord Thy God;

(Deuteronomy 29:29) The secret things belong unto the Lord our God: but those things which are revealed belong unto us and to our children for ever, <u>that we may do all</u> <u>the words of this law.</u>

(Deuteronomy 31:12) Gather the people together, men and women, and children, and thy stranger that is within thy gates, that they may hear, and that they may learn, and fear the Lord your God, <u>and observe to do all the words</u> of this law:

> (Joshua 3:9) And Joshua said unto the children of Israel, Come hither, <u>and hear the words of the Lord your God.</u>
>
> (Joshua 24:26) <u>And Joshua wrote these words in the book</u> of the law of God, and took a great stone, and set it up there under an oak, that was by the sanctuary of the Lord.
>
> (Joshua 24:27) And Joshua said unto all the people, Behold, this stone shall be a witness unto us; <u>for it hath heard all</u> the words of the Lord which he spake unto us: it shall be therefore a witness unto you, lest ye deny your God.

I could go on forever, it seems, showing that the word is all that God com- manded, or all of his law. So when we look at John 1:1-14, we can actually see that all of God's laws became flesh.

Okay, now we move on to the next verse that confuses people.

> (John 10) 30 I and my Father are one. 31 Then the Jews took up stones again to stone him. 32 Jesus answer them, Many good works have I shewed you from my Father; for which of those works do ye stone me? 33 The Jews answered him, saying, For a good work we stone thee not; but for blasphemy; and because that thou, being a man, makest thyself God.

If we just look at these few verses without looking at the rest of the chapter it can be hard to separate the truth. So let us listen to the entire chapter so we can understand what we are being told.

> (John 10) Verily, verily, I say unto you, He that entereth not by the door into the sheepfold, but climbeth up some other way, the same is a thief and a robber. 2 But

he that entereth in by the door is the shepherd of the sheep. 3 To him the porter openeth; and the sheep hear his voice: and he calleth his own sheep by name, and leadeth them out. 4 And when he putteth forth his own sheep, he goeth before them, and the sheep follow him: for they know his voice. 5 And a stranger will they not follow, but will flee from him: for they know not the voice of strangers. 6 This par- able spake Jesus unto them: but they understood not what things they were which he spake unto them. 7 Then said Jesus unto them again, Verily, verily, I say unto you, I am the door of the sheep. 8 All that ever came before me are thieves and robbers: but the sheep did not hear them. 9 I am the door: by me if any man enter in, he shall be saved, and shall go in and out, and find pasture. 10 The thief cometh not, but for to steal, and to kill, and to destroy: I am come that they might have life, and that they might have it more abundantly. 11 I am the good shepherd: the good shepherd giveth his life for the sheep. 12 But he that is an hireling, and not the shepherd, whose own the sheep are not, seeth the wolf coming, and leaveth the sheep, and fleeth: and the wolf catcheth them, and scattereth the sheep. 13 The hireling fleeth, because he is an hireling, and careth not for the sheep. 14 I am the good shepherd, and know my sheep, and am known of mine. 15 As the Father knoweth me, even so know I the Father: and I lay down my life for the sheep. 16 And other sheep I have, which are not of this fold: them also I must bring, and they shall hear my voice; and there shall be one fold, and one shepherd. 17 Therefore doth my Father love me, because I lay down my life, that I might take it again. 18 No man taketh it from me, but I lay it down of myself. I have power to lay it down, and I have power to take it again. This commandment have I received of my Father. 19 There was a division therefore again among the Jews for these sayings. 20 And many of them said, He hath a devil, and is mad; why hear ye him? 21 Others said, These are not the words of him that hath a devil. Can a devil open the eyes of the blind? 22 And it was at Jerusalem the feast of the dedication, and it was winter. 23 And Jesus walked in the temple in Solomon's porch. 24 Then came the Jews round about him, and said unto him, How long dost thou make us to doubt? If thou be the Christ, tell us plainly. 25 Jesus answered them, I told you, and ye believed not: the works that I do in my Father's name, they bear witness of me. 26 But ye believe not, because ye are not of my sheep, as I said unto you. 27 My sheep hear my voice, and I know them, and they follow me: 28 And I give unto them eternal life; and they shall never perish, neither shall any man pluck them out of my hand. 29 My Father, which gave them me, is greater than all; and no man is able to pluck them out of my Father's hand. 30 I and my Father are one. 31 Then the Jews took up stones again to stone him. 32 Jesus answered them, Many good works have I shewed you from my Father; for which of those works do ye stone me? 33 The Jews answered him, saying, For a good work we stone thee not; but for blasphemy; and because that thou, being a man, makest thyself God. 34 Jesus answered them, Is it not written in your law, I said, Ye are gods? 35 If he called them gods, unto whom the word of God came, and the scripture cannot be broken; 36 Say ye of him, whom the Father hath sanctified, and sent into the world, Thou blas- phemest; because I said, I am the Son of God? 37 If I do not the works of my Father, believe me not. 38 But if I do, though ye believe not me, believe the works: that ye may know, and believe,

> that the Father is in me, and I in him. 39 Therefore they sought again to take him: but he escaped out of their hand, 40 And went away again beyond Jordan into the place where John at first baptized; and there he abode. 41 And many resorted unto him, and said, John did no miracle: but all things that John spake of this man were true. 42 And many believed on him there.

I will break this chapter down from the beginning. As we learned from John 1, we have seen that all of God's law became flesh. Now we hear Jesus say that he is the door for the sheep. The sheep are not scared of him because he is their shepherd. He is explaining that because he is of the Father, that he follows all of God's laws. The sheep will follow him by obeying God's laws, as well. In verse 8 he is letting us know that all those that come before He actually comes back are not genuine. If he wasn't walking with the desire to be completely obedient, then his disobedience is what would scare the sheep off. Someone trying to get into God's house by being dis- obedient would be that thief he refers to. This disobedience comes from the lack of love for our Father. The sheep would know that the disobedient shepherd would lead them to their death.

In verse 9, when he states 'by me if any man enters', we should be hearing 'by the law' if any man enters. He is also telling us that only those that know who he is, and why he walked the earth, will be the ones to follow him. Those that hear him will not attend these churches that are teaching us **ANYTHING** other than **all** of the truth. We will not follow anyone that teaches that all of God's laws are not the way of life; or we will at least start requesting that the church change directions of their teaching our Father's word. These churches are leading **MANY** to their own destruction. When we listen to the parable as a whole, we can hear that our works are not what is going to get us eternal life. It is our love for our Father which leads to eternal life. We can't just think that if we obey the law or his voice, we will automatically be rewarded with eternal life. That is who the thief is that he is talking about. They are trying to get in without truly listening to our Father and loving Him with all of their heart, soul, and minds.

Next topic in the chapter is when Jesus was talking about laying down his life. He declares that no man can take his life, but he has the power to lay down his life and take it again. He clearly tells us that this power, or commandment, has been received from his Father. He is clearly separating himself from his Father. If we listen to what Jesus is saying, he is clearly saying that he had to follow commandments given by his Father.

Now we need to move down to verses 25-32. Jesus, right away here, tells us that the works that he does are in his Father's name. He is also let- ting us know that there are a lot that won't believe because they are not his sheep or, should we say, his true followers. In verse 29 Jesus is telling us that his Father gives him his sheep (or people that follow him) and no man will pluck them out of His hand. Those that the Father gave Jesus will be explained later in the message.

In verse 30 Jesus clearly states that he and the Father are one. Now we know that Jesus was created by the seed of God and not by the seed of man. We know that Jesus walked and talked all of God's law perfectly. Now we need to remember that a man and wife are to do just that. They are to become one. That does not mean that my wife is to take my first name and become a man, does it? No, of course not, it means that we are two sepa- rate people but we live our lives as one. Everything in my life becomes our life and everything in her life becomes our life. This is what Jesus is saying about his relationship with His Father. They work hand and hand, or in per- fect harmony. Remember that Jesus, being in complete compliance with the Father, thought of himself as an equal to the Father. Philippians 2:5 tells us, "Let this mind be in you, which was also in Christ Jesus: 6 Who, being in the form of God, thought it not robbery to <u>be equal with God</u>."

Remember that Lucifer was cast from heaven because he **thought** he was mightier than God. Jesus feared his Father and knew not to think he was better than God. Are we not saying the same thing the Jews did? Aren't we making Jesus out to be a God? Jesus himself explains in verse 36 that the Father sanctified him. I do have to mention that in verse 36, Jesus himself states that he is the Son of God. To say that he is anything other than the Son of God would make him out to be a liar or, at best, delusional.

Now we need to look at John 8:58. I will also use a few verses around this verse to explain this.

> (John 8) 52 Then said the Jews unto him, Now we know that thou hast a devil. Abraham is dead, and the prophets; and thou sayest, If a man keep my saying, he shall never taste of death. 53 Art thou greater than our father Abraham, which is dead? and the prophets are dead: whom makest thou thyself? 54 Jesus answered, If I honour myself, my honour is nothing: it is my Father that honoureth me; of whom ye say, that he is your God: 55 Yet ye have not known him; but I know him: and if I should say, I know him not, I shall be a liar like unto you: but I know him, and keep his saying. 56 Your father Abraham rejoiced to see my day: and he saw it, and was glad. 57 Then said the Jews unto him, Thou art not yet fifty years old, and hast thou seen Abraham? 58 Jesus said unto them, Verily, verily, I say unto you, Before Abraham was, I am.

Now I understand that this can be very tricky if we don't listen to every- thing our Father is saying. We need to remember that God said that He will rise up a prophet in Deuteronomy 18:15, "The Lord thy God will raise up unto thee a Prophet from the midst of thee, of thy brethren, like unto me; unto him ye shall hearken." We also know that all things the prophets said was inspired by God, as shown in Hebrews 1:1, "God, who at sundry times and in divers manners spake in time past unto the fathers by the prophets."

As we can see in John 8:54 Jesus starts out telling the Jews that he honors his Father and that he seeks not his own glory. He is already trying to explain that he is not God. In verse 55 he tells the Jews that they have not known the Father, but he knows the Father and that he keeps His sayings. Then we move to verse 56 where he mentions that Abraham rejoiced to see his day and that he saw and rejoiced. Now in verse 58 he states "before Abraham was, I am", so we have to go back to before Abraham. I would like to take us back to Genesis.

> (Genesis 13) 14 And the Lord said unto Abraham, after that Lot was separated from him. Lift up now thin eyes, and look from the place where thou art northward, and southward, and eastward, and westward:15 For all The land which thou seest, to thee will I give it, and to thy seed for ever.16 And I will make thy seed as the dust of the earth: so that if a man can number the dust of the earth, then shall thy seed also be numbered.17 Arise, walk through the land in the length of it and in the breadth of it; for I will give it unto thee.18 Then Abram removed his tent, and came and dwelt in the plain of Mamre, which is in Hebron, and built there an altar unto the Lord.

We can see here that Abram was shown what he would be rewarded with. Now we will move to Revelation.

> (Revelation 7) 9 After this I beheld, and, lo, a great multi- tude, which no man could number, of all nations, and kin- dreds, and people, and tongues, stood before the throne, and before the Lamb, clothed with white robes, and palms in their hands; 10 And cried with a loud voice, saying, Salvation to our God which sitteth upon the throne, and unto the Lamb. 11 And all the angels stood round about the throne, and about the elders and the four beasts, and fell before the throne on their faces, and worshipped God, 12

> Saying, Amen: Blessing, and glory, and wisdom, and thanksgiving, and honour, and power, and might, be unto our God for ever and ever. Amen. 13 And one of the elders answered, saying unto me, What are these which are arrayed in white robes? and whence came they? 14 And I said unto him, Sir, thou knowest. And he said to me, These are they which came out of great tribulation, and have washed their robes, and made them white in the blood of the Lamb. 15 Therefore are they before the throne of God, and serve him day and night in his temple: and he that sit- teth on the throne shall dwell among them. 16 They shall hunger no more, neither thirst any more; neither shall the sun light on them, nor any heat. 17 For the Lamb which is in the midst of the throne shall feed them, and shall lead them unto living fountains of waters: and God shall wipe away all tears from their eyes.

We need to look back in verse 56 of John 8, and pay attention to what Jesus actually said. He said your father Abraham rejoiced to see his day and he saw it. This is the vision Abram was shown before God changed his name to Abraham. It is pretty clear here that Abram was shown this great multitude of people from all over, and these people would be of his seed. This mul- titude of people isn't founded yet and will not be until the 1000 year reign with Christ. This is how Jesus is able to declare that he is 'before Abraham, I am'. Abram was shown the day, or the 1000 year reign, of Christ. This is where Abram was shown all the land he would inherit and his seed, which is as great as the number of stars. He was shown this before he became Abraham. Hence, Jesus was saying that I am the King of the Kingdom which is to come and I will be the King in that day, or that 1000 year reign. This is where all of Abram's land and seed will be. Remember, a day with the Lord is like a thousand years as stated in 2Peter 3:8, "But, beloved, be not ignorant of this one thing, that one day is with the Lord as a thousand years, and a thousand years as one day."

Something else we haven't been listening to, that we need to draw attention to, is the difference in the Father saying that He is 'I AM' and Jesus saying 'I am'. In Exodus 3:14, "God said unto Moses, **I AM THAT I AM:** and he said, thus shalt thou say unto the children of Israel, **I AM** hath sent me." Now when we listen to what Jesus is saying in John 8:58, "Jesus said unto them, Verily, verily, I say unto you, Before Abraham **was, I am.**" Can we all see the difference in the capitalization? This just further shows that we have not been listening to what our Father has been trying to tell us all along.

Now let us look in Acts 20:28, "Take heed therefore unto yourselves, and to all the flock, over the which the Holy Ghost hath made you overseers, to feed the church of God, which he hath purchased with his own blood." Now if you have children are they not your own blood? Remember Jesus is the only begotten of the Father, which makes him of God's blood. In a spiritual sense, that is. We all know the Holy Ghost comes from our Father.

So now let us look at John 20:28, "And Thomas answered and said unto him, My Lord and my God." If we read this verse by itself, yes it does sound like Thomas is declaring that Jesus is also God. However, when we read the rest of the verses of the chapter, there is a completely different picture painted for us. So let us do just that.

> (John 20) 28 And Thomas answered and said unto him, My Lord and my God. 29 Jesus saith unto him, Thomas, because thou hast seen me, thou hast believed: blessed are they that have not seen, and yet have believed. 30 And many other signs truly did Jesus in the presence of his disciples, which are not written in this book: 31 But these are written, that ye might believe that <u>Jesus is the Christ,</u> <u>**the Son of God;**</u> and that believing ye might have life through his name.

Now, as we have already seen that the word of God became flesh and the word being Jesus, or the law of God, became flesh. We all know that Jesus loves his Father with all of his heart, soul, and mind. He strived to obey EVERYTHING that the father commanded, with honor. This is why the Father gave him the powers of performing miracles through the Holy Spirit. As Jesus said many times, everything he does comes from his Father. This is also why we are being told that we are to believe that Jesus is the Christ and that he is the Son of God. We are specifically being told that we should believe that he is the only begotten Son of God.

Now let us look at Titus 2:13, "Looking for that blessed hope, and the glorious appearing of the great God and our Saviour Jesus Christ." The first thing that sticks out like a sore thumb to me is the separation of God and our Saviour Jesus Christ. Just because the conjunction "and" is used here does not mean that they are the same thing. An example that comes to mind is seeing a balloon that is pink **and** purple. Yes, the same balloon consists of two different colors. But if we see two balloons, one being pink **and** one being purple, it means something completely different than seeing one balloon with two colors. Now that we are starting to picture them being dif- ferent, let us look at the scriptures that tell us that they both will be present in the thousand year reign.

> (Ezekiel 46) Thus saith the Lord God; The gate of the inner court that looketh toward the east shall be shut the six working days; but on the sabbath it shall be opened, and in the day of the new moon it shall be opened.2 And the prince shall enter by the way of the porch of that gate without, and shall stand by the post of the gate, and the priests shall prepare his burnt offering and his peace offer- ings, and he shall worship at the threshold of the gate: then he shall go forth; but the gate shall not be shut until the evening.3 Likewise the people of the land shall worship at the door of this gate before the Lord in the sabbaths and in the new moons.

This is a quick glimpse of the sanctuary that our Father will be residing in during the 1000 year reign, and Christ is the prince that shall enter by the way to the porch of the gate. There will be a lot more on the 1000 year reign with Christ coming later in this message. Now let us look at 2 Peter:

> (2Peter 1) 2 Simon Peter, a servant and an apostle of Jesus Christ, to them that have obtained like precious faith with us through the righteousness of God and our Saviour Jesus Christ: 2 Grace and peace be multiplied unto you through the knowledge of God, and of Jesus our Lord, 3 According as his divine power hath given unto us all things that per- tain unto life and godliness, through the knowledge of him that hath called us to glory and virtue: 4 Whereby are given unto us exceeding great and precious promises: that by these ye might be partakers of the divine nature, having escaped the corruption that is in the world through lust.

Once again we have to note how this is worded, 'through the righteousness of God **and** our Saviour Jesus Christ'. The same wording in verse 2 tells us that Grace and peace will be multiplied through the knowledge of God **and** of Jesus Christ. Once we start looking at Jesus as someone that strived to obey all of God's laws, and that this is why he was given power to perform miracles (because of his desire to be in complete obedience), we start to see that when we strive to follow with obedience, we will be given exceedingly great and precious promises.

Next we need to look at Hebrew 1:8, but to explain this I will show the entire chapter.

> (Hebrews 1) God, who at sundry times and in divers man- ners spake in time past unto the fathers by the prophets, 2 Hath in these last days spoken unto us by his Son, whom he hath appointed heir of all things,

by whom also he made the worlds; 3 Who being the brightness of his glory, and the express image of his person, and upholding all things by the word of his power, when he had by himself purged our sins, sat down on the right hand of the Majesty on high: 4 Being made so much better than the angels, as he hath by inheritance obtained a more excellent name than they. 5 For unto which of the angels said he at any time, Thou art my Son, this day have I begotten thee? And again, I will be to him a Father, and he shall be to me a Son? 6 And again, when he bringeth in the firstbegotten into the world, he saith, And let all the angels of God worship him. 7 And of the angels he saith, Who maketh his angels spirits, and his ministers a flame of fire. 8 But unto the Son he saith, Thy throne, O God, is for ever and ever: a sceptre of righ- teousness is the sceptre of thy kingdom. 9 Thou hast loved righteousness, and hated iniquity; therefore God, even thy God, hath anointed thee with the oil of gladness above thy fellows. 10 And, Thou, Lord, in the beginning hast laid the foundation of the earth; and the heavens are the works of thine hands: 11 They shall perish; but thou remainest; and they all shall wax old as doth a garment; 12 And as a vesture shalt thou fold them up, and they shall be changed: but thou art the same, and thy years shall not fail. 13 But to which of the angels said he at any time, Sit on my right hand, until I make thine enemies thy footstool? 14 Are they not all ministering spirits, sent forth to minister for them who shall be heirs of salvation?

Notice how God has spoken to us in these last days through His Son. We then see in verse 5 that God is separating His begotten from the angels. God is clarifying that the angels of God are to worship His begotten Son. We see that Jesus was made much better than the angels.

In verse 8 we can see that this is being said unto the Son, the throne of God is forever. Okay the law of God is forever, also; so unto the Son (all the law) of God is forever. We see in verse 9 that THOU SON HAS LOVED RIGHTEOUSNESS AND HATED INIQUITY. Because of this we can see that God HATH ANOINTED THEE WITH THE OIL OF GLADNESS ABOVE THY FELLOWS. If we have been listening, we should be hearing that Jesus is a fellow angel.

> (Exodus 23) 20 Behold, I send an Angel before thee, to keep thee in the way, and to bring thee into the place which I have prepared.21 Beware of him, and obey his voice, pro- voke him not; for he will not pardon your transgressions: for my name is in him.22 But if thou shalt indeed obey his voice, and do all that I speak; then I will be an enemy unto thine enemies, and an adversary unto thine adversaries.23 For mine Angel shall go before thee, and bring thee in unto the Amorites, and the Hittites, and the Perizzites, and the Canaanites, the Hivites, and the Jebusites: and I will cut them off.24 Thou shalt not bow down to their gods, nor serve them, nor do after their works: but thou shalt utterly overthrow them, and quite break down their images.

Remember that if we truly follow Jesus we, too, will learn to love righteousness and hate iniquity. Iniquity is being anything that goes against **any and all** of our Father's laws.

All this chapter is doing is showing us that God has placed His Son above all, including the angels. He is doing this because Jesus hated iniquity and loved righteousness. Remember iniquity is anything other than God's laws. From e-sword, Iniquity G458 ἀνομία anomia an-om-ee'-ah From G459; illegality, that is, violation of law or (generally) wickedness: - iniquity, X transgress (-ion of) the law, unrighteousness.

Next we look at 1 John 2:2 but to do this I will show the first seven verses.

> (1 John 2) My little children, these things write I unto you, that ye sin not. And if any man sin, we have an advocate with the Father, Jesus Christ the righteous: 2 And he is the propitiation for our sins: and not for ours only, but also for the sins of the whole world. 3 And hereby we do know that we know him, if we keep his commandments. 4 He that saith, I know him, and keepeth not his commandments, is a liar, and the truth is not in him. 5 But whoso keepeth his word, in him verily is the love of God perfected: hereby know we that we are in him. 6 He that saith he abideth in him ought himself also so to walk, even as he walked. 7 Brethren, I write no new commandment unto you, but an old commandment which ye had from the beginning. The old commandment is the word which ye have heard from the beginning.

We are told in the very beginning of the chapter that we have an advocate with the Father. So we need to look at what the definition of advocate is. To do this we will go to e-sword. Advocate G387 παράκλητος paraklētos par-ak'-lay-tos An intercessor, consoler: - advocate, comforter.

Jesus is the one that will talk to the Father and tell Him if we have tried to be obedient and that it actually came from the heart, or if we just obeyed because we thought that is what we had to do to get into the Father's house. If we have tried to be obedient to the Father out of love for the Father, then Jesus will comfort the Father and advise Him whether or not we will do well in His house. Notice in verse 5, we are being told that whoso keep his word (law) is where the love of God is. In verse 6 we are being advised that if we say that we abide in him, that we should be walking as he did. Then we move to verse 7 and we are clearly being told that this is not a new commandment, but rather a commandment that we had from the beginning. **The commandment is the word, or all the laws, of God.** Remember us learning that all of the law of God became flesh? Notice, too, how this com- mandment is the same one we have heard from the beginning.

Next we will go to 2 Corinthians 5:21 but to do this we will look at a few verses leading up to it.

> (2 Corinthians 5) 18 And all things are of God, who hath reconciled us to himself by Jesus Christ, and hath given to us the ministry of reconciliation; 19 To wit, that God was in Christ, reconciling the world unto himself, not imputing their trespasses unto them; and hath committed unto us the word of reconciliation. 20 Now then we are ambassadors for Christ, as though God did beseech you by us: we pray you in Christ's stead, be ye reconciled to God. 21 For he hath made him to be sin for us, who knew no sin; that we might be made the righteousness of God in him.

We will start out with what we are being told in verse 17. If any man be in Christ, he is a new creature. Remember, if any man claims to be in Christ, he should walk as Christ did. We are told in verse 18 that all things are of God and that He hath reconciled us unto Himself by Jesus Christ (by the law). Now we see in verse 19 that God was in Christ. We know that Christ was God's only begotten. We know that because of Christ's love for the Father he knew no sin; he hated sin or iniquity. We see that Jesus committed unto us the word, or the law, of reconciliation. Paul is praying, in Christ sake, that we be reconciled to God. Remember that Christ walked desiring with all of his heart, in complete obedience, with honor and we need him to be an advocate for us. Christ will only do this if we love the Father with all of our heart, soul, and mind. This is why he prays that we might be made the righteousness of God in Jesus, as stated in verse 21. Now let us look at 1Tim 6:14-16, with surrounding verses.

> (1 Timothy 6)11 But thou, O man of God, flee these things; and follow after righteousness, godliness, faith, love, patience, meekness. 12 Fight the good fight of faith, lay hold on eternal life, whereunto thou art also called, and hast professed a good profession before many witnesses. 13 I give thee charge in the sight of God, who quickeneth all things, and before Christ Jesus, who before Pontius Pilate witnessed a good confession; 14 That thou keep this com- mandment without spot, unrebukable, until the appearing of our Lord Jesus Christ: 15 Which in his times he shall shew, who is the blessed and only Potentate, the King of kings, and Lord of lords; 16 Who only hath immortality, dwelling in the light which no man can approach unto; whom no man hath seen, nor can see: to whom be honour and power everlasting. Amen. 17 Charge them that are rich in this world, that they be not highminded, nor trust in uncertain riches, but in the living God, who giveth us richly all things to enjoy.

Once again we see the conjunction 'and' in verse 13. Not only do we see the conjunction here, we see that they are separated by pointing out that Jesus is the one that witnessed a good confession at the time of Pontius, who authorized his crucifixion. Then we move to verse 14 and see that the confession that Jesus made was for us to keep the commandment that was just quoted in verses 11 and 12. Then we see that verse 15 is stating 'in his times'. This is referring to the time Jesus will be King of all Kings. This is Jesus' time, The 1000 Year Reign. Then in verse 16 we are being told that Jesus is dwelling in the light. Remember when God said no man can see Him? We go back to Exodus 33:20, "And he said, <u>Thou canst not see my face: for there shall no man see me</u>, and live." After Jesus was resurrected, he went to dwell at the right side of the Almighty. See how in verse 16, after Paul is lead to the place, Jesus is dwelling in the light or at the right side of

God? We see that Paul describes the light that Jesus is dwelling in. And to the light is the one that is to be honor and power everlasting. Amen. We need to see here that all honor and power goes to GOD.

Now as I go down the list, I see there is some confusion on John 15:13. Once again, we will use the verses surrounding verse 13 so that we can listen to everything we are being told here.

> (John 15) 9 As the Father hath loved me, so have I loved you: continue ye in my love. 10 If ye keep my command- ments, ye shall abide in my love; even as I have kept my Father's commandments, and abide in his love. 11 These things have I spoken unto you, that my joy might remain in you, and that your joy might be full. 12 This is my commandment, That ye love one another, as I have loved you. 13 Greater love hath no man than this, that a man lay down his life for his friends. 14 Ye are my friends, if ye do whatsoever I command you. 15 Henceforth I call you not servants; for the servant knoweth not what his lord doeth: but I have called you friends; for all things that I have heard of my Father I have made known unto you. 16 Ye have not chosen me, but I have chosen you, and ordained you, that ye should go and bring forth fruit, and that your fruit should remain: that whatsoever ye shall ask of the Father in my name, he may give it you. 17 These things I command you, that ye love one another.

Right away in verse 9 we hear Jesus separating the identity of the Father and himself. In verse 10 he is telling us that we are to obey all his com- mandments as he has obeyed all of his Father's commandments. This is how we abide in Jesus' love; as his obedience to his Father is how he abides in his Father's love. He is letting us know that if we obey everything, this is how we will be full of joy. 1 John 5:1 says, "Whosoever believeth that Jesus is the Christ is born of God: and every one that loveth him that begat loveth him also that is begotten of him. 2 By this we know that we love the children of God, when we love God, and keep his commandments. 3 **For this is the love of God, that we keep his commandments: and his commandments are not grievous.**"

Now when we go to verse 14, we are clearly being told that we are his friends if we **obey** whatsoever he commands us. In verse 15 he is saying that we are not his servants, because those servants knoweth not what he does. Being his friend, he is making us known of the Father. In verse 16 he is letting us know that we have not chosen him but that he has chosen us, those that obey everything because of their love for the Father. He is also telling those that obey to bring forth fruit. That fruit is the people whom we teach that it is actually our love for the Father that is the reason we become obedient to the Father. Not because obedience is what gives us eternal life, but rather obedience because of our love for the Father and EVERYTHING He has done for us, is doing for us, and has promised to do for us.

Now we move down the list to Romans 5:8. This verse does not need many surrounding verses. Romans 5:8 states, "But God commendeth his love toward us, in that, while we were yet sinners, Christ died for us. 9 Much more then, being now justified by his blood, we shall be saved from wrath through him." We are being told in verse 8 that God loves us so much that He sent His only begotten Son to live and die for us while we were still sinners. We need to try and remember that Jesus will only justify us through his blood if we have the same compassion as he did. As I have been trying to illustrate, Jesus walked the law perfectly and we are to follow Him. We are to walk the law as well as we can. When we love the Father with all of our heart, soul, and mind we will naturally be obedient to the Father, as Jesus was. When we do all that the Father commanded because of our love for the Father, then we become sinless in the Father's eyes. Not because we walked perfectly, but because we desired with all of our hearts to be obedient. This is why James tells us that faith without works is dead in James 2:17, "Even so <u>faith, if it hath not works, is dead, being alone</u>." If we truly have faith that the Father's way is what will lead us to eternal life with God, then we will be obedient. Not because we have to, but because we trust the Father and have faith that His ways are the perfect way to that perfect eternal life with Him. This same obedience is what keeps us from the wrath of God.

Next on the list is 1 Timothy 3:16, "And without controversy great is the mystery of godliness: God was manifest in the flesh, justified in the Spirit, seen of angels, preached unto the Gentiles, believed on in the world, received up into glory."

First we need to ask what he means by saying without controversy. We go back to e-sword: G3672 ὁμολογουμένως homologoumenōs hom- ol-og-ow-men'-oce Adverb of present passive participle of G3670; con- fessedly: - without controversy. Now because this definition just mainly tell us what we are looking up we need to look at what it is a participle of. G3670 ὁμολογέω homologeō hom-ol-og-eh'-o From a compound of the base of G3674 and G3056; to assent, that is, covenant, acknowledge: - con- (pro-) fess, <u>confession is made</u>, give thanks, promise.

From here we can see that Paul is making a confession that great is the mystery of godliness. He is confessing that godliness is going to be difficult to figure out.

Now let us see what manifest in the flesh means by using e-sword again. Manifest G5319 φανερόω phaneroō fan-er-o'-o From G5318; to render apparent (literally or figuratively): - appear, manifestly declare, (make) manifest (forth), shew (self). Okay we see this comes from G5318 φανερός phaneros fan-er-os' From G5316; shining, that is, apparent (lit- erally or figuratively); neuter (as adverb) publicly, externally: - abroad, + appear, **known,** manifest, open [+ -ly], outward ([+ -ly]).

After doing the research for the proper definition, we can see that God was made known in the flesh. Jesus walked this earth to do just that; make his Father known and what his Father wanted from all that would listen.

Then we see that God is justified in the Spirit. We need to understand what justified means. G1344 δικαιόω dikaioō dik-ah-yo'-o From G1342; **to render** (that is, show or regard as) **just or innocent**: - free, justify (-ier), be righteous. We see it comes from G1342 δίκαιος dikaios dik'-ah-yos From G1349; **equitable** (in character or act); by implication innocent, holy (absolutely or relatively): - just, meet, right (-eous). Then we see this comes from G1349 δίκη dikē dee'-kay Probably from G1166; right (as self-ev- ident), that is, justice (the principle, a decision, or its execution): - **judg- ment, punish, vengeance.**

Now after seeing all these definitions, we can see that God is justified in the Spirit. It is by God's Holy Spirit which all of the books of the bible have been written. The Spirit is what has inspired the prophets to write everything down as they have done. Acts 3:21 tells us, "Whom the heaven must receive until the times of restitution of all things, which God hath spoken by the mouth of all his holy prophets since the world began." They have let us know what we are to do to gain eternal life. They have let us know that we have a choice. We must do things the way God said they must be done in order for us to enter into heaven. They, at the same time, let us know what will happen if we choose not to live by God's rules. By giving us the knowledge and choice, God is justified. He could have just put us here on earth and said figure it out on you own, but because of His gra- cious love for us He has left us His instructions and has given us a choice of whether we want to love Him and be obedient or not.

Then we are being told that God is also seen of the angels. We all know the angels live in God's house already and are obedient. This is how they stay in His house. If they chose a different way, other than God's, they would be cast out of His house. Isaiah 14:12 says, "How art thou fallen from heaven, O Lucifer, son of the morning! how art thou cut down to the ground, which didst weaken the nations! 13 For **thou hast said in thine heart,** I will ascend into heaven, I will exalt my throne above the stars of God: I will sit also upon the mount of the congregation, in the sides of the north."

Satan **thinks** he can do things better than God. The only way to do this is by **thinking** that his way of running the show is better than God's way. God will **NOT** tolerate this from anyone, not even one of the angels that used to live in God's house. Is this not the same thing we do? If we do any- thing other than what God commanded, then we are being just like Satan. Then we see that God is preached unto the Gentiles. What is preached?

G2784 κηρύσσω kērussō kay-roos'-so Of uncertain affinity; to herald (as a public crier), especially divine truth (the gospel): - preach (-er), **proclaim, publish.** We can see that **all** the things God told the Gentiles is being pro- claimed, or published, within our bibles.

Next we see the phrase believed on in the world. What is Paul saying that believed on is? G4100 πιστεύω pisteuō pist-yoo'-o From G4102; to **have faith** (in, upon, or with respect to, a person or thing), that is, credit; by implication to entrust (especially one's spiritual well being to Christ): - believe (-r), **commit** (to trust), **put in trust with**.

We can see that once Gentiles have faith, that Christ has told us all we need to do to obtain eternal life. They that put their trust in him, and commit themselves to EVERYTHING he has commanded, will be received up into glory.

Next we go to Acts 4:12, "Neither is there salvation in any other: for there is none other name under heaven given among men, whereby we must be saved." We are simply being told, straight up, that Jesus is the only way for us to be saved. As I have been illustrating, Jesus represents all of God's word or law. **THE ONLY WAY WE CAN BE SAVED IS THROUGH ALL OF GOD'S LAW.**

Next we need to look at Matthew 1:23, "Behold, a virgin shall be with child, and shall bring forth a son, and they shall call his name Emmanuel, which being interpreted is, God with us." Now without going to e-sword and breaking the definitions down, I will ask that we all think of the person Jesus is. He represents all of God's laws. He did everything that his Father commanded. He was made perfect through his complete obedience to the Father. God is perfect and we will be made perfect through our obedience to the Father, as well. Now when we truly think about it, we can hear that God sent His Son to represent to us everything that the Father is about and this is why he is called 'God with us'. Something we should also take note of is that Jesus was not perfect while he was a man. Because of his desire to walk all of his Father's law perfectly, he was made perfect, just as we will be if, and only if, we do the same as he did. This will be further illustrated later on.

Next we go to John 5:17, "But Jesus answered them, My Father wor- keth hitherto, and I work. 18 Therefore the Jews sought the more to kill him, because he not only had broken the sabbath, but said also that God was his Father, making himself equal with God." Here we do not need to go into depths of the verses because clearly Jesus is just simply stating that his Father has been working, and that he, too, works. No problem separating the two of them. We can see that the Jews sought to kill him not because he was the Father, but they wanted to kill him because he was an equal to the Father. We know that Jesus obeyed everything that the Father commanded. This is also telling us that Jesus was not actually breaking the Sabbath by God's laws, but rather by man's laws. The Father blesses him because of his obedience. Giving him all authority, all the power, and all the wisdom of God is why he was considered an equal with God. He obtained all of this wisdom because he feared God. Proverbs 9:10 says, "<u>The fear of the</u> <u>Lord is the beginning of wisdom: and the knowledge of the holy is under- standing</u>." We can know that he feared the Father by looking at Hebrews 5:7, "**Who in the days of his flesh, when he had offered up prayers and supplications with strong crying and tears unto him that was able to save him from death, and was heard in that he feared.**"

Next we need to look at John 5:23, "That all men should honour the Son, even as they honour the Father. He that honoureth not the Son hono- ureth not the Father which hath sent him." Now here we are being told that we should be honoring the Son, as well the Father. We are being told that if we do not honor the Son, then we do not honor the Father. If we do not obey everything that Jesus commanded, then obviously we do not obey the Father. Everything that Jesus commanded came from the Father.

Next we need to look at John 8:24, "I said therefore unto you, that ye shall die in your sins: for if ye believe not that I am he, ye shall die in your sins." Now before I show the surrounding verses, that give a very clear understanding of everything he is saying, I want to point out that he is saying 'if ye not believe I am he'. I am he is stating what? Is he saying he is God? No, he is saying he is the only begotten of the Father that represents all of God's laws and that he is the only way to salvation.

Now that I have said that, let us look at the surrounding verses so that you can see that this is not me giving you my opinion.

> (John 8) 18 I am one that bear witness of myself, and the Father that sent me beareth witness of me. 19 Then said they unto him, Where is thy Father? Jesus answered, Ye neither know me, nor my Father: if ye had known me, ye should have known my Father also. 20 These words spake Jesus in the treasury, as he taught in the temple: and no man laid hands on him; for his hour was not yet come. 21 Then said Jesus again unto them, I go my way, and ye shall seek me, and shall die in your sins: whither I go, ye cannot come. 22 Then said the Jews, Will he kill himself? because he saith, Whither I go, ye cannot come. 23 And he said unto them, Ye are from beneath; I am from above: ye are of this world; I am not of this world. 24 I said therefore unto you, that ye shall die in your sins: for if ye believe not that I am he, ye shall die in your sins. 25 Then said they unto him, Who art thou? And Jesus saith unto them, Even the same that I said unto you from the beginning. 26 I have many things to say and to judge of you: but he that sent me is true; and I speak to the world those things which I have heard of him. 27 They understood not that he spake to them of the Father. 28 Then said Jesus unto them, When ye have lifted up the Son of man, then shall ye know that I am he, and that I do nothing of myself; but as my Father hath taught me, I speak these things. 29 And he that sent me is with me: the Father hath not left me alone; for I do always those things

> that please him. 30 As he spake these words, many believed on him. 31 Then said Jesus to those Jews which believed on him, If ye continue in my word, then are ye my disciples indeed; 32 And ye shall know the truth, and the truth shall make you free.

Jesus starts out telling us that he bears witness of himself and that the Father bears witness of him. In verse 19 Jesus is telling us that if we truly knew who he was, and why he was the person he was, then we would know the Father. Remember that Jesus came here to show that we are to walk as he did. He represented all of God's laws as the way to redemption, or our way into the Father's house. When we go down to verse 21, we hear Jesus telling us that he is going his way. He is telling us that if we do not get to know who he really is, we will keep walking in our own ways. We will continue to sin, and that those sinful ways in which we live are what will keep us from eternal life with the Father. In verse 23 he is telling us that the ways of this world are not God's ways, which of course we know that Jesus is in God's house, which is of no sin. Jesus had no desire to do any- thing other than what his Father commanded. (This world doesn't want to obey God at all). This is why Jesus is not of this world. This world that we live in now is Satan's world if we remember from 2Corinthians 4:4, "In whom the god of this world hath blinded the minds of them which believe not, lest the light of the glorious gospel of Christ, who is the image of God, should shine unto them."

Then in verse 24 He is simply saying if we do not believe that he rep- resents all of God's laws, we will not follow his ways. The desire to live any way other than God's ways will prevent us from living in God's house, which also means that we will perish if we do not learn to love our Father with all of our heart, soul, and mind. In verse 26, Jesus is letting us know that he has many things to say and judge. He is saying that he has many things that he could say and judge us for 'but' he does not because he is only speaking and judging from what he has heard from the Father.

In verse 28 we hear Jesus saying that when we realize who Jesus really is and everything that he is about, then we will know that he is the only way to God. We will realize that everything that Jesus is all about comes from the Father. This is how, in verse 29, Jesus can say that the Father is with him at all times. Because of Jesus's obedience to everything that the Father commanded, his Father will never leave him because his true obedience always pleases the Father. Then, when we move to verse 31, we hear Jesus telling us that when we walk as he did then we will be his true disciples.

In verse 32 he is telling us that when we truly follow him and obey everything that the Father commands, we will be free. We will no longer feel like the law is something we have to do, but all that the Father com- manded will be done naturally because of our love and respect for the Father. The way I like to say it is, because of our love for the Father we will respect EVERYTHING that He commands. Once we start to love our Father with all of our heart, soul, and mind, we will stop worrying, hurting, getting angry and so much more. We will be set free of all evil, as stated in John 8:32, "And ye shall know the truth, and the truth shall make you free." Next on the list is John 14:6-7 and 14:9-11. Instead of just showing these verses I will show the surrounding verses again and break them down.

> (John 14) 6 Jesus saith unto him, I am the way, the truth, and the life: no man cometh unto the Father, but by me. 7 If ye had known me, ye should have known my Father also: and from henceforth ye know him, and have seen him. 8 Philip saith unto him, Lord, show us the Father, and it sufficeth us. 9 Jesus saith unto him, Have I been so long time with you, and yet hast thou not known me, Philip? he that hath seen me hath seen the Father; and how sayest thou then, Show us the Father? 10 Believest thou not that I am in the Father, and the Father in me? the words that I speak unto you I speak not of myself: but the Father that dwelleth in me, he doeth the works. 11

> Believe me that I am in the Father, and the Father in me: or else believe me for the very works' sake. 12 Verily, verily, I say unto you, He that believeth on me, the works that I do shall he do also; and greater works than these shall he do; because I go unto my Father. 13 And whatsoever ye shall ask in my name, that will I do, that the Father may be glorified in the Son. 14 If ye shall ask any thing in my name, I will do it. 15 If ye love me, keep my commandments.

Okay we start from verse 6, Jesus is telling us that he is the way, the truth, and the life. So we then look in our bibles to hear what we are being told that the way is. Proverbs 6:23 tells us, "For the commandment is a lamp; and the law is light; and reproofs of instruction are the way of life."

As we can see, the commandment is the lamp and the law is the light that shows us the **way** of life. All of the law and the commandments are the way to eternal life. To further illustrate this, we look in Psalms 119:142, "Thy righteousness is an everlasting righteousness <u>and thy law is the truth</u>." This is why Jesus is telling us that no one can come to the Father but by him. He is saying no one can come to the Father but by the command- ments and **all** of the law. This is why he is telling us in verse 7 that if we know who Jesus is and what Jesus represents, being someone that strives to follow all of the laws of God, then we know the Father as well as we know Jesus. We, too, have seen everything about the Father through seeing His only begotten Son.

In verse 9 Jesus is relating the fact that he does not understand why Philip doesn't yet understand who Jesus is and what Jesus is all about. Jesus is EVERYTHING that the Father is about; and because he is everything that the Father is about is why he tells us in verse 10 that he speaks not of himself but of the Father that dwelleth in him. He is actually giving glory to the Father here at the end of the verse and stating that it is the love for his Father that drives him to do the works that makes him the person he is.

Then, when we look at verses 11 and 12, he is telling us to believe that he is all that the Father is about. He is also letting us know if we believe in who Jesus is, and realize that his obedience to the Father is what he is all about, that we, too, will do the same. We will be obedient to the Father as Jesus was. Then he goes on to tell us that our works will be greater because we no longer have the living example in front of us. Our works will be greater because these works come from true faith. We have the faith that all of God's laws are the way to eternal life with the Father. We trust that all the ways of the Father will lead us to eternal life with the Father.

In verse 13 and 14 he is simply telling us that when we truly believe who Jesus is, and ask for anything in his name, then (and only when we come to truly trust in all of God's ways) we can ask for anything that coex- ists with all desire to obey all of God's ways, then it will be given to us. Then in verse 15, that if we truly love him we will keep his commandments. Yes this does mean all of the city, county, state, federal government laws must we obey as well.

Next we look into Hebrews 2:17-18 but to do this we will look at the surrounding verses again.

> (Hebrews 2) 12 Saying, I will declare thy name unto my brethren, in the midst of the church will I sing praise unto thee. 13 And again, I will put my trust in him. And again, Behold I and the children which God hath given me. 14 Forasmuch then as the children are partakers of flesh and blood, he also himself likewise took part of the same; that through death he might destroy him that had the power of death, that is, the devil; 15 And deliver them who through fear of death were all their lifetime subject to bondage. 16 For verily he took not on him the nature of angels; but he took on him the seed of Abraham. 17 Wherefore in all things it behoved him to be made like unto his brethren, that he might be a merciful and faithful high priest in things pertaining to God, to

> make reconciliation for the sins of the people. 18 For in that he himself hath suffered being tempted, he is able to succour them that are tempted.

Now when we read this as a whole, we can start to hear all of what we are being told. We hear in verse 14 that God took a partaker of the flesh and blood. No, not God Himself; but rather God's only begotten Son, which is a part of God. God's own flesh and blood, as we would say about our children today, went through death that he might destroy the power of death. We escape death by loving our Father with all of our heart, soul, and minds and then becoming obedient to the Father, just as Jesus was. His love and obedience to the Father is how Jesus overcame death. In verse 16 we are being told again that Jesus took on not the form of angels, but man. Remember that God placed Jesus over the angels, and that Jesus is also an angel as we learned earlier. This was done so that man himself could see exactly what will happen to him if we do as Jesus did. We are being told that he (Jesus) will be a high priest for us if we do as Jesus did and that he will be the one that reconciles our sins with the Father. We are being shown that Jesus walked this earth being tempted, as we are; but because of his love for the Father, he overcame that temptation. As we can also do, but this only comes from the love we have for the Father.

Hebrews 4:15-16 is where we need to look next. Hebrews 4:15 says, "For we have not an high priest which cannot be touched with the feeling of our infirmities; but was in all points tempted like as we are, yet without sin. 16 Let us therefore come boldly unto the throne of grace, that we may obtain mercy, and find grace to help in time of need." We are being told that we have a high priest that can feel our infirmities and that he was tempted like a man. So let us look up what infirmities is on e-sword. G769 ἀσθένεια astheneia as-then'-i-ah From G772; **feebleness (of body or mind);** by implication malady; **moral frailty:** - disease, infirmity, sickness, **weakness**.

Now after everything that we have been learning, we should be starting to hear that Jesus can be touched by our weakness. He can be touched by us when we break down mentally, physically and emotionally, and realize that we have been wrong all this time. When we are being told to come unto the throne of grace boldly, this does not mean that we have a free ticket to do whatever we want. This grace comes from us lowering ourselves down and finally doing things the way our Father needs us to do them. If we turn back to our Father's ways he will, at any time, have mercy on us and be gracious enough not to just throw us to the curb. Yes, our Father has that much love for us. He will never keep us from his house, but we have to meet His conditions.

Okay, we need to move to Philippians 2:5-7 with a few verses around them.

> (Philippians 2) 5 Let this mind be in you, which was also in Christ Jesus: 6 Who, being in the form of God, thought it not robbery to be equal with God: 7 But made himself of no reputation, and took upon him the form of a servant, and was made in the likeness of men: 8 And being found in fashion as a man, he humbled himself, and became obe- dient unto death, even the death of the cross. 9 Wherefore God also hath highly exalted him, and given him a name which is above every name.

We note in verse 6 that Christ is in the form of God and not actually God. Remember that he is everything that God is about. We are being told in verse 7 that he made no reputation of the matter. This means he is in no way saying, nor even hinting, that he is God. We are being told that he thought it not robbery to be equal to God. Being equal to God is in complete compli- ance with all of God's ways. Remember that is why Satan was cast out of heaven, because he thought that his ways would be better than God's. Jesus is only being an equal to his Father, not robbing God of any of His glory. Jesus is nothing more than his Father and nothing less; complete obedi- ence. In verse 8 we are being told that he was fashioned as a man and, even though God had placed him above all, that he humbled himself. Humbling himself is lowering himself, knowing that he is NOTHING without the Father, as I have shown in previous verses. Then, in verse 9, we are being told that because of his obedience even unto death, his Father exalted him and gave him a name above all. Now just try to imagine ourselves having to be obedient unto our own deaths just so we could show our fellow brethren how they need to live. I think it is fair to say that none of us have that kind of love within ourselves. Yes we might give our life for our children, but do we think we would be crucified as Jesus was for all mankind? Remember, Jesus is placed above the angels and will be the King of God's Kingdom when he comes back to set up the 1000 year reign with Christ.

We need to move on to 1 Peter 2:24, but I will show the surrounding verses so we can hear what we are being told.

> (1 Peter 2) 21 For even hereunto were ye called: because Christ also suffered for us, leaving us an example, that ye should follow his steps: 22 Who did no sin, neither was guile found in his mouth: 23 Who, when he was reviled, reviled not again; when he suffered, he threatened not; but committed himself to him that judgeth righteously: 24 Who his own self bare our sins in his own body on the tree, that we, being dead to sins, should live unto righteousness: by whose stripes ye were healed. 25 For ye were as sheep going astray; but are now returned unto the Shepherd and Bishop of your souls.

Now when we start with verse 21, we are told exactly what Jesus did for us. He suffered for us, to leave us an example that we are to **follow** in his steps. Remember, he desired to walk in perfect obedience and we are to follow him. Then, notice how in verse 23 Jesus committed himself to the one that judges righteously; that one being his Father. In verse 24 we are being told that Jesus died on the cross for our sins. Not because he sinned, but for the sin of those that understand and follow him. He took on the weight of sin for the souls that understand who he was and what he was all about. He did not take on the weight of sin for all just so they can be in total disre- gard to our Father. He died leaving us an example of what happens to us when we follow him. This is NOT telling us that we can sin all we want; but if we try to walk in complete obedience to the Father, this obedience is because we love the Father and not because this is what must be done to get to the Father. Once we understand this, then he becomes the Shepherd and Bishop of our souls.

Now I want to look at a few times in Revelations that people are hearing the wrong message. I wanted to place Revelation toward the back of this chapter because by now we are starting to understand who Jesus is. First, let us look at Rev 1:1-3, "The Revelation of Jesus Christ, which God gave unto him, to shew unto his servants things which must shortly come to pass; and he sent and signified it by his angel unto his servant John: 2 Who bare record of the word of God, and of the testimony of Jesus Christ, and of all things that he saw. 3 Blessed is he that readeth, and they that hear the words of this prophecy, and keep those things which are written therein: for the time is at hand."

Here we hear that John is being given the Revelation of Jesus Christ by God. John is baring record of the word of God; baring record of all the laws of God, and the testimony of Jesus. Jesus was the living testimony of God by walking in complete obedience, then dying on the cross and being res- urrected to eternal life. We get his testimony by seeing exactly how things will work for us if we do as Jesus did. Then we are being told blessed is he that reads this and understands. Blessed are those that keep the saying of this prophecy. In other words, blessed are those that hear the law and obey the law, because they are the ones that will gain eternal life with the Father. There is another message here, but if we are truly listening to our Father we already know what it is.

Next we move to Revelation 1:5-6. Rev 1:5 says, "And from Jesus Christ, who is the faithful witness, and the first begotten of the dead, and the **prince** of the kings of the earth. Unto him that loved us, and washed us from our sins in his own blood, 6 And hath made us kings and priests unto God and his Father; to him be glory and dominion for ever and ever. Amen."

Okay we have been hearing that Jesus was completely obedient to his Father, which allowed him to be the ultimate faithful witness. By now we should be hearing that Jesus is the way that our sins are washed away and he shows us how that is done. Once that is done, then, and only then, we become priests unto God and his Father. All glory goes to the Father because of what the Father has done, is doing, and will do for us.

Next we go to Revelation 5: 8-9, but to do this I need to show sur- rounding verses.

> (Revelation 5) 7 And he came and took the book out of the right hand of him that sat upon the throne; 8 And when he had taken the book, the four beasts and four and twenty elders fell down before the Lamb, having every one of them harps, and golden vials full of odours, which are the prayers of saints. 9 And they sung a new song, saying, Thou art worthy to take the book, and to open the seals thereof: for thou wast slain, and hast redeemed us to God by thy blood out of every kindred, and tongue, and people, and nation; 10 And hast made us unto our God kings and priests: and we shall reign on the earth.

We can see in verse 7 that John saw Jesus take the book out of the right hand of the one that sat on throne. Remember that Jesus is sitting at the right side of the Almighty.

Now we need to look at Revelation 1:5, "And from Jesus Christ, who is the faithful witness, and the first begotten of the dead, **and the prince of the kings of the earth.** Unto him that loved us, and washed us from our sins in his own blood, 6 **And hath made us kings and priests unto God and his Father**; to him be glory and dominion for ever and ever. Amen." We can see here that this is a prophecy of a future time. This is once the kingdom has been established. This is when Jesus will be the prince of the kings of the earth. And this is the time that certain ones of us will be made into kings and priests unto our Father. We again need to realize that Jesus only washes us from our sins if we are trying to be obedient to the Father because of our love for our Father.

Next we move to Revelation 1:17, "And when I saw him, I fell at his feet as dead. And he laid his right hand upon me, saying unto me, Fear not; I am the first and the last: 18 I am he that liveth, and was dead; and, behold, I am alive for evermore, Amen; and have the keys of hell and of death."

We hear Jesus saying he is the first and the last, right? We know God declares that He is the first and the last in Isaiah 44:6, "Thus saith the Lord the King of Israel, and his redeemer the Lord of hosts; I am the first, and I am the last; and beside me there is no God." At first glance we hear Jesus declaring he is the same as God, which causes people to think that he is God. When we start listening to everything, we can hear something completely different. Let us listen to what Paul is telling us about Jesus in Philippians 2:5, "Let this mind be in you, which was also in Christ Jesus: 6 Who, being in the form of God, thought it not robbery to be equal with God: 7 But made himself of no reputation, and took upon him the form of a servant, and was made in the likeness of men."

We can hear that Jesus thought it not robbery to be equal with God. Jesus thought it not being robbery to be equal with God because Jesus loves his Father and in all ways is completely obedient to the Father. At the same time, we know Jesus acknowledged that the Father is greater than he is. John 14: 28 states, "Ye have heard how I said unto you, I go away, and come again unto you. If ye loved me, ye would rejoice, because I said, I go unto the Father: for my Father is greater than I." When we listen to what we are being told, we hear that Jesus knows that he is in complete compliance with the Father, and nothing he does is anything other than the Father's will, so he can know that it is not robbery of the Father for Jesus to consider himself an equal to Him. He is stating that he is the first and last way to the Father. He is the first one that the Father has ever redeemed and he is stating that he is the last way anyone can be redeemed. Without Jesus there is no way anyone can be redeemed. No man comes unto the Father but by him, as shown in

John 14:6, "Jesus saith unto him, I am the way, the truth, and the life: no man cometh unto the Father, but by me."

Next we want to listen to what the Father has to say in Isaiah 43:10, "Ye are my witnesses, saith the Lord, and my servant whom I have chosen: that ye may know and believe me, and understand that I am he: before me there was no God formed, neither shall there be after me. 11 I, even I, am the Lord; and beside me there is no saviour." Something I need to point out here is that God Himself said that besides him there is no savior. We have just seen that Jesus sits at the right side of the Almighty. This is our Father telling us that Jesus is not a god. Jesus is not the one that saves us. Jesus is the one that leads us to the one that can save us. **ALL GLORY GOES TO THE FATHER**.

When we hear this we should know that there is no other God, other than the Father. Unless we think that the Father does not know what he is talking about, we hear Him say loud and clear **that there is no** God before Him and that there will **never be** a God after Him. **God is the only God.** Remember that Jesus even knew that the Father was the one that could save him. Hebrews 5:7 says, "Who in the days of his flesh, when he had offered up prayers and supplications with strong crying and tears unto him that was able to save him from death, and was heard in that he feared; 8 Though he were a Son, yet learned he obedience by the things which he suffered." We can surly hear that even Jesus, the Son of God, knew that the Father is the only one that could save him, and that he feared the Father. If we think Jesus is God, then how could there be someone else that could save him? Why would he fear that one that could save him?

Now I know that a lot of people think that Jesus is the one that redeems us, but I would like to show to all that Jesus is actually the one that leads us to our redemption and not the one that redeems us. To do this, I want to show Zechariah's prophecy in Luke 1 starting with verse 67.

> (Luke 1) 67 And his father Zechariah was filled with the Holy Ghost, and prophesied, saying, 68 **Blessed**

be the Lord God of Israel; for he hath visited and redeemed his people, 69 And hath raised up an horn of salvation for us in the house of his servant David; 70 As he spake by the mouth of his holy prophets, which have been since the world began: 71 That we should be saved from our ene- mies, and from the hand of all that hate us; 72 To perform the mercy promised to our fathers, and to remember his holy covenant; 73 The oath which he sware to our father Abraham, 74 That he would grant unto us, that we being delivered out of the hand of our enemies might serve him without fear, 75 In holiness and righteousness before him, all the days of our life. 76 And thou, child, shalt be called the **prophet** of the Highest: for thou shalt go before the face of the Lord to prepare his ways; 77 To give knowl- edge of salvation unto his people by the remission of their sins, 78 Through the tender mercy of our God; whereby the dayspring from on high hath visited us, 79 To give light to them that sit in darkness and in the shadow of death, to guide our feet into the way of peace. 80 And the child grew, and waxed strong in spirit, and was in the deserts till the day of his shewing unto Israel.

Now we start out hearing that this is a prophecy, so we know that this is referring to a time that is yet to come. We hear Zechariah blessing the Lord God of Israel. In verse 69 he is blessing the one that raised up a horn of sal- vation for us in the house of his servant David. Now note how he is saying that God raised up a horn. He did not say that God raised up our redemption. We know that Jesus came through the house of David by listening to what he said in Revelation 22:16, "I Jesus have sent mine angel to testify unto you these things in the churches. I am the root and the offspring of David, and the bright and morning star."

Then in verse 70 he is reassuring us that God has spoken to us through the prophets since the world began. In verse 71 he is also letting us know that we shall be saved from our enemies and from the hand of all that hate us through the **horn** which God raised up, that horn being the law in the flesh. Now in verse 72 he is continuing his blessing of the promise to our fathers, that promise of the holy covenant to come. Note the holy covenant is not here yet.

Then in verse 76 he is referring back to Jesus, who is also a prophet. This is noted in Acts 3:21, "Whom the heaven must receive until the times of restitution of all things, which God hath spoken by the mouth of all his holy prophets since the world began. **22 For Moses truly said unto the fathers, A prophet shall the Lord your God raise up unto you of your brethren, like unto me; him shall ye hear in all things whatsoever he shall say unto you. 23 And it shall come to pass, that every soul, which will not hear that prophet, shall be destroyed from among the people.**"

Then in verse 77 we are being told that the prophet will give knowl-edge of salvation; not that that prophet is salvation. In verse 78 we are being reminded that through the tender mercies of God He has raised up this prophet, or God's only begotten Son.

We know that Jesus is the only way one can be redeemed by God, because of his complete love and obedience to the Father. Not one soul, other than Jesus', is redeemed yet and will not be until they learn to love the Father with all of their heart, soul, and mind. There is no other way to redemption but by doing as he does. We see pretty much the same thing being said in Rev 2:8, "And unto the angel of the church in Smyrna write; These things saith the first and the last, which was dead, and is alive."

Then we look at Revelation 19:10 but we will also listen to what verse 9 is saying. Revelation 19:9 says, "And he saith unto me, Write, Blessed are they which are called unto the marriage supper of the Lamb. And he saith unto me, These are the true sayings of God. 10 And I fell at his feet to worship him. And he said unto me, See thou do it not: I am thy fellows- ervant, and of thy brethren that have the testimony of Jesus: worship God: for the testimony of Jesus is the spirit of prophecy."

Okay, we should remember this is an angel that is revealing all of this to John. This is why John is told not to fall to his feet to worship him. The angel is not worthy of worship. The angel is a fellow of the brethren that have received the testimony of Christ. For the testimony of Jesus Christ is what the entire bible is about. It is a book of instructions leading us to the Father's house. God's spirit, if you remember me mentioning earlier, is what inspired all the prophets to write what they have written for us.

Next we need to look at Revelation 22:13-14. Revelation 22:13 tells us, "I am Alpha and Omega, the beginning and the end, the first and the last. 14 Blessed are they that do his commandments, that they may have right to the tree of life, and may enter in through the gates into the city."

We can hear Christ, once again, say that he is the beginning and the end. He is saying that he is the law of God from the beginning of creation to the end. He is the only way to the Father. We, too, can get to our Father by completely loving the Father with all of our heart, soul, and minds which leads to complete obedience. That is exactly what is being said in verse 14. Blessed are those that do his commandments; or actually blessed are those that do all the law of God. Now, also notice how he is saying blessed are they that do the commandments, that they **may** have the right to the tree of life. He is letting us know that if we think all of God's laws are what we have to do, rather than we do the commandments because of our love for the Father, we are not going to have the right to the tree of life.

This is where something else should be brought to our attention. We hear a lot of churches say that once you're saved, you're always saved. First, we need to remember that Lucifer was already with the Father and was cast out of heaven. Then we also hear the Father telling us that even though you might be chosen, you can still fall. This is shown in 1 Samuel 15:10, "Then came the word of the Lord unto Samuel, saying, 11 **It repen- teth me that I have set up Saul to be king: for he is turned back from following me, and hath not performed my commandments.** And it grieved Samuel; and he cried unto the Lord all night." If we read the rest of the chapter, we can hear that our Father dethroned Saul. This is why we are told, once we know the truth, to work out our salvation with fear and trembling. This is told in Philippians 2:12, "Wherefore, my beloved, as ye have always obeyed, not as in my presence only, but now much more in my absence, work out your own salvation with fear and trembling." It is very easy to fall away from our Father's perfection. Just because we have been saved or chosen, we can still fall. After we have been saved, or chosen, by God we can always turn back to the ways of the people instead of the ways of God. We need to hearken to the voice of our Father at all times, and at no time hearken to voice of the people. We need to look at Colossians 1:16 and the surrounding verses.

> (Colossians 1) 3 We give thanks to God and the Father of our Lord Jesus Christ, praying always for you, 4 Since we heard of your faith in Christ Jesus, and of the love which ye have to all the saints, 5 For the hope which is laid up for you in heaven, whereof ye heard before in the word of the truth of the gospel; 6 Which is come unto you, as it is in all the world; and bringeth forth fruit, as it doth also in you, since the day ye heard of it, and knew the grace of God in truth: 7 As ye also learned of Epaphras our dear fellowservant, who is for you a faithful minister of Christ; 8 Who also declared unto us your love in the Spirit.9 For this cause we also, since the day we heard it, do not cease to pray for you, and to desire that ye might be filled with the knowledge of his will in all wisdom and spiri- tual understanding; 10 That ye might walk worthy of the Lord unto all pleasing, being fruitful in every good work, and increasing in the knowledge of God; 11 Strengthened with all might, according to his glorious power, unto all patience and longsuffering with joyfulness; 12 Giving thanks unto the Father, which hath made us meet to be partakers of the inheritance of the saints in light: 13 Who hath delivered us from the power of darkness, and

> hath translated us into the kingdom of his dear Son: 14 In whom we have redemption through his blood, even the forgive- ness of sins: 15 Who is the image of the invisible God, the firstborn of every creature: 16 For by him were all things created, that are in heaven, and that are in earth, visible and invisible, whether they be thrones, or dominions, or principalities, or powers: all things were created by him, and for him: 17 And he is before all things, and by him all things consist. 18 And he is the head of the body, the church: who is the beginning, the firstborn from the dead; that in all things he might have the preeminence. 19 For it pleased the Father that in him should all fulness dwell.

Once we start listening to who Jesus really is, this isn't that hard to under- stand; but it can be very confusing if we still haven't listened to all we are being told. So I will start with verse 3. Right away Paul is letting us know that God and Jesus are not the same character. He does this by saying we give thanks to God and the Father <u>of our Lord</u> **Jesus Christ,** not because Christ is God or the Father.

Notice how in verses 5 and 6 Paul is praying for faith in Christ Jesus and of the love ye have to all the saints. He then states that he is praying for the hope of things which are laid up in heaven that we heard before in the word of the truth of the gospel. Remember how I showed the word is all of God's law? Remember what the truth is? It is explained in Psalms 119:142, "Thy righteousness is an everlasting righteousness and thy law is the truth." Notice how he is also letting us know that the grace of God is in truth or, we can actually say, all of the law of God.

In verse 9, he is praying that ye might be filled with the knowledge of his will; that is God's will, in all wisdom and spiritual understanding. In verse 10 he is letting us know that our knowledge, wisdom, and under- standing will bring in good works. In verse 12 he is praying that the knowl- edge, wisdom, and spiritual understanding gives us a chance to be partakers of the inheritance of the saints in light; in which has delivered us from darkness and has translated us into the kingdom of his dear Son. Notice how he is praying that we will be translated into the kingdom. This is referring, once again, to the 1000 year reign with Christ. Note here that Paul is praying for us to be with the Son, which is the Father's Son.

Then, in verse 15, Paul is stating that the Son is in the image of the invisible God. Once again, he is just an image of God and not God himself. Now in verse 16, when we realize that Christ is all about God's laws, we can see how all things were created by him (by the law of God). To show this, we need to go back to the beginning, in Genesis 2, "Thus the heavens and the earth were finished, and all the host of them. 2 And on the seventh day God ended his work which he had made; and he rested on the seventh day from all his work which he had made. 3 **And God blessed the sev- enth day, and sanctified it: because that in it he had rested from all his work which God created and made.**" Now we can see from the time of creation, all things were created by all of God's laws. This is why Paul is saying all things were made by him and for him. All things being for him are the things to come in his day. John 8:56 tells us, "Your father Abraham rejoiced to see my day: and he saw it, and was glad." We all know Jesus is going to be the King of all Kings in God's kingdom.

Now in verse 17 we see this confirmed. The law is before all things and by the law all things consist. All of God's laws always have been and always will be. This is how God's house is already functioning and we will not be allowed in until we become completely aware that we must do all the laws of God, as he wants them done, so that His house will continue functioning perfectly. We do this by first loving the Father with all of our heart, soul, and mind. In verse 18 we hear Paul saying he is the head of the church, the King of the Kingdom. And then in verse 19 we are being told that it pleased the Father that all fullness dwells in Jesus. That is the full- ness of love for, and obedience to, the Father.

Now I want to take some time and listen to a few times that Jesus him- self acknowledges that nothing he does is of his own will but only done by the Father's will.

> (John 5) 19 Then answered Jesus and said unto them, Verily, verily, I say unto you, The Son can do nothing of himself, but what he seeth the Father do: for what things soever he doeth, these also doeth the Son likewise. 20 For the Father loveth the Son, and sheweth him all things that himself doeth: and he will shew him greater works than these, that ye may marvel. 21 For as the Father raiseth up the dead, and quickeneth them; even so the Son quickeneth whom he will. 22 For the Father judgeth no man, but hath committed all judgment unto the Son:

We can see here that Jesus is separating himself from the Father. He further illustrates this in verse 30 "I can of mine own self do nothing: as I hear, I judge: and my judgment is just; because I seek not mine own will, but the will of the Father which hath sent me."

> (John 14) 9 Jesus saith unto him, Have I been so long time with you, and yet hast thou not known me, Philip? he that hath seen me hath seen the Father; and how sayest thou then, Show us the Father? 10 Believest thou not that I am in the Father, and the Father in me? the words that I speak unto you I speak not of myself: but the Father that dwelleth in me, he doeth the works. 11 Believe me that I am in the Father, and the Father in me: or else believe me for the very works' sake. 12 Verily, verily, I say unto you, He that believeth on me, the works that I do shall he do also; and greater works than these shall he do; because I go unto my Father.

Now I know this is where a lot will say that Jesus is saying he is God, but we need to listen to what he is really saying. He is saying that he is in his Father and his Father is in him. This comes from Jesus being created by the Father. With Jesus being in complete compliance with all that his Father commanded, is how the Father was in him and he was in the Father. Let us think back to the beginning of the world. When God created everything, he created everything within His own laws. He created everything within six days and then rested on the seventh. We know that God Himself would not have broken any of his own laws because we all know that God is perfect. So I am asking that we start thinking of how perfectly His son walked in all of God's laws, as we should be trying with all of our heart to do the same as Jesus did, for he was our example for us. We now jump down to John 14:

> (John 14) 26 But the Comforter, which is the Holy Ghost, whom the Father will send in my name, he shall teach you all things, and bring all things to your remembrance, what- soever I have said unto you. 27 Peace I leave with you, my peace I give unto you: not as the world giveth, give I unto you. Let not your heart be troubled, neither let it be afraid. 28 Ye have heard how I said unto you, I go away, and come again unto you. If ye loved me, ye would rejoice, because I said, I go unto the Father: for my Father is greater than I.

We first hear Jesus telling us that his Father will send the Holy Ghost and then the Holy Ghost will bring all things to our remembrance, all that Jesus has said to us. He is telling us that the Holy Ghost will bring remembrance to our souls. The peace that Jesus has left with us is not the peace of this world. He is letting us know that there is no need to worry about the things which are to come. He is letting us know that if we truly love him, and know who he really is and what he is about, that we should be rejoicing. When we listen to the whole message in this passage, we can hear that no man that claims that he is Jesus is a true prophet; for Jesus said he is going unto the Father and that the Holy Ghost will be amongst us. No man will see Jesus again until he comes back to set up his Father's kingdom.

> (John 6)35 And Jesus said unto them, I am the bread of life: he that cometh to me shall never hunger; and he that believeth on me shall never thirst. 36 But I said unto you, That ye also have seen me, and believe not. 37 All that the Father giveth me shall come to me; and him that cometh to me I will in no wise cast out. 38 For I came down from heaven, not to do mine own will, but the will of him that sent me. 39 And this is the Father's will which hath sent me, that of all which he hath given me I should lose nothing, but should raise it up again at the last day. 40 And this is the will of him that sent me, that every one which seeth the Son, and believeth on him, may have everlasting life: and I will raise him up at the last day.

We can hear Jesus telling us that whoever comes to him will never hunger or thirst. He is saying that all those that truly follow him and love the Father with all of their heart, soul, and minds will always be taken care of. No matter how rocky things might look right now, we will never go hungry or be thirsty. He tells that if we truly come to him, there is no way that he will cast us away. Then he reassures us that he came down from heaven to do his Father's will and not his own. Then, when he talks about all that the Father has given him, he is talking about the children of Israel. Remember when God scattered the Israelites? I am going to include the curse that we are under still, so we can get the whole grasp of why our Father has scattered us.

> (Deuteronomy 28) 15 But it shall come to pass, if thou wilt not hearken unto the voice of the Lord thy God, to observe to do all his commandments and his statutes which I com- mand thee this day; that all these curses shall come upon thee, and overtake thee: 16 Cursed shalt thou be in the city, and cursed shalt thou be in the field. 17 Cursed shall be thy basket and thy store. 18 Cursed shall be the fruit of thy body, and

the fruit of thy land, the increase of thy kine, and the flocks of thy sheep. 19 Cursed shalt thou be when thou comest in, and cursed shalt thou be when thou goest out. 20 The Lord shall send upon thee cursing, vexation, and rebuke, in all that thou settest thine hand unto for to do, until thou be destroyed, and until thou perish quickly; because of the wickedness of thy doings, whereby thou hast forsaken me. 21 The Lord shall make the pestilence cleave unto thee, until he have consumed thee from off the land, whither thou goest to possess it. 22 The Lord shall smite thee with a consumption, and with a fever, and with an inflammation, and with an extreme burning, and with the sword, and with blasting, and with mildew; and they shall pursue thee until thou perish. 23 And thy heaven that is over thy head shall be brass, and the earth that is under thee shall be iron. 24 The Lord shall make the rain of thy land powder and dust: from heaven shall it come down upon thee, until thou be destroyed. 25 The Lord shall cause thee to be smitten before thine enemies: thou shalt go out one way against them, and flee seven ways before them: and shalt be removed into all the kingdoms of the earth. 26 And thy carcase shall be meat unto all fowls of the air, and unto the beasts of the earth, and no man shall fray them away. 27 The Lord will smite thee with the botch of Egypt, and with the emerods, and with the scab, and with the itch, whereof thou canst not be healed. 28 The Lord shall smite thee with madness, and blindness, and aston- ishment of heart: 29 And thou shalt grope at noonday, as the blind gropeth in darkness, and thou shalt not prosper in thy ways: and thou shalt be only oppressed and spoiled evermore, and no man shall save thee. 30 Thou shalt betroth a wife, and another man shall lie with her: thou shalt build an house, and thou shalt not dwell therein: thou shalt plant a vineyard, and shalt not gather the grapes thereof. 31 Thine ox shall be slain before thine eyes, and thou shalt not eat thereof: thine ass shall be violently taken away from before thy face, and shall not be restored to thee: thy sheep shall be given unto thine enemies, and thou shalt have none to rescue them. 32 Thy sons and thy daughters shall be given unto another people, and thine eyes shall look, and fail with longing for them all the day long; and there shall be no might in thine hand. 33 The fruit of thy land, and all thy labours, shall a nation which thou knowest not eat up; and thou shalt be only oppressed and crushed alway: 34 So that thou shalt be mad for the sight of thine eyes which thou shalt see. 35 The Lord shall smite thee in the knees, and in the legs, with a sore botch that cannot be healed, from the sole of thy foot unto the top of thy head. 36 The Lord shall bring thee, and thy king which thou shalt set over thee, unto a nation which neither thou nor thy fathers have known; and there shalt thou serve other gods, wood and stone. 37 And thou shalt become an astonishment, a proverb, and a byword, among all nations whither the Lord shall lead thee. 38 Thou shalt carry much seed out into the field, and shalt gather but little in; for the locust shall consume it. 39 Thou shalt plant vineyards, and dress them, but shalt neither drink of the wine, nor gather the grapes; for the worms shall eat them. 40 Thou shalt have olive trees throughout all thy coasts, but thou shalt not anoint thyself with the oil; for thine olive shall cast his fruit. 41 Thou shalt beget sons and daughters, but thou shalt not enjoy them; for they shall go into captivity. 42 All thy trees and fruit of thy land shall the locust consume. 43 The stranger that is within thee shall get up above thee very high; and thou shalt come down very low. 44 He shall lend to thee, and thou shalt not lend to him: he shall be the head, and thou shalt be the tail. 45 Moreover all these curses shall come upon thee, and shall pursue thee, and overtake thee, till thou be destroyed; because thou hear- kenedst not unto the voice of the Lord thy God, to keep his commandments and his statutes which he commanded thee: 46 And they shall be upon thee for a sign and for a wonder, and upon thy seed for ever. 47 Because thou servedst not the Lord thy God with joyfulness, and with gladness of heart, for the abundance of all things; 48 Therefore shalt thou serve thine enemies which the Lord shall send against thee, in hunger, and in thirst, and in nakedness, and in want of all things: and he shall put a yoke of iron upon thy neck, until he have destroyed thee. 49 The Lord shall bring a nation against thee from far, from the end of the earth, as swift as the eagle flieth; a nation whose tongue thou shalt not understand; 50 A nation of fierce countenance, which shall not regard the person of the old, nor shew favour to the young: 51 And he shall eat the fruit of thy cattle, and the fruit of thy land, until thou be destroyed: which also shall not leave thee either corn, wine, or oil, or the increase of thy kine, or flocks of thy sheep, until he have destroyed thee. 52 And he shall besiege thee in all thy gates, until thy high and fenced walls come down, wherein thou trustedst, throughout all thy land: and he shall besiege thee in all thy gates throughout all thy land, which the Lord thy God hath given thee. 53 And thou shalt eat the fruit of thine own body, the flesh of thy sons and of thy daughters, which the Lord thy God hath given thee, in the siege, and in the strait- ness, wherewith thine enemies shall distress thee: 54 So that the man that is tender among you, and very delicate, his eye shall be evil toward his brother, and toward the wife of his bosom, and toward the remnant of his children which he shall leave: 55 So that he will not give to any of them of the flesh of his children whom he shall eat: because he hath nothing left him in the siege, and in the straitness, wherewith thine enemies shall distress thee in all thy gates. 56 The tender and delicate woman among you, which would not adventure to set the sole of her foot upon the ground for delicateness and tenderness, her eye shall be evil toward the husband of her bosom, and toward her son, and toward her daughter, 57 And toward her young one that cometh out from between her feet, and toward her children which she shall bear: for she shall eat them for want of all things secretly in the siege and straitness, wherewith thine enemy shall distress thee in thy gates. 58 If thou wilt not observe to do all the words of this law that are written in this book, that thou mayest fear this glorious and fearful name, The Lord Thy God; 59 Then the Lord will make thy plagues wonderful, and the plagues of thy seed, even great plagues, and of long continuance, and sore sicknesses, and of long continuance. 60 Moreover he will bring upon thee all the diseases of Egypt, which thou wast afraid of; and they shall cleave unto thee. 61 Also every sickness, and every plague, which is not written in the book of this law, them will the Lord bring upon thee, until thou be destroyed. 62 And ye shall be left few in number, whereas ye were as the stars of heaven for multi- tude; because thou wouldest not obey the voice of the Lord thy God. 63 And it shall come to pass, that as the Lord rejoiced over you to do you good, and to multiply you; so the Lord will rejoice over you to destroy you, and to bring you to nought; and ye shall be plucked from off the land whither thou goest to possess it. 64 **And the Lord shall scatter thee among all people, from the one end of the earth even unto the other; and there thou shalt serve other gods, which neither thou nor thy fathers have known, even wood and stone.** 65 And among these nations shalt thou find no ease, neither shall the sole of thy foot have rest: but the Lord shall give thee there a trem- bling heart, and failing of eyes, and sorrow of mind: 66 And thy life shall hang in doubt before thee; and thou shalt fear day and night, and shalt have none assurance of thy life: 67 In the morning thou shalt say, Would God it were even! and at even thou shalt say, Would God it were morning! for the fear of thine heart wherewith thou shalt fear, and for the sight of thine eyes which thou shalt see. 68 And the Lord shall bring thee into Egypt again with ships, by the way whereof I spake unto thee, Thou shalt see it no more again: and there ye shall be sold unto your enemies for bondmen and bondwomen, and no man shall buy you.

When we start listening to everything that our Father is telling us, we can start to realize that our souls are the same souls that have been here since the time of Moses. Our souls are the original Israelites that our Father has scattered because of our disobedience. Then Jesus talks about raising all that the Father has given him at the last day. That last day is the 1000 year reign with Christ. He goes on to say that it is the will of his Father that all who believe in Jesus, for who he really is, **may** have eternal life. Jesus will raise all that truly believe, and have a love for our Father, up at the last day. Notice how Jesus says "may have eternal life". Just because we make it to the kingdom does not mean we are guaranteed eternal life. There will be more explanation on the 1000 year reign, and God scattering the Israelites, later on in this message.

> (John 7) 16 Jesus answered them, and said, My doctrine is not mine, but his that sent me. 17 If any man will do his will, he shall know of the doctrine, whether it be of God, or whether I speak of myself. 18 He that speaketh of himself seeketh his own glory: but he that seeketh his glory that sent him, the same is true, and no unrighteousness is in him. 19 Did not Moses give you the law, and yet none of you keepeth the law? Why go ye about to kill me?

Jesus, himself, is telling us if we do the will of the Father then we will stay away from false doctrine, or man's doctrine that we see all over in our bibles. Only the words of God need to be taken note of, nothing more and nothing less. I ask that we pay close attention to what Jesus said here in verse 19. Remember that we are being told that all of what Moses gave to us is the old covenant. Now we should be realizing that there is nothing old about it, rather it is the covenant that we are still in.

> (John 8) 42 Jesus said unto them, If God were your Father, ye would love me: for I proceeded forth and came from God; neither came I of myself, but he sent me. 43 Why do ye not understand my speech? even because ye cannot hear my word. 44 Ye are of your father the devil, and the lusts of your father ye will do. He was a murderer from the beginning, and abode not in the truth, because there is no truth in him. When he speaketh a lie, he speaketh of his own: for he is a liar, and the father of it.

Jesus here is clearly saying that he came from God. He said he did not come of himself. If we say that he is God, then we do not know who he is. This, in return, means that we don't love him either. How can we truly love him if we believe that he is someone he is not? He is letting us know that if we don't understand his speech, that our father is the devil. We will then follow after the lusts of the devil. He is letting us know that we will not abide in truth; and yes, if there is no truth in us then we, too, will speak lies.

Matthew 24:36 says, "But of that day and hour knoweth no man, no, not the angels of heaven, but my Father only." Mark 13:32 tells us, "But of that day and that hour knoweth no man, no, not the angels which are in heaven, neither the Son, but the Father."

Note here that Jesus said himself that he does not know the day nor the hour, but only the Father. He specifically said that the Son of God did not know. I have heard well known pastors say that God made himself not know while he was in the human form. If that is the case, then that would make God a character that likes to trick or deceive people (NOT A CHANCE). This also helps us understand what Jesus meant when he asked his Father why He had forsaken him in Matthew 27:46, "And about the ninth hour Jesus cried with a loud voice, saying, Eli, Eli, lama sabachthani? that is to say, My God, my God, why hast thou forsaken me?" Our scripture does not say this exactly, but when we listen to everything we can't help but imagine that Jesus thought that his death would have come sooner than the 9th hour. He had to be thinking that our Father was not going to take the Ghost from him. Remember that Jesus also feared the one who could save him, as shown again in Hebrews5:7, "<u>Who in the days of his flesh, when</u> he had offered up prayers and supplications with strong crying and tears unto him that was able to save him from death, and was heard in that he feared." We do know that Jesus was in complete compliance with his Father. He couldn't understand why his Father hadn't taken the Ghost from him. Also remember how we are to work out our salvation with trembling and fear. If Jesus, being God's Son, feared the one who could save him, then we need to realize how **much we should fear the one who can save us, also.**

Let us note a few times that Jesus himself gave thanks to the Father.

> (Matthew11) 25 At that time Jesus answered and said, I thank thee, O Father, Lord of heaven and

earth, because thou hast hid these things from the wise and prudent, and hast revealed them unto babes. 26 Even so, Father: for so it seemed good in thy sight. 27 All things are delivered unto me of my Father: and no man knoweth the Son, but the Father; neither knoweth any man the Father, save the Son, and he to whomsoever the Son will reveal him.

Jesus is letting us know, in this prayer, that the prudent will not be able to understand what is going on. Remember what we are told in Matthew 24:43, "But know this, that if the goodman of the house had known in what watch the thief would come, he would have watched, and would not have suffered his house to be broken up." Jesus is letting us know that all things are delivered unto him by his Father. Then he is telling us that no man understands that the Father is the one who saved the Son, except the babes. Matthew 14:23 says, "And when he had sent the multitudes away, he went up into a mountain apart to pray: and when the evening was come, he was there alone." Remember how we are to take our prayers to the closet? We never hear or see Jesus praying in public. We hear him thanking the Father for making a small amount of food enough to feed a large multitude of people, but not praying before he eats. More examples of Jesus praying in private are found in Luke 6:12, "And it came to pass in those days, that he went out into a mountain to pray, and continued all night in prayer to God." And Luke 22:41, "And he was withdrawn from them about a stone's cast, and kneeled down, and prayed, 42 Saying, Father, if thou be willing, remove this cup from me: nevertheless not my will, but thine, be done. 43 And there appeared an angel unto him from heaven, strengthening him. 44 And being in an agony he prayed more earnestly: and his sweat was as it were great drops of blood falling down to the ground." Now we see here that after Jesus was withdrawn from them, and while praying, an angel appeared unto him. Now we should note that someone from above, whom he was praying to, sent that angel. Then Jesus clearly asked that this cup be removed, if it is the Father's will and not his own will.

John 11:41 says, "Then they took away the stone from the place where the dead was laid. And Jesus lifted up his eyes, and said, Father, I thank thee that thou hast heard me. 42 And I knew that thou hearest me always: but because of the people which stand by I said it, that they may believe that thou hast sent me." If we listen to Jesus here, we hear him saying that the people did not believe that God had sent him. Are we not doing the same thing when we think of Jesus as being God, or a god? If we think Jesus is God, then we do not actually give glory to the Father that has created him. We take away the only begotten out of the equation. Therefore, if the only begotten is taken out of the picture, then there is no need for John 3:16, "For God so loved the world, that he gave his only begotten Son, that whosoever believeth in him should not perish, but have everlasting life."

We should also be making note how Jesus is constantly praying for the Father's will. If Jesus is God then there is no need for the Fathers will, because it would be his own will.

> (John 17) These words spake Jesus, and lifted up his eyes to heaven, and said, Father, the hour is come; glorify thy Son, that thy Son also may glorify thee: 2 As thou hast given him power over all flesh, that he should give eternal life to as many as thou hast given him. 3 And this is life eternal, that they might know thee the only true God, and Jesus Christ, whom thou hast sent. 4 I have glorified thee on the earth: I have finished the work which thou gavest me to do. 5 And now, O Father, glorify thou me with thine own self with the glory which I had with thee before the world was. 6 I have manifested thy name unto the men which thou gavest me out of the world: thine they were, and thou gavest them me; and they have kept thy word. 7 Now they have known that all things whatsoever thou hast given me are of thee. 8 For I have given unto them the words which thou gavest me; and they have received them, and have known surely that

I came out from thee, and they have believed that thou didst send me. 9 I pray for them: I pray not for the world, but for them which thou hast given me; for they are thine. 10 And all mine are thine, and thine are mine; and I am glorified in them. 11 And now I am no more in the world, but these are in the world, and I come to thee. Holy Father, keep through thine own name those whom thou hast given me, that they may be one, as we are. 12 While I was with them in the world, I kept them in thy name: those that thou gavest me I have kept, and none of them is lost, but the son of perdition; that the scripture might be fulfilled. 13 And now come I to thee; and these things I speak in the world, that they might have my joy fulfilled in themselves. 14 I have given them thy word; and the world hath hated them, because they are not of the world, even as I am not of the world. 15 I pray not that thou shouldest take them out of the world, but that thou shouldest keep them from the evil. 16 They are not of the world, even as I am not of the world. 17 Sanctify them through thy truth: thy word is truth. 18 As thou hast sent me into the world, even so have I also sent them into the world. 19 And for their sakes I sanctify myself, that they also might be sanctified through the truth. 20 Neither pray I for these alone, but for them also which shall believe on me through their word; 21 That they all may be one; as thou, Father, art in me, and I in thee, that they also may be one in us: that the world may believe that thou hast sent me. 22 And the glory which thou gavest me I have given them; that they may be one, even as we are one: 23 I in them, and thou in me, that they may be made perfect in one; and that the world may know that thou hast sent me, and hast loved them, as thou hast loved me. 24 Father, I will that they also, whom

> thou hast given me, be with me where I am; that they may behold my glory, which thou hast given me: for thou lovedst me before the foundation of the world. 25 O righteous Father, the world hath not known thee: but I have known thee, and these have known that thou hast sent me. 26 And I have declared unto them thy name, and will declare it: that the love wherewith thou hast loved me may be in them, and I in them.

The first thing we should notice is how Jesus is praying that the Father will glorify the Son, so that the Son can glorify the Father. Then we start hearing Jesus praying that the Father will give eternal life to all that the Father has given him. In his prayer he is asking that these flesh that the Father has given know that Jesus is the one the Father has sent. In verse 4 when Jesus said he had finished the work he came here to do, we can hear him say that he has finished leaving the foot work for the Father's children. This is also the rest of the bible for all of his people that he is in charge of.

This helps explain what he meant when he said **it is done** on the cross. We hear him saying this in John 19:30, "When Jesus therefore had received the vinegar, he said, It is finished: and he bowed his head, and gave up the ghost." His testimony was finished. Remember I said I would explain the scattered children a bit ago? Well these children are what the Father has given to Jesus. Remember how our Father wanted to destroy us?

> (Exodus 32) 7 **And the Lord said unto Moses, Go, get thee down; for thy people, which thou broughtest out of the land of Egypt, have corrupted themselves: 8 They have turned aside quickly out of the way which I com- manded them: they have made them a molten calf, and have worshipped it, and have sacrificed thereunto, and said, These be thy gods, O Israel, which have brought thee up out of the land of Egypt. 9 And the Lord said unto**

Moses, I have seen this people, and, behold, it is a stiffnecked people: 10 Now therefore let me alone, that my wrath may wax hot against them, and that I may consume them: and I will make of thee a great nation. 11 And Moses besought the Lord his God, and said, Lord, why doth thy wrath wax hot against thy people, which thou hast brought forth out of the land of Egypt with great power, and with a mighty hand? 12 Wherefore should the Egyptians speak, and say, For mischief did he bring them out, to slay them in the mountains, and to consume them from the face of the earth? Turn from thy fierce wrath, and repent of this evil against thy people. 13 Remember Abraham, Isaac, and Israel, thy servants, to whom thou swarest by thine own self, and saidst unto them, I will multiply your seed as the stars of heaven, and all this land that I have spoken of will I give unto your seed, and they shall inherit it for ever. **14 And the Lord repented of the evil which he thought to do unto his people.**

Our father has been getting fed up with us constantly disobeying Him. Have you ever wondered what it means when we are told that no man will remember from the past or the future?

> (Ecclesiastes 1) 9 The thing that hath been, it is that which shall be; and that which is done is that which shall be done: and there is no new thing under the sun.10 Is there any thing whereof it may be said, See, this is new? it hath been already of old time, which was before us.11 <u>**There is no remembrance of former things; neither shall there be any remembrance of things that are to come with those that shall come after.**</u>

Now in verse 5 it may sound as if Jesus is saying that he was here before the world existed, but when we truly listen we hear him saying that perfection is what the Father had with him before the world was. Now in verse 6 we hear Jesus praying about those that the Father have given him. So now we need to journey back into our Old Testament to see what Jesus is talking about.

> (Exodus 32) 9 And the Lord said unto Moses, I have seen this people, and, behold, it is a stiffnecked people: 10 **Now therefore let me alone, that my wrath may wax hot against them, and that I may consume them:** and I will make of thee a great nation. 11 And Moses besought the Lord his God, and said, Lord, why doth thy wrath wax hot against thy people, which thou hast brought forth out of the land of Egypt with great power, and with a mighty hand?

We need to remember that our Father wanted to destroy us for our lack of obedience. It is kind of like when a husband comes home from work and the wife is fed up with the children. She tells him that they are his children and he can take care of them now. This is what our Father has done with Jesus. Here, Jesus, you get them now; I am fed up with them (in a sense). Then in verse 8 Jesus is praying that he has given us the words that his Father has given him so that his children will know that it is Jesus that our Father has sent. These words have been placed in our letter from our Father. Then in verse 9 Jesus is praying only for those that the Father has given him; he is not praying for the entire world. Much of this world will never hear the words that our Father gave to Jesus to leave for us. Jesus, in verse 11, is praying that those that the Father has given Jesus may be as one, as he and the Father are one.

Now notice in verse 12, Jesus is saying that none of the children that the Father has given to Jesus is lost. I have to ask if you remember anytime in your lifetime that you felt that you came out extremely lucky or something. In some way or another, things should have turned out a lot worse than they did. Like an 'almost died' moment if this would have happened a different way. Well when we listen to Jesus, we can see in verse 15 that Jesus asked our Father not to take us out of this world, but to keep us from evil. This is how we know that we are not lost. Our Father has been protecting us from evil all this time. Our Father now has placed us exactly where He has wanted us our entire life. Then in verses 18 and 19 he is asking the Father to sanctify his children through truth, or should we say the law. Then in verse 20 is where Jesus is also praying for anyone that believes on him. This is where we are being told that it is not just the original Israelites that are welcome to come to the truth. We are being told that all can be as one, just as the Father and Jesus are one.

Now in verse 24 Jesus makes it sound as if he was here before the foun- dation, but we should listen to how Jesus prays in John 17:24, "Father, I will that they also, whom thou hast given me, be with me where I am; that they may behold my glory, which thou hast given me: for thou lovedst me before the foundation of the world." We can start to understand by now that the Father loved perfection before the foundation of the world. In his prayer, Jesus finishes by stating that he has declared unto the children the name in which has sent him. Jesus is stating that he has declared that the only begotten Son of the Father has left these words and he prays that the love that our Father has for him, and him for the Father, is also abiding in all of the children that our Father has given to Jesus.

Now we start to understand what Jesus was saying in John when he stated that he is the truth. John 14:6 says, "Jesus saith unto him, I am the way, the truth, and the life: no man cometh unto the Father, but by me." So we look in our bibles to see what the truth is, which we find in Psalms 119:142, "Thy righteousness is an everlasting righteousness, **and thy law is the truth."**

Now we can see that the law is the truth. We see that Jesus, himself, is telling us that he is all about the law. We need to see what else Jesus said about himself when it comes to the truth.

> (Jeremiah 7) 22 For I spake not unto your fathers, nor com- manded them in the day that I brought them out of the land of Egypt, concerning burnt offerings or sacrifices: 23 But this thing commanded I them, saying, Obey my voice, and I will be your God, and ye shall be my people: and walk ye in all the ways that I have commanded you, that it may be well unto you. 24 But they hearkened not, nor inclined their ear, but walked in the counsels and in the imagination of their evil heart, and went backward, and not forward.

As we can see here, God told His people to walk in His ways. His ways are everything that He has commanded. We can know that God's laws are the way God wishes all to walk by looking at verse 24 above. God Himself said that not walking in His ways is us walking backwards and not forward. We will never get to the place God desires us to be if we continue to desire to walk backwards. Proverbs 6:23 tells us, "For the commandment is a lamp; and the law is light; and reproofs of instruction are the way of life". Here we see that the commandment is a lamp and the law is light.

Jesus also said he is the light that leads us out of darkness in John 8: 12, "Then spake Jesus again unto them, saying, I am the light of the world: he that followeth me shall not walk in darkness, but shall have the light of life." Now after just looking at these few verses, again we can see that Jesus defined himself as the law of God, the law in which is the light that will show us the way to eternal life. Notice how he is letting us know that no man comes unto the Father but by him. Jesus is clearly telling us that no man comes unto the Father **but by the law.**

Now I ask that we think of our own children, or even ourselves, when we were young. You know how your child wants to be just like you? I am not talking about your teenagers, when they feel they know everything and that they can do it all themselves, but when your child is around five years old and thinks you are his or her world. They defend you at all cost. They brag on you at all times. They get so excited when you come home from work because they truly felt that they needed you with them at all times.

I remember a time when I was four or five and thought my dad was the best of everything. He was invincible in my eyes. He was everything to me. I am not sure if this is a true memory or if it is one that I have devel- oped because I have heard the story told so many times. But I remember we went swimming in some river in New York. My dad swam out in the deeper part of the river. I don't know how deep the water was, but I do know it was over his head. Without even thinking of the dangers involved with me swimming out there, I followed him. My mother went hysterical screaming, "David Charles get back in here". I remember yelling back to her, "Why? My dad is out here."

You see, I wanted to do everything that my dad was doing. He did no wrong in my eyes. This is the relationship that we need to realize that Jesus has with his Father. But in their relationship, there is absolutely no wrong. With Jesus recognizing that his Father created him and loved him, he desired to do everything that his Father commanded. This is what the Father desires from us.

We need to take note that we are also being instructed not to call another man Father. Matthew 23:9 says, "And call no man your father upon the earth: for one is your Father, which is in heaven." Yes we all have fathers, but there is no other than the Father. The Father in heaven receives all the glory, all the time. Our Father is in charge of everything. We should be starting to understand that all these bad things that happen to us are our own fault. This is said by Jesus in John 16:33, "These things I have spoken unto you, that in me ye might have peace. In the world ye shall have tribulation: but be of good cheer; I have overcome the world." He is saying that if we truly follow him we will have peace, but if we do not follow him whole- heartedly then there will be tribulation because we are in Satan's world. In 2 Corinthians 4:4 we are told, "In whom the god of this world hath blinded the minds of them which believe not, lest the light of the glorious gospel of Christ, who is the image of God, should shine unto them."

Matthew 16:24 says, "Then said Jesus unto his disciples, If any man will come after me, let him deny himself, and take up his cross, and follow me." I have explained that Jesus had all the desire to obey all that God has commanded and Jesus himself is telling us to follow him. We are to deny ourselves and take up our cross and follow him. We are to stop thinking that our ways are going to get us into heaven. We are to realize that being obedient to all of God's laws is the way to our salvation.

This is how Jesus was made perfect; he desired with all of his heart to be completely obedient to the Father. We should desire to be completely obedient to the Father. This is how Jesus is made perfect, as we will be. The desire that drove him to be completely obedient to the Father is what made him perfect. That is the love that Jesus felt for the Father and this is the love we need to grow into. This is the love that will also give us the desire to be completely obedient. This is how we will be made perfect in the Father's eyes.

That is how Jesus became the author of salvation and why we are to follow him. If we love the Father, as Jesus does, and we strive to learn obe- dience, as Jesus did, we will follow Jesus to his Father and then we will be adopted and made perfect, just as Jesus is. There is our salvation.

Now we need to look at when Jesus fasted for forty days.

> (Matthew 4) Then was Jesus led up of the Spirit into the wilderness to be tempted of the devil. 2 And when he had fasted forty days and forty nights, he was afterward an hungred. 3 And when the tempter came to him, he said, If thou be the Son of God, command that these stones be made bread. 4 But he answered and said, It is written, Man shall not live by bread alone, but by every word that pro- ceedeth out of the mouth of God. 5 Then the devil taketh him up into the holy city, and setteth him on a pinnacle of the temple, 6 And saith unto him, If thou be the Son of God, cast thyself down: for it is written, He shall give

his angels charge concerning thee: and in their hands they shall bear thee up, lest at any time thou dash thy foot against a stone. 7 Jesus said unto him, It is written again, Thou shalt not tempt the Lord thy God. 8 Again, the devil taketh him up into an exceeding high mountain, and sheweth him all the kingdoms of the world, and the glory of them; 9 And saith unto him, All these things will I give thee, if thou wilt fall down and worship me. 10 Then saith Jesus unto him, Get thee hence, Satan: for it is written, Thou shalt worship the Lord thy God, and him only shalt thou serve. 11 Then the devil leaveth him, and, behold, angels came and minis- tered unto him.

James 1:13 says, "Let no man say when he is tempted, I am tempted of God: **for God cannot be tempted with evil, neither tempteth he any man:** 14 But every man is tempted, when he is drawn away of his own lust, and enticed."

Now we just read that Jesus was tempted, but we can clearly hear that our Father cannot be tempted. This automatically rules Jesus out from being God. Now this also illustrates that Jesus was not perfect while he was a man, as perfect cannot be tempted, either. Deuteronomy 32:4 states, **"He is the Rock, his work is perfect: for all his ways are judgment: a God of truth and without iniquity, just and right is he."** We need to realize that Jesus was a man, just like you and me. He was tempted just as we are and he had the struggles that we do. But he loved his father with all of his heart, soul, and mind. He desired, in all ways imaginable, to be completely obedient to his Father. This is how he became perfect and this is how we will become perfect.

Satan, the Mark of the Beast, and the Beast

Now that I have brought up the forty day fast that Jesus did, I want to show how Satan gets us, what the mark of the beast will be and who will be the beast. To do this we need to go back to the beginning of our bibles.

(Genesis 3) Now the serpent was more subtil than any beast of the field which the Lord God had made. And he said unto the woman, Yea, hath God said, Ye shall not eat of every tree of the garden? 2 And the woman said unto the serpent, We may eat of the fruit of the trees of the garden: 3 But of the fruit of the tree which is in the midst of the garden, God hath said, Ye shall not eat of it, nei- ther shall ye touch it, lest ye die. 4 And the serpent said unto the woman, Ye shall not surely die: 5 For God doth know that in the day ye eat thereof, then your eyes shall be opened, and ye shall be as gods, knowing good and evil. 6 And when the woman saw that the tree was good for food, and that it was pleasant to the eyes, and a tree to be desired to make one wise, she took of the fruit thereof, and did eat, and gave also unto her husband with her; and he did eat. 7 And the eyes of them both were opened, and they knew that they were naked; and they sewed fig leaves together, and made themselves aprons. 8 And they heard the voice of the Lord God walking in the garden in the cool of the day: and Adam and his wife hid themselves from the presence of the Lord God amongst the trees of the garden. 9 And the Lord God called unto Adam, and said unto him, Where art thou? 10 And he said, I heard thy voice in the garden, and I was afraid, because I was naked; and I hid myself. 11 And he said, Who told thee that thou wast naked? Hast thou eaten of the tree, whereof I com- manded thee that thou shouldest not eat? 12 And the man said, The woman whom thou gavest to be with me, she gave me of the tree, and I did eat. 13 And the Lord God said unto the woman, What is this that thou hast done? And the woman said, The serpent beguiled me, and I did eat. **14 And the Lord God said unto the serpent, Because thou hast done this, thou art cursed above all cattle, and above every beast of the field; upon thy belly shalt thou go, and dust shalt thou eat all the days of thy life: 15 And I will put enmity between thee and the woman, and between thy seed and her seed; it shall bruise thy head, and thou shalt bruise his heel**.

Note that Satan is cursed above all the cattle and every beast of the field. Dust is what he shall eat all the days of his life. Now I want to draw your attention to Ephesians 2:2, "Wherein in time past ye walked according to the course of this world, **according to the prince of the power of the air, the spirit that now worketh in the children of disobedience**". I would like to point out that Satan is in the air. Satan gets in our thoughts, thoughts that go against anything that our Father has commanded. To further illus- trate this we need to look in the book of Job:

> (Job 2) Again there was a day when the sons of God came to present themselves before the Lord, and Satan came also among them to present himself before the Lord. 2 And the Lord said unto Satan, From whence

comest thou? And Satan answered the Lord, and said, <u>From going to and fro in the earth, and from walking up and down in it.</u> 3 And the Lord said unto Satan, Hast thou considered my ser- vant Job, that there is none like him in the earth, a perfect and an upright man, one that feareth God, and escheweth evil? and still he holdeth fast his integrity, although thou movedst me against him, to destroy him without cause. 4 And Satan answered the Lord, and said, Skin for skin, yea, all that a man hath will he give for his life. 5 But put forth thine hand now, and touch his bone and his flesh, and he will curse thee to thy face. 6 And the Lord said unto Satan, Behold, he is in thine hand; but save his life. 7 So went Satan forth from the presence of the Lord, and smote Job with sore boils from the sole of his foot unto his crown. 8 And he took him a potsherd to scrape himself withal; and he sat down among the ashes. 9 Then said his wife unto him, Dost thou still retain thine integrity? curse God, and die. 10 **But he said unto her, Thou speakest as one of the foolish women speaketh. What? shall we receive** good at the hand of God, and shall we not receive evil? <u>In all this did not Job sin with his lips</u>.

We hear that even though all this evil was falling upon Job, at no time would he let evil thoughts enter into his mind. Now we need to see what escheweth means in the concordance on e-sword. H5493 רוּשׂ סוּר sûr śûr soor, soor A primitive root; to turn off (literally or figuratively): - be [-head], bring, call back, **decline, depart**, eschew, get [you], go (aside), X grievous, lay away (by), leave undone, be past, pluck away, put (away, down), **rebel**, remove (to and fro), revolt, X be sour, take (away, off), turn (aside, away, in), **withdraw, be without**. Notice how Job would not let evil thoughts enter into his mind.

Let us look at a few other examples within our bibles. In John 13:26, "Jesus answered, He it is, to whom I shall give a sop, when I have dipped it. And when he had dipped the sop, he gave it to Judas Iscariot, the son of Simon. 27 **And after the sop Satan entered into him**. Then said Jesus unto him, That thou doest, do quickly. 28 Now no man at the table knew for what intent he spake this unto him." Now we have to ask how Satan, at the table, entered into Judas. It was into his thoughts.

We find another example in Acts 5:2, "And kept back part of the price, his wife also being privy to it, and brought a certain part, and laid it at the apostles' feet. 3 But Peter said, Ananias, why hath **Satan filled thine heart to lie to the Holy Ghost**, and to keep back part of the price of the land? 4 Whiles it remained, was it not thine own? and after it was sold, was it not in thine own power? why hast thou conceived this thing in thine heart? thou hast not lied unto men, but unto God." We must ask how Satan filled his heart to lie; it was because Ananias allowed satanic thoughts in his mind.

Let's read 2 Thessalonians 2:8, "And then shall that Wicked be revealed, whom the Lord shall consume with the spirit of his mouth, and shall destroy with the brightness of his coming: 9 Even him, whose coming is after the working **of Satan with all power and signs and lying wonders**, 10 And with all deceivableness of unrighteousness in them that perish; because they received not the love of the truth, that they might be saved." When we lie, do we not think of the lie first? We need to look at when Jesus fasted for forty day once again.

> (Matthew 4) Then was Jesus led up of the Spirit into the wilderness to be tempted of the devil. 2 And when he had fasted forty days and forty nights, he was afterward an hungred. 3 And when the tempter came to him, he said, If thou be the Son of God, command that these stones be made bread. 4 But he answered and said, It is written, Man shall not live by bread alone, but by every word that pro- ceedeth out of the mouth of God. 5 Then the devil taketh him up into the holy city, and setteth him on a pinnacle of the temple, 6 And saith unto him, If thou be the Son of God, cast thyself down: for it is written, He shall give his angels charge

concerning thee: and in their hands they shall bear thee up, lest at any time thou dash thy foot against a stone. 7 Jesus said unto him, It is written again, Thou shalt not tempt the Lord thy God. 8 Again, the devil taketh him up into an exceeding high mountain, and sheweth him all the kingdoms of the world, and the glory of them; 9 And saith unto him, All these things will I give thee, if thou wilt fall down and worship me. 10 Then saith Jesus unto him, Get thee hence, Satan: for it is written, Thou shalt worship the Lord thy God, and him only shalt thou serve. 11 Then the devil leaveth him, and, behold, angels came and minis- tered unto him.

Have you ever wondered how Satan was able to move Jesus to all these different locations on the 40th day of his fast? Notice how Jesus hungered after fasting 40 days. This is telling us that Jesus was completely worn out, as we are when we fast just a few days. Now being worn out and being incredibly hungry, his mind was at a weakened stage. This allowed the satanic thoughts to enter into his mind. This is how he was tempted, as we are tempted today. It is a power in the air that is going about this earth getting into our heads, suggesting that we do not have to obey every word that comes out of God's mouth.

The good news is that we have also been told how to keep these satanic thoughts out of our heads. 1Peter 5:8 says, "**Be sober, be vigilant**; because your adversary the devil, as a roaring lion, walketh about, seeking whom he may devour". Note how the devil is walking throughout the world seeking those whom he can devour. The only way he can do this is by traveling through the air. Ephesians 2:2 tells us, "Wherein in time past ye walked according to the course of this world, **according to the prince of the power of the air,** the spirit that now worketh in the children of disobedience." Notice how it is the spirit that works in the children of disobedience and not the children of obedience. So yes, that means that we have to give up all the beer that we consume and yes, that even means that we need to let go of all pot and all the other drugs we take these days that make us feel differently than our

Father wants us to feel at all times. We need to allow our minds to be open so that our Father can communicate with us. He speaks to us through our bibles. When we are always thinking of Him, and what He has said in the bible, then we hear Him more clearly. We learn what verses to recite when the tempter himself comes to us.

Notice what we are told in Ephesians 4:27, "Neither give place to the devil." We are not to allow the devil a foothold in our minds. Once he gets a foothold in our minds, he continues to make us **think** that we do not need to obey God. After a while of these thoughts being in our minds, and the more we think that we do not have to obey God, before we know it Satan has us wrapped around his little finger, getting us to do things against God's ways. If we are seeking God diligently, as we are told to do in Hebrews 11:6, "But without faith it is impossible to please him: for he that cometh to God must believe that he is, and that he is a **rewarder of them that dil- igently seek him**" and if we are praying constantly like we are told to do in 1 Thessalonians 5:17, "**Pray without ceasing.** 18 In every thing give thanks: for this is the will of God in Christ Jesus concerning you", then Satan will not have a chance to get a foothold in our minds. We are to study God's word without end so we know the scriptures as well as Jesus did. If we continually study and seek God we will have no problem throwing Satan to the curb when he tries to tempt us. When we commit our heart, soul, and minds to the Father, Satan will have no chance of getting in. That is where our Father desires all of us to be.

I told you that I would explain what the mark of the beast is. We start out by listening to what we are told in Revelation 13:18, "Here is wisdom. Let him that hath understanding count the number of the beast: for it is the number of a man; and his number is Six hundred threescore and six." Now, just in case there are some who do not understand what six hundred threescore and six means we will show the meaning in the concordance on e-sword. G5516 χξς chi xi stigma khee xee stig'-ma The 22nd, 14th and an obsolete letter (G4742 as a cross) of the Greek alphabet (intermediate between the 5th and 6th), used as numbers; denoting respectively 600, 60 and 6; 666 as a numeral: - six hundred threescore and six.

Now that we can understand that the number of the beast is 666, we need to go back in Genesis to see what day man was created on.

> (Genesis 1) 26 And God said, Let us make man in our image, after our likeness: and let them have dominion over the fish of the sea, and over the fowl of the air, and over the cattle, and over all the earth, and over every creeping thing that creepeth upon the earth. 27 So God created man in his own image, in the image of God created he him; male and female created he them. 28 And God blessed them, and God said unto them, Be fruitful, and multiply, and replenish the earth, and subdue it: and have dominion over the fish of the sea, and over the fowl of the air, and over every living thing that moveth upon the earth. 29 And God said, Behold, I have given you every herb bearing seed, which is upon the face of all the earth, and every tree, in the which is the fruit of a tree yielding seed; to you it shall be for meat. 30 And to every beast of the earth, and to every fowl of the air, and to every thing that creepeth upon the earth, wherein there is life, I have given every green herb for meat: and it was so. 31 And God saw every thing that he had made, and, behold, it was very good. **And the evening and the morning were the sixth day.**

So we know that our Father created us on the 6th day.

Now we need to look and see what the greatest commandment is again.

> (Matthew 22) 34 But when the Pharisees had heard that he had put the Sadducees to silence, they were gathered together. 35 Then one of them, which was a lawyer, asked him a question, tempting him, and saying, 36 Master, which is the great commandment

in the law? 37 Jesus said unto him, Thou shalt love the Lord thy God <u>with all thy heart</u>, and <u>with all thy soul</u>, and <u>with all thy mind</u>. 38 This is the first and great commandment. 39 And the second is like unto it, Thou shalt love thy neighbour as thyself. 40 On these two commandments hang all the law and the prophets.

Now throughout this entire book I have been showing that we are to love our Father with all of our heart, soul, and minds. This is because when a man or woman refuses to love God with all of their heart, soul, and mind, they have just taken the mark of the beast. To break it down a little more we can look at it this way; when a man refuses to love God with all of his heart, that is one 6; when a man refuses to love God with all of his soul, he has just obtained another 6; and when a man refuses to love God with all of his mind, this makes the third 6.

Now I know there is a lot of hype floating around out here wondering if the mark of the beast will be a computer chip or something like that, or a tattoo to show that they have taken the mark of the beast. But when we listen to what we are being told in the verses that come prior to when we are given the number of the beast, we get an entirely different picture.

(Revelation 13) 14 And deceiveth them that dwell on the earth by the means of those miracles which he had power to do in the sight of the beast; saying to them that dwell on the earth, that they should make an <u>image</u> to the beast, which had the wound by a sword, and did live. 15 And he had power to give life unto the <u>image</u> of the beast, that the <u>image</u> of the beast should both speak, and cause that as many as would not worship the <u>image</u> of the beast should be killed. 16 And he causeth all, both small and great, rich and poor, free and bond, to **receive a mark in their right hand, or in their foreheads:** 17 And that no man might buy or sell, save he that had the mark, or the name of the beast, or the number of his name. 18 Here is wisdom. Let him that hath understanding count the number of the beast: for it is the number of a man; and his number is Six hun- dred threescore and six.

We can now start to understand that because they choose not love our Father with all of their heart, soul, and mind, their works will be other than what our Father has commanded; this is how it will be in their hands. When their minds refuse to love our Father with all of their heart, soul, and mind is how the mark will be in their foreheads.

Now that we understand what the mark of the beast is going to be, it shouldn't be that hard to figure out who the beast is actually going to be. The beast is going to be all of the people that refuse to love our Father with all of their heart, soul, and mind. These are the people that think that God's ways are not the way to live. They will not submit themselves to our Father because their pride is too large. These people will continue to think that their ways of living are better than our Fathers, just like Lucifer did. Remember, he thought it possible to be better than God Almighty. Remember how we are told that those of us that will not worship the image of the beast will make it to the kingdom? The image is in our actions. Our actions are the image of worshipping Satan, or worshipping our Father. Our actions will give the image, or should we say our works will give the image. If we are obeying our Father, then we will be honoring the Sabbath as he has commanded. We will not take any part in man-made holidays. We will not eat or drink anything other than what our Father has said is okay to eat and drink. But if we obey Satan, then our works will go against what our Father has commanded. Our works will give off an image that we don't care about the true Sabbath, or we will continue to let money be our god and tell ourselves that we have to work on the Sabbath in order to make ends meet. We will continue believing that we need extra holidays, other than what our Father said we need. Now we can understand exactly what the image of the beast is and who and how the beast will rise.

God's Holy Days

In this chapter, we are going to dive into the neglect of God's Holy Days. Today, most don't even try to honor God's Holy days. I realize that there are some that do, but what are we called if we don't do what everyone else does? What I mean is that we are called legalists or something similar. We are told that we are free from the law, but if we look at the bible as a whole we see that everything that gives us eternal life is obedience to the law.

We have not found anywhere that tells us, in our letter from our Father, that if we choose to be disobedient we will be rewarded and gain eternal life in heaven. Churches today teach us that Jesus died for our sins and that he did away with the law. They teach us that we do not have to be obedient, unless it benefits them. They stand up in the synagogues, or churches, to be seen by other men. They tell us to keep the Sabbath holy, yet they disregard that the Sabbath never got changed in our bible from Saturday to Sunday. They neglect telling us that we should follow all the rules and regulations that we are told to do in order to honor the Sabbath.

They tell us to love God with all of our heart, soul, and mind, yet don't know how we are to do that when we are told how to love God within our own bibles. 1 John 5:3 tells us, **"For this is the love of God, that we keep his commandments: and his commandments are not grievous."** I know some think that this is just the Ten Commandments, but I disagree. When God instructed Moses how to build the Tabernacle, He commanded him how to do it. When God tells us to make fringes for ourselves in Numbers, he is not suggesting we make fringes.

> (Number 15) 37 And the Lord spake unto Moses, saying, 38 Speak unto the children of Israel, and bid them that **they make them fringes** in the borders of their garments throughout their generations, and that they put upon the fringe of the borders a ribband of blue: 39 And it shall be unto you for a fringe, that ye may look upon it, and **remember all the commandments** of the Lord, **and do them** ; and that ye seek not after your own heart and your own eyes, after which ye use to go a whoring: 40 That ye may remember, **and do all my commandments**, and be holy unto your God. 41 I am the Lord your God, which brought you out of the land of Egypt, to be your God: I am the Lord your God.

He is commanding us to make them. He is not telling us to buy them nor to make them for someone else. Each child of the Israelites is instructed to make their own fringes. We know it can't be too hard because our Father has commanded nothing that is too hard for us to do in Deuteronomy 30:11, **"For this commandment which I command thee this day, it is not hidden from thee, neither is it far off."**

Isn't that what having faith is all about? We should trust that God's ways of living are the best way to live and then have faith, no matter our circumstances, that this will lead us the right way. Everything that God has instructed us to do will give us the best life but only if, and I mean only if, we do everything God said to do. We need to follow His commandments, judgments, statutes, ordinances and all of His laws; nothing more and nothing less.

I bring all this up because I want to show people that just because a preacher tells you that he or she is teaching you the proper way to be of God, he or she is most likely wrong. Unless he or she is telling you to obey every word that proceeds out of the mouth of God, they are telling you to go against God's word. When do we hear the preachers telling us that we should try to observe God's Holy Days?

Let us take a look at God's Holy Days to see how the common church of today ignores them.

> (Leviticus 23) 1 And the LORD spake unto Moses, saying, 2 Speak unto the children of Israel, and say unto them, Concerning the feasts of the LORD, which ye shall pro- claim to be holy convocations, even these are my feasts. 3 Six days shall work be done: but the seventh day is the sabbath of rest, an holy convocation; ye shall do no work therein: it is the sabbath of the LORD in all your dwellings. 4 These are the feasts of the LORD, even holy convocations, which ye shall proclaim in their seasons. 5 In the fourteenth day of the first month at even is the LORD'S passover. 6 And on the fifteenth day of the same month is the feast of unleavened bread unto the LORD: seven days ye must eat unleavened bread. 7 In the first day ye shall have an holy convocation: ye shall do no servile work therein. 8 But ye shall offer an offering made by fire unto the LORD seven days: in the seventh day is an holy convocation: ye shall do no servile work therein. 9 And the LORD spake unto Moses, saying, 10 Speak unto the children of Israel, and say unto them, When ye be come into the land which I give unto you, and shall reap the harvest thereof, then ye shall bring a sheaf of the first- fruits of your harvest unto the priest: 11 And he shall wave the sheaf before the LORD, to be accepted for you: on the morrow after the sabbath the priest shall wave it. 12 And ye shall offer that day when ye wave the sheaf an he lamb without blemish of the first year for a burnt offering unto the LORD. 13 And the meat offering thereof shall be two tenth deals of fine flour mingled with oil, an offering made by fire unto the LORD for a sweet savour: and the drink

offering thereof shall be of wine, the fourth part of an hin. 14 And ye shall eat neither bread, nor parched corn, nor green ears, until the selfsame day that ye have brought an offering unto your God: it shall be a statute for ever throughout your generations in all your dwellings. 15 And ye shall count unto you from the morrow after the sabbath, from the day that ye brought the sheaf of the wave offering; seven sabbaths shall be complete: 16 Even unto the morrow after the seventh sabbath shall ye number fifty days; and ye shall offer a new meat offering unto the LORD. 17 Ye shall bring out of your habitations two wave loaves of two tenth deals: they shall be of fine flour; they shall be baken with leaven; they are the firstfruits unto the LORD. 18 And ye shall offer with the bread seven lambs without blemish of the first year, and one young bullock, and two rams: they shall be for a burnt offering unto the LORD, with their meat offering, and their drink offerings, even an offering made by fire, of sweet savour unto the LORD. 19 Then ye shall sacrifice one kid of the goats for a sin offering, and two lambs of the first year for a sacri- fice of peace offerings. 20 And the priest shall wave them with the bread of the firstfruits for a wave offering before the LORD, with the two lambs: they shall be holy to the LORD for the priest. 21 And ye shall proclaim on the self- same day, that it may be an holy convocation unto you: ye shall do no servile work therein: it shall be a statute for ever in all your dwellings throughout your generations. 22 And when ye reap the harvest of your land, thou shalt not make clean riddance of the corners of thy field when thou reapest, neither shalt thou gather any gleaning of thy harvest: thou shalt leave them unto the poor, and to the stranger: I am the LORD your God. 23 And the LORD spake unto

Moses, saying, 24 Speak unto the children of Israel, saying, In the seventh month, in the first day of the month, shall ye have a sabbath, a memorial of blowing of trumpets, an holy convocation. 25 Ye shall do no servile work therein: but ye shall offer an offering made by fire unto the LORD. 26 And the LORD spake unto Moses, saying, 27 Also on the tenth day of this seventh month there shall be a day of atonement: it shall be an holy con- vocation unto you; and ye shall afflict your souls, and offer an offering made by fire unto the LORD. 28 And ye shall do no work in that same day: for it is a day of atonement, to make an atonement for you before the LORD your God. 29 For whatsoever soul it be that shall not be afflicted in that same day, he shall be cut off from among his people. 30 And whatsoever soul it be that doeth any work in that same day, the same soul will I destroy from among his people. 31 Ye shall do no manner of work: it shall be a statute for ever throughout your generations in all your dwellings. 32 It shall be unto you a sabbath of rest, and ye shall afflict your souls: in the ninth day of the month at even, from even unto even, shall ye celebrate your sab- bath. 33 And the LORD spake unto Moses, saying, 34 Speak unto the children of Israel, saying, The fifteenth day of this seventh month shall be the feast of tabernacles for seven days unto the LORD. 35 On the first day shall be an holy convocation: ye shall do no servile work therein. 36 Seven days ye shall offer an offering made by fire unto the LORD: on the eighth day shall be an holy convocation unto you; and ye shall offer an offering made by fire unto the LORD: it is a solemn assembly; and ye shall do no servile work therein. 37 These are the feasts of the LORD, which ye shall proclaim to be holy convocations, to offer an offering made by fire unto the LORD, a burnt offering, and a meat offering, a sacrifice, and drink offerings, every thing upon his day: 38 Beside the sabbaths of the LORD, and beside your gifts, and beside all your vows, and beside all your freewill offerings, which ye give unto the LORD. 39 Also in the fifteenth day of the seventh month, when ye have gathered in the fruit of the land, ye shall keep a feast unto the LORD seven days: on the first day shall be a sabbath, and on the eighth day shall be a sabbath. 40 And ye shall take you on the first day the boughs of goodly trees, branches of palm trees, and the boughs of thick trees, and willows of the brook; and ye shall rejoice before the LORD your God seven days. 41 And ye shall keep it a feast unto the LORD seven days in the year. It shall be a statute for ever in your generations: ye shall celebrate it in the seventh month. 42 Ye shall dwell in booths seven days; all that are Israelites born shall dwell in booths: 43 That your generations may know that I made the children of Israel to dwell in booths, when I brought them out of the land of Egypt: I am the LORD your God. 44 And Moses declared unto the children of Israel the feasts of the LORD.

As we can see in the beginning of the chapter, God is sure to tell us about the Sabbath and command us to keep it Holy. He is not saying that we should keep any Sabbath day, nor is he suggesting we change the Sabbath to any other day and then keep it Holy. He is telling us to keep the Sabbath Holy, and nothing more or nothing less. Do exactly as He has commanded to do for the Sabbath.

Now that we have taken the time to look over the Holy Days that God has commanded us to keep, we will break each one down and show exactly how many ways the church of today ignores them, if not completely abol- ishes them.

First we see that we are keep Passover. This is on the 14th day of the first month of the year. Now we need to realize that January is not the first month of the year on the God's calendar. We then need to find out when the calendar that God ordained starts. At this time, I want to include some information that I have obtained from The Church of God website:

The first day of God's new year begins with the first new moon nearest the spring turn (equinox). We know this for several reasons: God instructed His people to keep the Feast of Ingathering (Tabernacles) at the "end [or turn] of the year" (Ex. 23 and 34). The Feast of Ingathering is kept in the seventh month of the year (Lev. 23) and so we know God is referring here to the end of the agricultural year-near the autumn turn (equinox) after the harvest. Seven months prior to the harvest is the spring. Thus God's year begins with the nearest new moon at the spring turn.

A New Moon Begins the Year

We know God's year begins with a new moon because the scriptures tells us so: "This month shall be your beginning of months; it shall be the first month of the year to you, God proclaimed to the Israelites" (Ex. 12:2). The actual word 'month," remember means 'moonth,'one complete luna- tion beginning with the new moon.

We also know we begin with the new moon nearest--before or after --- the spring turn (equinox) or else God's Feast of Ingathering could not always occur at the turn of the agricultural year!!

From here then the successive new moons of God's calendar can be obtained from an observatory or computer program showing when the last of the waning crescent moon ends and a dark moon begins. The observatory sources are superior to that of the local newspaper's in that they usually tell you the specific time of the new dark moon each month in Jerusalem time zone. This is important to someone in God's church. The world's calcula- tions are based on the Roman midnight-to midnight day. God's calculations are based on His sunset-to-sunset day calculated from Jerusalem time. All of God's holy convocations should be calculate based on this.

The first day of the year is the day which includes the new moon con- junction. Passover is kept at twilight at the beginning of the 14th day of the first month (immediately after sunset of the 13th). The Days of Unleavened Bread extend from the beginning of the 15th to sunset of the 21st. The Feast of Trumpets is observed on the very first day of the seventh moon or month. Atonement the 10th day. The Feast of Ingathering from the 15th to the 22nd. All of these dates can be worked out from Leviticus 23. (www. postponements.com)

Today, in this country anyway, the churches don't even try to recognize the Passover from a biblical stand point. I mean, they don't even tell us what God told us. The Passover is a very important day to God. This is the actual day that Jesus, His son, was to be crucified. Churches today say that Good Friday is the day Jesus died, but they lack a very important under- standing of God's word. Matthew12:40 tells us, "For as Jonas was three days and three nights in the whale's belly; so shall the Son of man be three days and three nights in the heart of the earth." Now Jesus himself said that he would be in the belly of the earth for three days and three nights, how can he be crucified on Friday and resurrected by sunrise Sunday?

Churches today think, or teach, that because Jesus had to be taken off the cross before the Sabbath began that it had to be Friday. However, this totally disregards the very next Holy Day after passover.

> (Leviticus 23) 6 And on the fifteenth day of the same month is the feast of unleavened bread unto the LORD: seven days ye must eat unleavened bread. 7 In the first day ye shall have an **holy convocation: ye shall do no servile work therein.** 8 But ye shall offer an offering made by fire unto the LORD seven days: in the seventh day is **an holy convocation: ye shall do no servile work therein.**

We see here that we are to start the feast of unleavened bread, and the first and last days of this feast shall be High Sabbaths. A High Sabbath is a Sabbath day that we are to observe, other than the weekly Sabbath. Remember when we started on the Holy Days we were told to proclaim holy convocations? Churches today completely ignore this fact. If they pay any attention at all to what God commanded, here we can easily see that Easter is a bogus holiday and has **NOTHING** to do with God or Jesus.

Let's look within the scriptures to find out what we are instructed to do for the Feast of unleavened bread. In Exodus 12:15 we are told, "Seven days shall ye eat unleavened bread; even the first day ye shall put away leaven out of your houses: for whosoever eateth leavened bread from the first day until the seventh day, that soul shall be cut off from Israel." Exodus 12:19 continues with, "Seven days shall there be no leaven found in your houses: for whosoever eateth that which is leavened, even that soul shall be cut off from the congregation of Israel, whether he be a stranger, or born in the land." Deuteronomy 16:3 states, "Thou shalt eat no leavened bread with it; seven days shalt thou eat unleavened bread therewith, even the bread of affliction; for thou camest forth out of the land of Egypt in haste: that thou mayest remember the day when thou camest forth out of the land of Egypt all the days of thy life."

We are instructed to get <u>all leaven</u> out of our house and out of our gates. Get it off of our property.

Now, also notice how we are told that the first and last day shall be a holy convocation and no servile work shall be done. This is what is called a High Sabbath. It is a day that God has set aside for rest to worship Him other than the weekly Sabbath. These are not days that God has asked us to keep; he commanded us to keep them.

Now I know some might not understand what it means to not eat leaven or even to get it out from your gates. We then need to look at e-sword or a Strong's Exhaustive Concordance to look up the definition of unleavened bread. H4682 הצמ matstsâh mats-tsaw' From H4711 in the sense of greedily devouring for sweetness; properly sweetness; concretely sweet (that is, <u>not soured or bittered with yeast</u>); specifically an unfermented cake or loaf, or (elliptically) the festival of Passover (because no leaven was then used): - unleavened (bread, cake), w<u>ithout leaven.</u>

Do we even know why God would have us do this? The answer is within our bibles. When we go to the New Testament, we can see that leaven also symbolized sin. Matthew 16:11 says, "How is it that ye do not under- stand that I spake it not to you concerning bread, that ye should beware of the leaven of the Pharisees and of the Sadducees?" Also 1 Corinthians 5:7, "Purge out therefore the old leaven, that ye may be a new lump, as ye are unleavened. For even Christ our passover is sacrificed for us".

As we can see, the leaven also symbolized our sin. We are to take leaven out from our gates. We still sin during this week, but we need to follow God's instructions so that he knows that we desire to take our sin from our lives. He needs to see our desires. Now we need to take note of what God tells us to do next.

> (Leviticus 23) 10 Speak unto the children of Israel, and say unto them, When ye be come into the land which I give unto you, and shall reap the harvest thereof, then ye shall bring a sheaf of the firstfruits of your harvest unto the priest: 11 And he shall wave the sheaf before the Lord, to be accepted for you: on the morrow after the sabbath the priest shall wave it. 12 And ye shall offer that day when ye wave the sheaf a he lamb without blemish of the first year for a burnt offering unto the Lord. 13 And the meat offering thereof shall be two tenth deals of fine flour min- gled with oil, an offering made by fire unto the Lord for a sweet savour: and the drink offering thereof shall be of wine, the fourth part of an hin. 14 And ye shall eat neither bread, nor parched corn, nor green ears, until the selfsame day that ye have brought an offering unto your God: it shall be a **statute for ever throughout your generations in all your dwellings.**

Next we have Pentecost which is explained in Leviticus 23:15-22, but I will only explain a few verses so that we can understand when and how we are to honor this day. Leviticus 23:15 tells us, "And ye shall count unto you from the morrow after the sabbath, from the day that ye brought the sheaf of the wave offering; seven sabbaths shall be complete: 16 Even unto the morrow after the seventh sabbath shall ye number fifty days; and ye shall offer a new meat offering unto the Lord." I will leave out the verses showing the offerings we are to make and will now show that this is also a holy convocation in which no servile work shall be done. Leviticus 23:21 lets us know, "And ye shall proclaim on the selfsame day, that it may be an holy convocation unto you: ye shall do no servile work therein: it shall be a statute for ever in all your dwellings throughout your generations." We need to be honoring this day because this is the day that the Holy Spirit will be poured upon the true followers of God.

Next we find that we have the Day of Trumpets, which falls on the first day of the seventh month on God's calendar. We find this in Leviticus 23:24, "Speak unto the children of Israel, saying, In the seventh month, in the first day of the month, shall ye have a sabbath, a memorial of blowing of trumpets, an holy convocation."

The Day of Trumpets is another High Sabbath. This is not a day that will fall on the weekly Sabbath on a yearly basis. God has instructed his people that this will be an additional Sabbath for this day on a yearly basis, not a weekly basis. When do we hear churches of today teaching about this Sabbath?

Next we move to the Day of Atonement. This day is on the tenth day of the seventh month on God's calendar.

> (Leviticus 23) 27 Also on the tenth day of this seventh month there shall be a day of atonement: it shall be an **holy convocation** unto you; and ye shall afflict your souls, and offer an offering made by fire unto the Lord. 28 And ye shall do no work in that same day: for it is a day of atone- ment, to make an atonement for you before the Lord your God. 29 For whatsoever soul it be that shall not be afflicted in that same day, he shall be cut off from among his people. 30 And whatsoever soul it be that doeth any work in that same day, the same soul will I destroy from among his people. 31 Ye shall do no manner of work: it shall be **a statute for ever throughout your generations** in all your dwellings. 32 It shall be unto you a sabbath of rest, and ye shall afflict your souls: in the ninth day of the month at even, from even unto even, shall ye celebrate your sabbath.

The way this reads in verse 32 can be a little confusing. So let us look at the definition of ninth day on e-sword. H8672 עשׁת העשׂת têsha' tish'âh tay'- shah, tish-aw' The second form is the masculine of the first; perhaps from H8159 through the idea of a turn to the next or full number ten; nine or (ordinal) ninth: - nine (+ -teen, + -teenth, -th).

This shows us that even of the ninth day is actually going into the tenth day. We then need to look and see what the Hebrew definition of even is so we can better understand what exact time of the day we are to start our celebration and end, as well. H6153 ברע 'ereb eh'-reb From H6150; dusk: - + day, even (-ing, tide), night. As we can see here, even is when the night sets in. We can usually tell by the sun and when it is setting in the west. When the daylight starts to diminish, we know the day is ending and the next biblical day is beginning.

Now we move onto the next Holy Day that God has ordained for us.

> (Leviticus 23) 34 Speak unto the children of Israel, saying, The fifteenth day of this seventh month shall be the feast of tabernacles for seven days unto the Lord. 35 On the first day shall be **an holy convocation: ye shall do no servile work therein**. 36 Seven days ye shall offer an offering made by fire unto the Lord: on the eighth day shall be **an holy convocation** unto you; and ye shall offer an offering made by fire unto the Lord: it is a solemn assembly; and ye shall **do no servile work therein**. And ye shall take you on the first day the boughs of goodly trees, branches of palm trees, and the boughs of thick trees, and willows of the brook; and ye shall rejoice before the Lord your God seven days. Lev 23:41 And ye shall keep it a feast unto the Lord seven days in the year. It shall be **a statute for ever in your generations:** ye shall celebrate it in the seventh month. 42 Ye shall dwell in booths seven days; all that are Israelites born shall dwell in booths: 43 That your genera- tions may know that I made the

children of Israel to dwell in booths, when I brought them out of the land of Egypt: I am the Lord your God. When do we hear churches of today instructing us that we are to spend a week in tents or booths so we can remember the time that God brought the children of Israel out of the land of Egypt?

The disregard for God's Holy Days is a very strong subject, but I believe this is a subject that is going to destroy a lot of God's people. Matthew 7:13 says, "Enter ye in at the strait gate: for wide is the gate, and broad is the way, that leadeth to destruction, and many there be which go in thereat: 14 Because strait is the gate, and narrow is the way, which leadeth unto life, and few there be that find it." How can we possibly think that Jesus meant anything other than many will go down that path to their own destruction? We will not find anywhere in our letter from our Father giving any autho- rization to change the Sabbath. We will not find anywhere in our letter from our Father allowing us to do anything other than what He said to do on the Sabbath. We have refused to listen to the Father since the time of creation.

> (Genesis 2) 8 And the Lord God planted a garden eastward in Eden; and there he put the man whom he had formed. 9 And out of the ground made the Lord God to grow every tree that is pleasant to the sight, and good for food; the tree of life also in the midst of the garden, and the tree of knowl- edge of good and evil. 10 And a river went out of Eden to water the garden; and from thence it was parted, and became into four heads. 11 The name of the first is Pison: that is it which compasseth the whole land of Havilah, where there is gold; 12 And the gold of that land is good: there is bdellium and the onyx stone. 13 And the name of the second river is Gihon: the same is it that compasseth the whole land of Ethiopia. 14

> And the name of the third river is Hiddekel: that is it which goeth toward the east of Assyria. And the fourth river is Euphrates. 15 And the Lord God took the man, and put him into the garden of Eden to dress it and to keep it. 16 And the Lord God commanded the man, saying, Of every tree of the garden thou mayest freely eat: 17 But of the tree of the knowledge of good and evil, thou shalt not eat of it: for in the day that thou eatest thereof thou shalt surely die.

We can hear our Father telling Adam not to eat of the fruit. Now we go to Genesis 3:

> (Genesis 3) Now the serpent was more subtil than any beast of the field which the Lord God had made. And he said unto the woman, Yea, hath God said, Ye shall not eat of every tree of the garden? 2 And the woman said unto the serpent, We may eat of the fruit of the trees of the garden: 3 But of the fruit of the tree which is in the midst of the garden, God hath said, Ye shall not eat of it, neither shall ye touch it, lest ye die. 4 And the serpent said unto the woman, Ye shall not surely die: 5 For God doth know that in the day ye eat thereof, then your eyes shall be opened, and ye shall be as gods, knowing good and evil. 6 And when the woman saw that the tree was good for food, and that it was pleasant to the eyes, and a tree to be desired to make one wise, she took of the fruit thereof, and did eat, and gave also unto her husband with her; and he did eat. 7 And the eyes of them both were opened, and they knew that they were naked; and they sewed fig leaves together, and made themselves aprons. 8 And they heard the voice of the Lord God walking in the garden in the cool of the day: and Adam and his wife hid themselves from the pres- ence of the

> Lord God amongst the trees of the garden. 9 And the Lord God called unto Adam, and said unto him, Where art thou? 10 And he said, I heard thy voice in the garden, and I was afraid, because I was naked; and I hid myself. 11 And he said, Who told thee that thou wast naked? Hast thou eaten of the tree, whereof I commanded thee that thou shouldest not eat? 12 And the man said, The woman whom thou gavest to be with me, she gave me of the tree, and I did eat. 13 And the Lord God said unto the woman, What is this that thou hast done? And the woman said, The serpent beguiled me, and I did eat.

As we can hear our Father telling us in the very beginning of His letter to us, we are the authors of our own confusion. Now just bear with me and you will understand what I am talking about. Eve ate of the fruit, even though our Father told Adam and her not to. Adam then also ate of the fruit, even though it was our Father that just told him not to eat of the tree of knowledge. Then, when our Father approached them, they both put the blame on someone else. This isn't Satan's fault. If Adam and Eve would have just listened to our Father in the beginning, everything would have been just fine. But they chose to do other than what our Father commanded. Then they pushed their own faults onto someone else. Adam said it was Eve that gave him the fruit. Just as we do today. Was he not saying that it was her fault because she gave him the fruit? Now when our Father asked Eve why she ate, she pushed the blame onto the serpent. She said the serpent beguiled her, as to say it was the serpent's fault that she ate the fruit. I have to ask, if I tell you that you can jump off of a bridge and you do, is it my fault that you jumped? I did not physically force you to jump, nor did I imply in any way that you had to. The problem is that we just don't listen to our Father. We tend to think that every- thing that goes wrong with our lives is because of someone or is someone else's doing. We do this so much that we have made ourselves blind to our own sin. If we can't realize that everything that goes wrong within our own lives is because of something that we have done, then it will be very hard to listen to our Father. Our Father has been telling us all along what we need to do to gain eternal salvation, but we get so caught up with our ways we don't take the time to listen. We are the authors of our own confusion and it is our ignorance that has gotten us in the position we are in today.

When it comes to any holidays that we celebrate other than what God commanded, we are in complete disobedience of our Father. When we cel- ebrate Christmas, New Years, birthdays, Valentine's day, Easter, Memorial day, Mother's day, Father's day, 4th of July, Labor Day, Halloween, and Thanksgiving. There are more days that I am not going to list, but we all know that these days are not listed anywhere in our bibles. Why do we think we need any other day to celebrate other than what our Father has given us to celebrate? We are told a few times within our bibles that we are not to add anything to our Father's word. Each day that we add to what God has com- manded is telling Him that we think we need more than what He gave us. We are saying we need more than perfect. Deuteronomy 4:2 states, "Ye shall **not add unto the word which I command you**, neither shall ye diminish ought from it, that ye may keep the commandments of the Lord your God which I command you." When we are adding days to celebrate, we are adding to God's word because His word does not instruct us to honor these days. This is the same thing with the Sabbath. If we change the Sabbath, are we now adding or taking away from our Father's word? I mean He did instruct us to only keep the Sabbath and gave the instructions for keeping the Sabbath.

Now we all need to think about when we celebrate days like Christmas and Easter. We need to think of the damage that it is doing to ourselves and to our children for generations to come. We tell our children that at certain times of the year a fictional character is going to bring them gifts or candy. We go all out to prove this lie to our children and are very disappointed when they find out the truth. Our children look forward to a character that has no biblical grounds. We are teaching our children how to lie. We are teaching our children to look forward to something other than our Father. I mean, we are instructed to teach our children about our Father all the time.

> (Deuteronomy 6) 3 Hear therefore, O Israel, and observe to do it; that it may be well with thee, and that ye may increase mightily, as the Lord God of thy fathers hath promised thee, in the land that floweth with milk and honey.
>
> 4 Hear, O Israel: The Lord our God is one Lord: 5 And thou shalt love the Lord thy God with all thine heart, and with all thy soul, and with all thy might. 6 **And these words, which I command thee this day, shall be in thine heart: 7 And thou shalt teach them diligently unto thy chil- dren, and shalt talk of them when thou sittest in thine house, and when thou walkest by the way, and when thou liest down, and when thou risest up.** 8 And thou shalt bind them for a sign upon thine hand, and they shall be as frontlets between thine eyes.

Now I mentioned in the beginning of this message that I would be bringing my birthday up again. I received a gift from our Father on my birthday that no man could ever come close to matching. We are to get our gifts from our Father and not man, but because we have been stuck on doing things our own way we have not allowed these gifts to come from our Father. When we set our children up with all the lies that come with these man- made holidays, how can we be teaching them anything about our Father? We are to teach them to obey every word that proceeds out of God's mouth.

NOTHING MORE AND NOTHING LESS!!!

The 1000 Year Reign with Christ

Now I know that there are a lot of people that think when Jesus comes back, it's going to be a great thing. We are now going to look at what our Father has told us it will be like when His Son comes back. Before we start, we need to try and remember that a day is like a thousand years, as shown in 2 Peter 3:8, "But, beloved, be not ignorant of this one thing, <u>that one day is with the Lord as a thousand years, and a thousand years as one day</u>." Do we remember in John that Jesus said before Abraham I am? Remember how Abram rejoiced to see his day? Now we are going to look into what his day is all about. This might be very offensive to some, so please just be patient because this is the road to heaven. These 1000 years are not going to be pleasant, as many think. After this time, and after all have learned to love the Father with all their heart, soul, and minds, we will be adopted into our Father's family and become perfect, but not until we to learn to love our Father with all of our heart, soul, and mind.

> (Zechariah 12) The burden of the word of the Lord for Israel, saith the Lord, which stretcheth forth the heavens, and layeth the foundation of the earth, and formeth the spirit of man within him. 2 Behold, I will make Jerusalem a cup of trembling unto all the people round about, when they shall be in the siege both against Judah and against Jerusalem. 3 And in that day will I make Jerusalem a burdensome stone for all people: all that burden themselves with it shall be cut in pieces, though all the people of the earth be gathered together against it. 4 In that day, saith

the Lord, I will smite every horse with astonishment, and his rider with madness: and I will open mine eyes upon the house of Judah, and will smite every horse of the people with blindness. 5 And the governors of Judah shall say in their heart, The inhabitants of Jerusalem shall be my strength in the Lord of hosts their God. 6 In that day will I make the governors of Judah like an hearth of fire among the wood, and like a torch of fire in a sheaf; and they shall devour all the people round about, on the right hand and on the left: and Jerusalem shall be inhabited again in her own place, even in Jerusalem. 7 The Lord also shall save the tents of Judah first, that the glory of the house of David and the glory of the inhabitants of Jerusalem do not mag- nify themselves against Judah.8 In that day shall the Lord defend the inhabitants of Jerusalem; and he that is feeble among them at that day shall be as David; and the house of David shall be as God, as the angel of the Lord before them. 9 And it shall come to pass in that day, that I will seek to destroy all the nations that come against Jerusalem. 10 And I will pour upon the house of David, and upon the inhabitants of Jerusalem, the spirit of grace and of sup- plications: and they shall look upon me whom they have pierced, and they shall mourn for him, as one mourneth for his only son, and shall be in bitterness for him, as one that is in bitterness for his firstborn. 11 In that day shall there be a great mourning in Jerusalem, as the mourning of Hadadrimmon in the valley of Megiddon. 12 And the land shall mourn, every family apart; the family of the house of David apart, and their wives apart; the family of the house of Nathan apart, and their wives apart; 13 The family of the house of Levi apart, and their wives apart; the family of Shimei apart, and their wives apart; 14 All the families that remain, every family apart, and their wives apart.

Remember that this day that our Father is referring to is the day of the Lord. This is going to be the 1000 year reign with Jesus.

> (Zechariah 13) In that day there shall be a fountain opened to the house of David and to the inhabitants of Jerusalem for sin and for uncleanness. 2 And it shall come to pass in that day, saith the Lord of hosts, that I will cut off the names of the idols out of the land, and they shall no more be remembered: and also I will cause the prophets and the unclean spirit to pass out of the land. 3 And it shall come to pass, that when any shall yet prophesy, then his father and his mother that begat him shall say unto him, Thou shalt not live; for thou speakest lies in the name of the Lord: and his father and his mother that begat him shall thrust him through when he prophesieth. 4 And it shall come to pass in that day, that the prophets shall be ashamed every one of his vision, when he hath prophesied; neither shall they wear a rough garment to deceive: 5 But he shall say, I am no prophet, I am an husbandman; for man taught me to keep cattle from my youth. 6 And one shall say unto him, What are these wounds in thine hands? Then he shall answer, Those with which I was wounded in the house of my friends. 7 Awake, O sword, against my shepherd, and against the man that is my fellow, saith the Lord of hosts: smite the shepherd, and the sheep shall be scattered: and I will turn mine hand upon the little ones. 8 And it shall come to pass, that in all the land, saith the Lord, two parts therein shall be cut off and die; but the third shall be left therein. 9 And I will bring the third part through the fire, and will refine

them as silver is refined, and will try them as gold is tried: they shall call on my name, and I will hear them: I will say, It is my people: and they shall say, The Lord is my God.

When we listen to what is going on here, we can hear that two thirds of the people shall be cut off and die. Remember that this is during the day of the Lord and not before. There is going to be people that are not going to do things God's way, no ifs, ands or buts about it. Remember this is the time that Satan will be locked up for 1000 years.

> (Revelation 20) And I saw an angel come down from heaven, having the key of the bottomless pit and a great chain in his hand. 2 And he laid hold on the dragon, that old serpent, which is the Devil, and Satan, and bound him a thousand years, 3 And cast him into the bottomless pit, and shut him up, and set a seal upon him, that he should deceive the nations no more, till the thousand years should be fulfilled: and after that he must be loosed a little season. 4 And I saw thrones, and they sat upon them, and judg- ment was given unto them: and I saw the souls of them that were beheaded for the witness of Jesus, and for the word of God, and which had not worshipped the beast, neither his image, neither had received his mark upon their fore- heads, or in their hands; and they lived and reigned with Christ a thousand years. 5 But the rest of the dead lived not again until the thousand years were finished. This is the first resurrection.

We can hear now that those that have already chosen to refuse to love our Father with all of their heart, soul, and mind will not even make it to the 1000 year reign with Jesus. They will stay asleep until the great white throne judgement. There will still be those who will resist God's word and that is what we are told in Isaiah.

(Isaiah 2) 3 And many people shall go and say, Come ye, and let us go up to the mountain of the Lord, to the house of the God of Jacob; and he will teach us of his ways, and we will walk in his paths: for out of Zion shall go forth the law, and the word of the Lord from Jerusalem. 4 And he shall judge among the nations, and shall rebuke many people: and they shall beat their swords into plowshares, and their spears into pruninghooks: nation shall not lift up sword against nation, neither shall they learn war any more. 5 O house of Jacob, come ye, and let us walk in the light of the Lord. And there are other areas of our letter where we are told the same thing. Why would we be beat our swords into plowshares if Satan is locked up and there is no more wars between nations going on?

(Zechariah 14) Behold, the day of the Lord cometh, and thy spoil shall be divided in the midst of thee. 2 For I will gather all nations against Jerusalem to battle; and the city shall be taken, and the houses rifled, and the women rav- ished; and half of the city shall go forth into captivity, and the residue of the people shall not be cut off from the city. 3 Then shall the Lord go forth, and fight against those nations, as when he fought in the day of battle. 4 And his feet shall stand in that day upon the mount of Olives, which is before Jerusalem on the east, and the mount of Olives shall cleave in the midst thereof toward the east and toward the west, and there shall be a very great valley; and half of the mountain shall remove toward the north, and half of it toward the south. 5 And ye shall flee to the valley of the mountains; for the valley of the mountains shall reach unto Azal: yea, ye shall flee, like as ye fled from before the earthquake in the days of Uzziah king of Judah: and the Lord my

God shall come, and all the saints with thee. 6 And it shall come to pass in that day, that the light shall not be clear, nor dark: 7 But it shall be one day which shall be known to the Lord, not day, nor night: but it shall come to pass, that at evening time it shall be light. 8 And it shall be in that day, that living waters shall go out from Jerusalem; half of them toward the former sea, and half of them toward the hinder sea: in summer and in winter shall it be. 9 And the Lord shall be king over all the earth: in that day shall there be one Lord, and his name one. 10 All the land shall be turned as a plain from Geba to Rimmon south of Jerusalem: and it shall be lifted up, and inhab- ited in her place, from Benjamin's gate unto the place of the first gate, unto the corner gate, and from the tower of Hananeel unto the king's winepresses. 11 And men shall dwell in it, and there shall be no more utter destruction; but Jerusalem shall be safely inhabited. 12 And this shall be the plague wherewith the Lord will smite all the people that have fought against Jerusalem; Their flesh shall con- sume away while they stand upon their feet, and their eyes shall consume away in their holes, and their tongue shall consume away in their mouth. 13 And it shall come to pass in that day, that a great tumult from the Lord shall be among them; and they shall lay hold every one on the hand of his neighbour, and his hand shall rise up against the hand of his neighbour. 14 And Judah also shall fight at Jerusalem; and the wealth of all the heathen round about shall be gathered together, gold, and silver, and apparel, in great abundance. 15 And so shall be the plague of the horse, of the mule, of the camel, and of the ass, and of all the beasts that shall be in these tents, as this plague. 16 And it shall come to pass, that every one that is left of all the nations which came against Jerusalem shall even go up from year to year to worship the King, the Lord of hosts, and to keep the feast of tabernacles. 17 And it shall be, that whoso will not come up of all the families of the earth unto Jerusalem to worship the King, the Lord of hosts, even upon them shall be no rain. 18 And if the family of Egypt go not up, and come not, that have no rain; there shall be the plague, wherewith the Lord will smite the heathen that come not up to keep the feast of tabernacles. 19 This shall be the punishment of Egypt, and the punishment of all nations that come not up to keep the feast of tabernacles. 20 In that day shall there be upon the bells of the horses, Holiness Unto The Lord; and the pots in the Lord's house shall be like the bowls before the altar. 21 Yea, every pot in Jerusalem and in Judah shall be holiness unto the Lord of hosts: and all they that sacrifice shall come and take of them, and seethe therein: and in that day there shall be no more the Canaanite in the house of the Lord of hosts.

As we can hear towards the end of the chapter, we can clearly tell that this is not heaven yet. There will be punishment and there will be nations that will go through periods of no rain, which causes drought and hunger. At the same time, we are starting to understand what Jesus will be doing in this time period. Jesus is the King of all kings, or the prince. The priests will be reporting to Jesus before they are allowed to enter the sanctuary, where the Father will be. Next I will be showing in more detail what it is going to look like during this time period and exactly where Jesus will be.

> (Ezekiel 40) In the five and twentieth year of our captivity, in the beginning of the year, in the tenth day of the month, in the fourteenth year after that the city was smitten, in the selfsame day the hand of the Lord

was upon me, and brought me thither. 2 In the visions of God brought he me into the land of Israel, and set me upon a very high mountain, by which was as the frame of a city on the south. 3 And he brought me thither, and, behold, there was a man, whose appearance was like the appearance of brass, with a line of flax in his hand, and a measuring reed; and he stood in the gate. 4 And the man said unto me, Son of man, behold with thine eyes, and hear with thine ears, and set thine heart upon all that I shall shew thee; for to the intent that I might shew them unto thee art thou brought hither: declare all that thou seest to the house of Israel. 5 And behold a wall on the outside of the house round about, and in the man's hand a measuring reed of six cubits long by the cubit and an hand breadth: so he measured the breadth of the building, one reed; and the height, one reed. 6 Then came he unto the gate which looketh toward the east, and went up the stairs thereof, and measured the threshold of the gate, which was one reed broad; and the other threshold of the gate, which was one reed broad. 7 And every little chamber was one reed long, and one reed broad; and between the little chambers were five cubits; and the threshold of the gate by the porch of the gate within was one reed. 8 He measured also the porch of the gate within, one reed. 9 Then measured he the porch of the gate, eight cubits; and the posts thereof, two cubits; and the porch of the gate was inward. 10 And the little chambers of the gate eastward were three on this side, and three on that side; they three were of one measure: and the posts had one measure on this side and on that side. 11 And he measured the breadth of the entry of the gate, ten cubits; and the length of the gate, thirteen cubits. 12 The space also before the little chambers was one cubit on this side, and the space was one cubit on that side: and the little chambers were six cubits on this side, and six cubits on that side. 13 He measured then the gate from the roof of one little chamber to the roof of another: the breadth was five and twenty cubits, door against door. 14 He made also posts of threescore cubits, even unto the post of the court round about the gate. 15 And from the face of the gate of the entrance unto the face of the porch of the inner gate were fifty cubits. 16 And there were narrow windows to the little chambers, and to their posts within the gate round about, and likewise to the arches: and windows were round about inward: and upon each post were palm trees. 17 Then brought he me into the outward court, and, lo, there were chambers, and a pavement made for the court round about: thirty chambers were upon the pavement. 18 And the pave- ment by the side of the gates over against the length of the gates was the lower pavement. 19 Then he measured the breadth from the forefront of the lower gate unto the fore- front of the inner court without, an hundred cubits east- ward and northward. 20 And the gate of the outward court that looked toward the north, he measured the length thereof, and the breadth thereof. 21 And the little chambers thereof were three on this side and three on that side; and the posts thereof and the arches thereof were after the mea- sure of the first gate: the length thereof was fifty cubits, and the breadth five and twenty cubits. 22 And their windows, and their arches, and their palm trees, were after the measure of the gate that looketh toward the east; and they went up unto it by seven steps; and the arches thereof were before them. 23 And the gate of the inner court was over against the gate toward the north, and toward the east; and he measured from gate to gate an hundred cubits. 24 After that he brought me toward the south, and behold a gate toward the south: and he measured the posts thereof and the arches thereof according to these measures. 25 And there were windows in it and in the arches thereof round about, like those windows: the length was fifty cubits, and the breadth five and twenty cubits. 26 And there were seven steps to go up to it, and the arches thereof were before them: and it had palm trees, one on this side, and another on that side, upon the posts thereof. 27 And there was a gate in the inner court toward the south: and he mea- sured from gate to gate toward the south an hundred cubits. 28 And he brought me to the inner court by the south gate: and he measured the south gate according to these mea- sures; 29 And the little chambers thereof, and the posts thereof, and the arches thereof, according to these mea- sures: and there were windows in it and in the arches thereof round about: it was fifty cubits long, and five and twenty cubits broad. 30 And the arches round about were five and twenty cubits long, and five cubits broad. 31 And the arches thereof were toward the utter court; and palm trees were upon the posts thereof: and the going up to it had eight steps. 32 And he brought me into the inner court toward the east: and he measured the gate according to these measures. 33 And the little chambers thereof, and the posts thereof, and the arches thereof, were according to these measures: and there were windows therein and in the arches thereof round about: it was fifty cubits long, and five and twenty cubits broad. 34 And the arches thereof were toward the outward court; and palm trees were upon the posts thereof, on this side, and on that side: and the going up to it had eight steps. 35 And he brought me to the north gate, and measured it according to these measures; 36 The little chambers thereof, the posts thereof, and the arches thereof, and the windows to it round about: the length was fifty cubits, and the breadth five and twenty cubits. 37 And the posts thereof were toward the utter court; and palm trees were upon the posts thereof, on this side, and on that side: and the going up to it had eight steps. 38 And the chambers and the entries thereof were by the posts of the gates, where they washed the burnt offering. 39 And in the porch of the gate were two tables on this side, and two tables on that side, to slay thereon the burnt offering and the sin offering and the trespass offering. 40 And at the side without, as one goeth up to the entry of the north gate, were two tables; and on the other side, which was at the porch of the gate, were two tables. 41 Four tables were on this side, and four tables on that side, by the side of the gate; eight tables, whereupon they slew their sacrifices. 42 And the four tables were of hewn stone for the burnt offering, of a cubit and an half long, and a cubit and an half broad, and one cubit high: whereupon also they laid the instruments wherewith they slew the burnt offering and the sacrifice. 43 And within were hooks, an hand broad, fastened round about: and upon the tables was the flesh of the offering. 44 And without the inner gate were the chambers of the singers in the inner court, which was at the side of the north gate; and their prospect was toward the south: one at the side of the east gate having the prospect toward the north. 45 And he said unto me, This chamber, whose prospect is toward the south, is for the priests, the keepers of the charge of the house. 46 And the chamber whose prospect is toward the north is for the priests, the keepers of the charge of the altar: these are the sons of Zadok among the sons of Levi, which come near to the Lord to minister unto him. 47 So he measured the court, an hundred cubits long, and an hundred cubits broad, foursquare; and the altar that was before the house. 48 And he brought me to the porch of the house, and measured each post of the porch, five cubits on this side, and five cubits on that side: and the breadth of the gate was three cubits on this side, and three cubits on that side. 49 The length of the porch was twenty cubits, and the breadth eleven cubits, and he brought me by the steps whereby they went up to it: and there were pillars by the posts, one on this side, and another on that side.

(Ezekiel 41) Afterward he brought me to the temple, and measured the posts, six cubits broad on the one side, and six cubits broad on the other side, which was the breadth of the tabernacle. 2 And the breadth of the door was ten cubits; and the sides of the door were five cubits on the one side, and five cubits on the other side: and he measured the length thereof, forty cubits: and the breadth, twenty cubits. 3 Then went he inward, and measured the post of the door, two cubits; and the door, six cubits; and the breadth of the door, seven cubits. 4 So he measured the length thereof, twenty cubits; and the breadth, twenty cubits, before the temple: and he said unto me, This is the most holy place. 5 After he measured the wall of the house, six cubits; and the breadth of every side chamber, four cubits, round about the house on every side. 6 And the side chambers were three, one over another, and thirty in order; and they entered into the wall which was of the house for the side chambers round about, that they might have hold, but they had not hold in the wall of the house. 7 And there was an enlarging, and a winding about still upward to the side chambers: for the winding about of the house went still upward round about the house: therefore the breadth of the house was still upward, and so increased from the lowest chamber to the highest by the midst. 8 I saw also the height of the house round about: the foundations of the side chambers were a full reed of six great cubits. 9 The thickness of the wall, which was for the side chamber without, was five cubits: and that which was left was the place of the side chambers that were within. 10 And between the chambers was the wideness of twenty cubits round about the house on every side. 11 And the doors of the side chambers were toward the place that was left, one door toward the north, and another door toward the south: and the breadth of the place that was left was five cubits round about. 12 Now the building that was before the separate place at the end toward the west was seventy cubits broad; and the wall of the building was five cubits thick round about, and the length thereof ninety cubits. 13 So he measured the house, an hundred cubits long; and the separate place, and the building, with the walls thereof, an hundred cubits long; 14 Also the breadth of the face of the house, and of the sep- arate place toward the east, an hundred cubits. 15 And he measured the length of the building over against the sepa- rate place which was behind it, and the galleries thereof on the one side and on the other side, an hundred cubits, with the inner temple, and the porches of the court; 16 The door posts, and the narrow windows, and the galleries round about on their three stories, over against the door, cieled with wood round about, and from the ground up to the win- dows, and the windows were covered; 17 To that above the door, even unto the inner house, and without, and by all the wall round

> about within and without, by measure. 18 And it was made with cherubims and palm trees, so that a palm tree was between a cherub and a cherub; and every cherub had two faces; 19 So that the face of a man was toward the palm tree on the one side, and the face of a young lion toward the palm tree on the other side: it was made through all the house round about. 20 From the ground unto above the door were cherubims and palm trees made, and on the wall of the temple. 21 The posts of the temple were squared, and the face of the sanctuary; the appear- ance of the one as the appearance of the other. 22 The altar of wood was three cubits high, and the length thereof two cubits; and the corners thereof, and the length thereof, and the walls thereof, were of wood: and he said unto me, This is the table that is before the Lord. 23 And the temple and the sanctuary had two doors. 24 And the doors had two leaves apiece, two turning leaves; two leaves for the one door, and two leaves for the other door. 25 And there were made on them, on the doors of the temple, cherubims and palm trees, like as were made upon the walls; and there were thick planks upon the face of the porch without. 26 And there were narrow windows and palm trees on the one side and on the other side, on the sides of the porch, and upon the side chambers of the house, and thick planks.

What we have been reading about in these last two chapters of Ezekiel is the description of our Father's sanctuary. The Most Holy Place is where our Father will reside while the 1000 year reign with Christ is going on. We will continue from here.

> (Ezekiel 42) Then he brought me forth into the outer court, the way toward the north: and he brought me into the chamber that was over against the separate

place, and which was before the building toward the north. 2 Before the length of an hundred cubits was the north door, and the breadth was fifty cubits. 3 Over against the twenty cubits which were for the inner court, and over against the pave- ment which was for the utter court, was gallery against gallery in three stories. 4 And before the chambers was a walk to ten cubits breadth inward, a way of one cubit; and their doors toward the north. 5 Now the upper chambers were shorter: for the galleries were higher than these, than the lower, and than the middlemost of the building. 6 For they were in three stories, but had not pillars as the pillars of the courts: therefore the building was straitened more than the lowest and the middlemost from the ground. 7 And the wall that was without over against the chambers, toward the utter court on the forepart of the chambers, the length thereof was fifty cubits. 8 For the length of the chambers that were in the utter court was fifty cubits: and, lo, before the temple were an hundred cubits. 9 And from under these chambers was the entry on the east side, as one goeth into them from the utter court. 10 The cham- bers were in the thickness of the wall of the court toward the east, over against the separate place, and over against the building. 11 And the way before them was like the appearance of the chambers which were toward the north, as long as they, and as broad as they: and all their goings out were both according to their fashions, and according to their doors. 12 And according to the doors of the cham- bers that were toward the south was a door in the head of the way, even the way directly before the wall toward the east, as one entereth into them. 13 Then said he unto me, The north chambers and the south chambers, which are before the separate place, they be holy chambers, where the priests that approach unto the Lord shall eat the most holy things: there shall they lay the most holy things, and the meat offering, and the sin offering, and the trespass offering; for the place is holy. 14 When the priests enter therein, then shall they not go out of the holy place into the utter court, but there they shall lay their garments wherein they minister; for they are holy; and shall put on other garments, and shall approach to those things which are for the people. 15 Now when he had made an end of mea- suring the inner house, he brought me forth toward the gate whose prospect is toward the east, and measured it round about. 16 He measured the east side with the measuring reed, five hundred reeds, with the measuring reed round about. 17 He measured the north side, five hundred reeds, with the measuring reed round about. 18 He measured the south side, five hundred reeds, with the measuring reed. 19 He turned about to the west side, and measured five hundred reeds with the measuring reed. 20 He measured it by the four sides: it had a wall round about, five hundred reeds long, and five hundred broad, to make a separation between the sanctuary and the profane place.

Now we need to pause just a short minute to make sure that everyone reading is actually listening to what we are being told. There will be sacri- fices for our sins again during the reign of Christ. These will not take away our sins, but will be a symbol of us desiring to rid ourselves of **ALL** sin. Remember the punishment that will be given to those that do not come to worship on certain days? This is where all that have desired to be with God but did not understand, or did not ever have the opportunity to learn what they needed to learn, will have the chance to learn to love our Father with all of their heart, soul, and minds.

(Ezekiel 43) Afterward he brought me to the gate, even the gate that looketh toward the east: 2 And, behold, the glory of the God of Israel came from the way of the east: and his voice was like a noise of many waters: and the earth shined with his glory. 3 And it was according to the appearance of the vision which I saw, even according to the vision that I saw when I came to destroy the city: and the visions were like the vision that I saw by the river Chebar; and I fell upon my face. 4 And the glory of the Lord came into the house by the way of the gate whose prospect is toward the east. 5 So the spirit took me up, and brought me into the inner court; and, behold, the glory of the Lord filled the house. 6 And I heard him speaking unto me out of the house; and the man stood by me. 7 And he said unto me, Son of man, the place of my throne, and the place of the soles of my feet, where I will dwell in the midst of the children of Israel for ever, and my holy name, shall the house of Israel no more defile, neither they, nor their kings, by their whoredom, nor by the carcases of their kings in their high places. 8 In their setting of their threshold by my thresholds, and their post by my posts, and the wall between me and them, they have even defiled my holy name by their abominations that they have com- mitted: wherefore I have consumed them in mine anger. 9 Now let them put away their whoredom, and the carcases of their kings, far from me, and I will dwell in the midst of them for ever. 10 Thou son of man, shew the house to the house of Israel, that they may be ashamed of their iniquities: and let them measure the pattern. 11 And if they be ashamed of all that they have done, shew them the form of the house, and the fashion thereof, and the goings out thereof, and the comings in thereof, and all the forms thereof, and all the ordinances thereof, and all the forms thereof, and all the laws thereof: and write it in their sight, that they may keep the whole form thereof, and all the ordinances thereof, and do them. 12 This is the law of the house; Upon the top of the mountain the whole limit thereof round about shall be most holy. Behold, this is the law of the house. 13 And these are the measures of the altar after the cubits: The cubit is a cubit and an hand breadth; even the bottom shall be a cubit, and the breadth a cubit, and the border thereof by the edge thereof round about shall be a span: and this shall be the higher place of the altar. 14 And from the bottom upon the ground even to the lower settle shall be two cubits, and the breadth one cubit; and from the lesser settle even to the greater settle shall be four cubits, and the breadth one cubit. 15 So the altar shall be four cubits; and from the altar and upward shall be four horns. 16 And the altar shall be twelve cubits long, twelve broad, square in the four squares thereof. 17 And the settle shall be fourteen cubits long and fourteen broad in the four squares thereof; and the border about it shall be half a cubit; and the bottom thereof shall be a cubit about; and his stairs shall look toward the east. 18 And he said unto me, Son of man, thus saith the Lord God; These are the ordinances of the altar in the day when they shall make it, to offer burnt offerings thereon, and to sprinkle blood thereon. 19 And thou shalt give to the priests the Levites that be of the seed of Zadok, which approach unto me, to minister unto me, saith the Lord God, a young bullock for a sin offering. 20 And thou shalt take of the blood thereof, and put it on the four horns of it, and on the four corners of the settle, and upon the border round about: thus shalt thou cleanse and purge it. 21 Thou shalt take the bullock also of the sin offering, and he shall burn it in the appointed place of the house, without the sanctuary. 22 And on the second day thou shalt offer a kid of the goats without blemish for a sin offering; and they shall cleanse the altar, as they did cleanse it with the bullock. 23 When thou hast made an end of cleansing it, thou shalt offer a young bullock without blemish, and a ram out of the flock without blemish. 24 And thou shalt offer them before the Lord, and the priests shall cast salt upon them, and they shall offer them up for a burnt offering unto the Lord. 25 Seven days shalt thou prepare every day a goat for a sin offering: they shall also prepare a young bullock, and a ram out of the flock, without blemish. 26 Seven days shall they purge the altar and purify it; and they shall consecrate themselves. 27 And when these days are expired, it shall be, that upon the eighth day, and so forward, the priests shall make your burnt offerings upon the altar, and your peace offerings; and I will accept you, saith the Lord God.

Remember the verses showing before that we have been playing the whore, or harlot? All of us that have played the harlot but still have a love for our Father will make it to the kingdom, but not all of us will learn to love our Father with all of our heart, soul, and mind and desire with everything we have to be completely obedient to the Father. He lets us know in this chapter that no one will come near Him that has any iniquity. He will be dwelling behind the walls that Jesus will be guarding. He is not going to tolerate sin at all. We can further understand this when we look at Leviticus 10, "And Nadab and Abihu, the sons of Aaron, took either of them his censer, and put fire therein, and put incense thereon, and offered strange fire before the Lord, which he commanded them not.2 And there went out fire from the Lord, and devoured them, and they died before the Lord." Nothing that goes against what the Father has commanded will ever be allowed near Him. However, He is letting us know that even after the 1000 year reign with Christ begins, if we turn away from our sins He will still have mercy on us. We are the ones that make the choice whether or not to love Him and gain that desire to obey every jot and tittle of every letter of His law.

> (Ezekiel 44) Then he brought me back the way of the gate of the outward sanctuary which looketh toward the east; and it was shut. 2 Then said the Lord unto me; This gate shall be shut, it shall not be opened, and no man shall enter in by it; because the Lord, the God of Israel, hath entered in by it, therefore it shall be shut. **3 It is for the prince; the prince, he shall sit in it to eat bread before the Lord; he shall enter by the way of the porch of that gate, and shall go out by the way of the same.** 4 Then brought he me the way of the north gate before the house: and I looked, and, behold, the glory of the Lord filled the house of the Lord: and I fell upon my face. 5 And the Lord said unto me, Son of man, mark well, and behold with thine eyes, and hear with thine ears all that I say unto thee concerning all the ordinances of the house of the Lord, and all the laws thereof; and mark well the entering in of the house, with every going forth of the sanctuary. 6 And thou shalt say to the rebellious, even to the house of Israel, Thus saith the Lord God; O ye house of Israel, let it suffice you of **all your abominations,** 7 In that ye have brought into my sanctuary strangers, **uncircumcised in heart, and uncircumcised in flesh, to be in my sanctuary, to pol- lute it, even my house, when ye offer my bread, the fat and the blood, and they have broken my covenant because of all your abominations. 8 And ye have not kept the charge of mine holy things: but ye have set keepers of my charge in my sanctuary for**

yourselves. 9 Thus saith the Lord God; No stranger, uncircumcised in heart, nor uncircumcised in flesh, shall enter into my sanctuary, of any stranger that is among the children of Israel. 10 And the Levites that are gone away far from me, when Israel went astray, which went astray away from me after their idols; they shall even bear their iniquity. 11 Yet they shall be ministers in my sanctuary, having charge at the gates of the house, and ministering to the house: they shall slay the burnt offering and the sacrifice for the people, and they shall stand before them to minister unto them. 12 Because they ministered unto them before their idols, and caused the house of Israel to fall into iniquity; therefore have I lifted up mine hand against them, saith the Lord God, and they shall bear their iniquity. 13 And they shall not come near unto me, to do the office of a priest unto me, nor to come near to any of my holy things, in the most holy place: **but they shall bear their shame, and their abominations which they have committed.** 14 But I will make them keepers of the charge of the house, for all the service thereof, and for all that shall be done therein. 15 **But the priests the Levites, the sons of Zadok, that kept the charge of my sanctuary when the children of Israel went astray from me, they shall come near to me to minister unto me, and they shall stand before me to offer unto me the fat and the blood, saith the Lord God:** 16 They shall enter into my sanctuary, and they shall come near to my table, to minister unto me, and they shall keep my charge. 17 And it shall come to pass, that when they enter in at the gates of the inner court, they shall be clothed with linen garments; and no wool shall come upon them, whiles they minister in the gates of the inner court, and within. 18 They shall have linen bonnets upon their heads, and shall have linen breeches upon their loins; they shall not gird themselves with any thing that causeth sweat. 19 And when they go forth into the utter court, even into the utter court to the people, they shall put off their garments wherein they ministered, and lay them in the holy cham- bers, and they shall put on other garments; and they shall not sanctify the people with their garments. 20 <u>Neither shall they shave their heads, nor suffer their locks to grow</u> long; <u>they shall only poll their heads</u>. 21 Neither shall any priest drink wine, when they enter into the inner court. 22 Neither shall they take for their wives a widow, nor her that is put away: but they shall take maidens of the seed of the house of Israel, or a widow that had a priest before. 23 And they shall teach my people the difference between the holy and profane, and cause them to discern between the unclean and the clean. 24 And in controversy they shall stand in judgment; and they shall judge it according to my judgments: and they shall keep my laws and my statutes in all mine assemblies; and they shall hallow my sab- baths. 25 And they shall come at no dead person to defile themselves: but for father, or for mother, or for son, or for daughter, for brother, or for sister that hath had no husband, they may defile themselves. 26 And after he is cleansed, they shall reckon unto him seven days. 27 And in the day that he goeth into the sanctuary, unto the inner court, to minister in the sanctuary, he shall offer his sin offering, saith the Lord God. 28 And it shall be unto them for an inheritance: I am their inheritance: and ye shall give them no possession in Israel: I am their possession. 29 They shall eat the meat offering, and the sin offering, and the trespass offering: and every dedicated thing in Israel shall be theirs. 30 And

> the first of all the firstfruits of all things, and every oblation of all, of every sort of your oblations, shall be the priest's: ye shall also give unto the priest the first of your dough, that he may cause the blessing to rest in thine house. 31 The priests shall not eat of any thing that is dead of itself, or torn, whether it be fowl or beast.

We can hear in this chapter what the role of the priest will be. Remember a couple of chapters ago we were learning that there will be a specific spot for the Levites? We know now that there will still be a lot of preaching and teaching going on. We are told that there will be controversy and all that don't agree with our Father's ways will be judged by the priests, and they will judge according to the Father's judgements. Yes Satan is locked up for this time period, but there is still going to be a lot of people that will refuse to do things the way our Father said they must be done. I also put the verse about the prince in bold because the prince is Jesus. He will be the one outside the Most Holy Place and guarding it to make sure that there is NO iniquity whatsoever that passes through.

> (Ezekiel 45) Moreover, when ye shall divide by lot the land for inheritance, ye shall offer an oblation unto the Lord, an holy portion of the land: the length shall be the length of five and twenty thousand reeds, and the breadth shall be ten thousand. This shall be holy in all the borders thereof round about. 2 Of this there shall be for the sanc- tuary five hundred in length, with five hundred in breadth, square round about; and fifty cubits round about for the suburbs thereof. 3 And of this measure shalt thou measure the length of five and twenty thousand, and the breadth of ten thousand: and in it shall be the sanctuary and the most holy place. 4 The holy portion of the land shall be for the priests the ministers of the sanctuary, which

shall come near to minister unto the Lord: and it shall be a place for their houses, and an holy place for the sanctuary. 5 And the five and twenty thousand of length, and the ten thou- sand of breadth shall also the Levites, the ministers of the house, have for themselves, for a possession for twenty chambers. 6 And ye shall appoint the possession of the city five thousand broad, and five and twenty thousand long, over against the oblation of the holy portion: it shall be for the whole house of Israel. 7 And a portion shall be for the prince on the one side and on the other side of the oblation of the holy portion, and of the possession of the city, before the oblation of the holy portion, and before the possession of the city, from the west side westward, and from the east side eastward: and the length shall be over against one of the portions, from the west border unto the east border. 8 In the land shall be his possession in Israel: and my princes shall no more oppress my people; and the rest of the land shall they give to the house of Israel according to their tribes. 9 Thus saith the Lord God; Let it suffice you, O princes of Israel: remove violence and spoil, and execute judgment and justice, take away your exactions from my people, saith the Lord God. 10 Ye shall have just balances, and a just ephah, and a just bath. 11 The ephah and the bath shall be of one measure, that the bath may contain the tenth part of an homer, and the ephah the tenth part of an homer: the measure thereof shall be after the homer. 12 And the shekel shall be twenty gerahs: twenty shekels, five and twenty shekels, fifteen shekels, shall be your maneh. 13 This is the oblation that ye shall offer; the sixth part of an ephah of an homer of wheat, and ye shall give the sixth part of an ephah of an homer of barley: 14 Concerning the ordinance of oil, the bath of oil, ye shall offer the tenth part of a bath out of the cor, which is an homer of ten baths; for ten baths are an homer: 15 And one lamb out of the flock, out of two hundred, out of the fat pastures of Israel; for a meat offering, and for a burnt offering, and for peace offerings, to make recon- ciliation for them, saith the Lord God. 16 **All the people of the land shall give this oblation for the prince in Israel.** 17 And it shall be the prince's part to give burnt offerings, and meat offerings, and drink offerings, in the feasts, and in the new moons, and in the sabbaths, in all solemnities of the house of Israel: he shall prepare the sin offering, and the meat offering, and the burnt offering, and the peace offerings, to make reconciliation for the house of Israel. 18 Thus saith the Lord God; In the first month, in the first day of the month, thou shalt take a young bullock without blemish, and cleanse the sanctuary: 19 And the priest shall take of the blood of the sin offering, and put it upon the posts of the house, and upon the four corners of the settle of the altar, and upon the posts of the gate of the inner court. 20 And so thou shalt do the seventh day of the month for every one that erreth, and for him that is simple: so shall ye reconcile the house. 21 In the first month, in the fourteenth day of the month, ye shall have the passover, a feast of seven days; unleavened bread shall be eaten. 22 And upon that day shall the prince prepare for himself and for all the people of the land a bullock for a sin offering. 23 And seven days of the feast he shall prepare a burnt offering to the Lord, seven bullocks and seven rams without blemish daily the seven days; and a kid of the goats daily for a sin offering. 24 And he shall prepare a meat offering of an ephah for a bullock, and an ephah for a ram, and an hin of oil for an ephah. 25 In the seventh

> month, in the fifteenth day of the month, shall he do the like in the feast of the seven days, according to the sin offering, according to the burnt offering, and according to the meat offering, and according to the oil.

Remember how God's Holy Days are a foreshadow of things to come? Colossians 2:16 states, "Let no man therefore judge you in meat, or in drink, or in respect of an holyday, or of the new moon, or of the sabbath days: 17 <u>Which are a shadow of things to come; but the body is of Christ</u>." These are days we need to be observing now so we will not be struggling with them once the 1000 year reign is set up. All these days will be established again and there will be punishment for not obeying them. Yes, we will be sacri- ficing again just as they did in ancient times. The only difference will be that Satan will no longer be able to tempt us as he will be locked up during this time. Jesus was and is and will always be the final sacrifice, but not until we learn to love our Father with all of our heart, soul, and mind. Not until we have a complete desire to be completely obedient to the Father. As we have been reading, our Father will not allow anyone with any iniquity in his or her heart near Him. Once we get all that iniquity out of our hearts, then Jesus will be our advocator with the Father.

> (Ezekiel 46) Thus saith the Lord God; The gate of the inner court that looketh toward the east shall be shut the six working days; but on the sabbath it shall be opened, and in the day of the new moon it shall be opened. 2 And the prince shall enter by the way of the porch of that gate without, and shall stand by the post of the gate, and the priests shall prepare his burnt offering and his peace offer- ings, and he shall worship at the threshold of the gate: then he shall go forth; but the gate shall not be shut until the evening. 3 Likewise the people of the land shall worship at the door of this gate before the Lord in the sabbaths

and in the new moons. 4 And the burnt offering that the prince shall offer unto the Lord in the sabbath day shall be six lambs without blemish, and a ram without blemish. 5 And the meat offering shall be an ephah for a ram, and the meat offering for the lambs as he shall be able to give, and an hin of oil to an ephah. 6 And in the day of the new moon it shall be a young bullock without blemish, and six lambs, and a ram: they shall be without blemish. 7 And he shall prepare a meat offering, an ephah for a bullock, and an ephah for a ram, and for the lambs according as his hand shall attain unto, and an hin of oil to an ephah. 8 And when the prince shall enter, he shall go in by the way of the porch of that gate, and he shall go forth by the way thereof. 9 But when the people of the land shall come before the Lord in the solemn feasts, he that entereth in by the way of the north gate to worship shall go out by the way of the south gate; and he that entereth by the way of the south gate shall go forth by the way of the north gate: he shall not return by the way of the gate whereby he came in, but shall go forth over against it. 10 And the prince in the midst of them, when they go in, shall go in; and when they go forth, shall go forth. 11 And in the feasts and in the solemnities the meat offering shall be an ephah to a bullock, and an ephah to a ram, and to the lambs as he is able to give, and an hin of oil to an ephah. 12 Now when the prince shall prepare a voluntary burnt offering or peace offerings vol- untarily unto the Lord, one shall then open him the gate that looketh toward the east, and he shall prepare his burnt offering and his peace offerings, as he did on the sabbath day: then he shall go forth; and after his going forth one shall shut the gate. 13 Thou shalt daily prepare a burnt offering unto the Lord of a lamb of the first year without blemish: thou shalt prepare it every morning. 14 And thou shalt prepare a meat offering for it every morning, the sixth part of an ephah, and the third part of an hin of oil, to temper with the fine flour; a meat offering continually by a perpetual ordinance unto the Lord. 15 Thus shall they prepare the lamb, and the meat offering, and the oil, every morning for a continual burnt offering. 16 Thus saith the Lord God; If the prince give a gift unto any of his sons, the inheritance thereof shall be his sons'; it shall be their possession by inheritance. 17 But if he give a gift of his inheritance to one of his servants, then it shall be his to the year of liberty; after it shall return to the prince: but his inheritance shall be his sons' for them. 18 Moreover the prince shall not take of the people's inheritance by oppres- sion, to thrust them out of their possession; but he shall give his sons inheritance out of his own possession: that my people be not scattered every man from his possession. 19 After he brought me through the entry, which was at the side of the gate, into the holy chambers of the priests, which looked toward the north: and, behold, there was a place on the two sides westward. 20 Then said he unto me, This is the place where the priests shall boil the trespass offering and the sin offering, where they shall bake the meat offering; that they bear them not out into the utter court, to sanctify the people. 21 Then he brought me forth into the utter court, and caused me to pass by the four cor- ners of the court; and, behold, in every corner of the court there was a court. 22 In the four corners of the court there were courts joined of forty cubits long and thirty broad: these four corners were of one measure. 23 And there was a row of building round about in them, round about them four, and it was made with boiling places under the rows round about. 24 Then said he unto me, These are the places of them that boil, where the ministers of the house shall boil the sacrifice of the people.

Here we see a bigger picture of what Jesus will be doing during the 1000 year reign. We know that Jesus is the prince of kings because of what we read in Revelation 1:5, "And from Jesus Christ, who is the faithful witness, and the first begotten of the dead, and the prince of the kings of the earth. Unto him that loved us, and washed us from our sins in his own blood".

See now, when we listen to everything that our Father has been telling us all along, we can start putting the pieces of our bible together instead of picking and choosing pieces and trying to force them together.

We also know that the New Covenant will not be established until after the 1000 year reign with Christ because we read a few chapters ago that there will still be teaching going on. Not everyone will know all of God's laws and some will still resist it. This will help us understand Hebrews 10.

> (Hebrews 10) For the law having a shadow of good things to come, and not the very image of the things, can never with those sacrifices which they offered year by year con- tinually make the comers thereunto perfect. 2 For then would they not have ceased to be offered? because that the worshippers once purged should have had no more conscience of sins.3 But in those sacrifices there is a remembrance again made of sins every year. 4 For it is not possible that the blood of bulls and of goats should take away sins.5 Wherefore when he cometh into the world, he saith, Sacrifice and offering thou wouldest not, but a body hast thou prepared me:6 In burnt offerings and sacrifices for sin thou hast had no pleasure.7 Then said I, Lo, I come

(in the volume of the book it is written of me,) to do thy will, O God.8 Above when he said, Sacrifice and offering and burnt offerings and offering for sin thou wouldest not, neither hadst pleasure therein; which are offered by the law;9 Then said he, Lo, I come to do thy will, O God. He taketh away the first, that he may establish the second.10 By the which will we are sanctified through the offering of the body of Jesus Christ once for all. 11 And every **priest standeth daily ministering and offering oftentimes the same sacrifices**, which can never take away sins: 12 But this man, after he had offered one sacrifice for sins for ever, sat down on the right hand of God; 13 From hence- forth expecting till his enemies be made his footstool. 14 For by one offering he hath perfected **for ever them that are sanctified.**15 Whereof the Holy Ghost also is a wit- ness to us: for after that he had said before,16 **This is the covenant that I will make with them after those days, saith the Lord, I will put my laws into their hearts, and in their minds will I write them;**17 **And their sins and iniquities will I remember no more.**18 Now where remission of these is, there is no more offering for sin.19 Having therefore, brethren, boldness to enter into the holiest by the blood of Jesus.

Remember we will not be allowed into the holiest until we love the Father with all of our heart, soul, and mind and are willfully completely obedient to every jot, tittle, of every letter of every law of His.

Those that come to love the Father with all of their heart, soul, and mind, and are striving to be completely obedient to our Father, are the ones that Jesus will make priests to help in the kingdom. These priests will be teaching and preaching throughout the reign with Christ. Then, as others learn to love our Father with all of their heart, soul, and minds and strive to be completely obedient to our Father, Jesus becomes the final sac- rifice for our sins and mediates with the Father, which allows us into our Father's house. This is when the New Covenant will be established. God will write His laws in our minds and on our hearts and He will no longer remember our sins.

Reason for Animal Sacrifices

Do we really understand what the purpose of the animal sacrifices was? We today think this was just some ritual. Have we ever considered that these sacrifices were symbolic of our way of showing our love for our Father? This is what the Father has told us to do for the Sabbath keeping.

> (Ezekiel 20) 11 And I gave them my statutes, and shewed them my judgments, which if a man do, he shall even live in them.12 Moreover also I gave them my sabbaths, to be a sign between me and them, that they might know that I am the Lord that sanctify them.13 But the house of Israel rebelled against me in the wilderness: they walked not in my statutes, and they despised my judgments, which if a man do, he shall even live in them; and my sabbaths they greatly polluted: then I said, I would pour out my fury upon them in the wilderness, to consume them.

When they used to sacrifice animals it was supposed to symbolize to our Father their desire not to sin. When they would give their best animals, ani- mals without blemish, for their sin sacrifice this would symbolize a way of repentance and this should have made people truly sorry for their sin. When they raised a very nice animal it should have meant something to them, because it was the best eating or maybe it would sell for the most, but it got to a point that the people just figured they could sin all they wanted and then sacrifice their animals once a week or so and all would be good. They were missing the entire point of what our Father has been trying to say to them in this letter of His.

This was a like a step-by-step process. They were to first learn what God's laws were and then, when they would sin, they would offer the best of what they had to ask God to forgive their sins that went against Him. This is similar to what we see going on in the churches today. People go to church once a week or so and then go on living in sin. They are seeking mates outside of marriage. They are bar-hopping, seeking sex with same sex people, doing all kinds of illegal drugs, cheating on spouses and etc. They go to church once a week and give a little money and they go on living as if God is happy with them.

Well we should be paying attention to our Father when He tells us He is sick of it.

> (Isaiah 1) 10 Hear the word of the Lord, ye rulers of Sodom; give ear unto the law of our God, ye people of Gomorrah.11 To what purpose is the multitude of your sacrifices unto me? saith the Lord: I am full of the burnt offerings of rams, and the fat of fed beasts; and I delight not in the blood of bullocks, or of lambs, or of he goats.12 When ye come to appear before me, who hath required this at your hand, to tread my courts? 13 Bring no more vain oblations; incense is an abomination unto me; the new moons and sabbaths, the calling of assemblies, I cannot away with; it is iniquity, even the solemn meeting. 14 Your new moons and your appointed feasts my soul hateth: they are a trouble unto me; I am weary to bear them. 15 And when ye spread forth your hands, I will hide mine eyes from you: yea, when ye make many prayers, I will not hear: your hands are full of blood.

As we can hear our Father telling us, He is sick of the sacrifices and assemblies when we do nothing but continue to sin against Him. He does go on to say that if we obey He will be our God.

(Isaiah 1) 16 Wash you, make you clean; put away the evil of your doings from before mine eyes; cease to do evil;17 Learn to do well; seek judgment, relieve the oppressed, judge the fatherless, plead for the widow.18 Come now, and let us reason together, saith the Lord: though your sins be as scarlet, they shall be as white as snow; though they be red like crimson, they shall be as wool.19 If ye be willing and obedient, ye shall eat the good of the land:20 But if ye refuse and rebel, ye shall be devoured with the sword: for the mouth of the Lord hath spoken it.

Our Father has caused Israel to forget His feast days and Sabbaths. He did this because of her disobedience. Once He had scattered and made Israel forget the feast days, He has required that Israel seek these days and honor them to be a sign for Him. Hosea 2:11 says, "I will also cause all her mirth to cease, her feast days, her new moons, and her sabbaths, and all her solemn feasts." This all winds back to the same thing with the animals. It is a sign to Him that we love Him with all of our heart, soul, and minds.

Let Us Make Man in Our Own Image

I know that this is a question that all of us have misunderstood for thou- sands of years. If you're sitting down, I ask in humor that you strap yourself in because once you start to understand this it will probably knock you off your chair, as it did me once the Father gave me the knowledge to understand this. I am this day, and probably will be every day of the rest of my life, astonished with how much we are made in their image.

Let us listen to what the Father is telling us in Genesis 1:26, "And God said, <u>Let us make man in our image, after our likeness</u>: and let them have dominion over the fish of the sea, and over the fowl of the air, and over the cattle, and over all the earth, and over every creeping thing that creepeth upon the earth. 27 So God created man in his own image, in the image of God created he him; male and female created he them."

Now I know that a lot of people think or (I hope) used to think that God was saying 'let us' is pertaining to His Son, but by now I think we should have a pretty good understanding of who Jesus is and realize that at no time did he exist in the Old Testament. Yes he was prophesied about, but he did not exist. Instead of me going on about all of that again, we should be listening to the Father and hear who "us" is that He was refer- ring to. 1 Timothy 3:16 says, "And without controversy great is the mystery of godliness: God was manifest in the flesh, justified in the Spirit, <u>seen of</u> <u>angels</u>, preached unto the Gentiles, believed on in the world, received up into glory."

Luke 1:26 tells us, "And in the sixth month the <u>angel Gabriel</u> <u>was sent</u> <u>from God</u> unto a city of Galilee, named Nazareth". Also in

Luke2:9, "And, lo, <u>the angel of the Lord</u> came upon them, and the glory of the Lord shone round about them: and they were sore afraid."

Now we can start to understand the angels are dwelling with God as we speak. This is why God said let us make man in our image. The Father is the creator and all glory goes to the Father and not the angels. To further illustrate this, we need to think of when someone invents a product of any kind. Let us think of Henry Ford and the invention of the automobile. Yes, he gets the credit for inventing the car. Today we still manufacture Fords, and other types of vehicles, but we are not the inventors. Henry Ford still gets the glory for inventing the automobile. So at no time can we give any glory to the angels, because the Father is the mastermind behind everything. After reading all that we have read in this book, we can start to understand that we should live every day in obedience. Ecclesiastes 12:13 tells us, "<u>Let us hear the conclusion of the whole matter: Fear God, and keep his com- mandments: for this is the whole duty of man.</u>" It does not matter who you are or what you do. We live in obedience to whatever we do. Let us look at a few examples to show you exactly what I am talking about. Once you come to understand this you will realize that the Father has hid nothing, and I mean nothing, from us. We live life by the very way He is telling us we need to throughout our entire lives.

I will start with an example of my life. I am a truck driver and I have to obey city, state, and federal laws at all times. If I do not I will be pun- ished some way or another. I will say I am breaking the speed limit and get a ticket. I have to pay a fine and there are points that will be acquired on my license. If I continue to speed I will get more tickets and fines. If I don't repent from doing things my way, the state of Missouri will take my license away from me. They will no longer let me drive in their house, their house being the state of Missouri. Now let me say that I do not get a speeding ticket, but get a log book violation. The federal Department of Transportation will fine me and shut down my truck for an uncertain amount of hours.

Now let us imagine that I ignore the maintenance on my truck and it becomes a safety issue. The Department of Transportation will shut me and the truck down until the issue (or issues) is fixed.

Now to give a little description of what is going on here without going into too much detail, I will explain. The federal government has this thing called a CSA score. Each time I get any infraction on my license or a safety violation, I accumu- late points on this score. After I accumulate so many points, the company that I am driving for will not allow me to be employed there anymore. This is because the higher the score the driver has indicates that the driver is an unsafe driver. Now the company also gets graded on this score, but their score is on all of their drivers and all of their equipment. Now if I accumu- late enough points the company will not allow me in their house anymore, the company being the house. They will fire me. On top of that, now very few other companies will hire me because it will have an effect on their score. The company will not want drivers with high scores, because after they accumulate too high of a score the federal government can shut their company down. The federal government will not allow them in their house anymore, the house being the United States.

Before I move on to the next example, we should also realize every- body involved with me and my driving in this example is also following the same guidelines, or unwritten laws, for whatever they do. The officer that issues me tickets is just being obedient to his or her boss. It just goes down the list with the state and federal government. Please keep this in mind on each example that I use.

I will use someone that works in a factory now. When they go in to work every day, they must be there at the scheduled starting time. They must produce a quota per hour, or per day, or they will be reprimanded. They are not allowed to take breaks other than specific times scheduled for breaks. Now if this person is late several times, or this person does not meet the quota expectations, they will be reprimanded, as well. If this person takes breaks other than the specific times scheduled, they will be repri- manded. If they continue to do things their own way the punishment gets worse. Eventually it gets to the point that the factory either forces them to repent of doing things their way or they will not be welcome in their house anymore, the factory being the house.

Now let us think of a waitress or waiter. Let us say that they are waiting on tables at a very well-known local steak house in your location. If the person waiting on tables is very rude, the customer will complain and most likely lessen the tip, which is the first form of punishment. If this person continues to be rude for a number of customers, the complaints will find their way back to management. Then management will inquire of the person and reprimand them for their rudeness. No telling what the repercussions will be for that person, but we do know that if this person continues in his or her ways, they will finally be asked to leave their house, the restaurant being the house. Now we should realize why the house is forced to ask this person to leave. If they continue to do things their own way, it will hurt their reputation and they will lose customers. Eventually that loss of customers could cause the restaurant to close its doors.

This is the same reason the Father needs us to be completely compliant with all that He has commanded us. If He allows anyone with any sin within their heart in His house, they will eventually think that some other way, other than God's, is better. Then His house becomes no longer perfect, as we all know it is now. Then His house will no longer exist. God will not, and cannot, allow imperfection in His house.

Now I want to use a child going through school. Let us think of a child in the 1st grade. The work they do in school is pretty easy for us, but not for them. Several times through the year this child is graded on their perfor- mance in the classroom. At the end of the school year the teacher decides if their performance has been satisfactory to advance to the next level of the house, the school being the house. If their performance is not good enough, they are held back until they are ready to advance. That is their repercus- sion. If their performance is satisfactory then they advance to a new room, being the 2nd grade. This procedure is repeated throughout the entire 12 grades of school. If this child has problems in, let's say, the 7th grade and is held back too many years, the school will eventually tell the parents that they are not capable of teaching the child. Then the child is no longer wel- come into the house at all. The child must obey all of the school guidelines in order to stay in their house. We can see this better if we say this child is constantly skipping class, hitting other students, or just always being very hostile towards the teachers. They will be given the opportunity to repent from their ways or they will be asked to leave the house, the school being the house.

We now think about a college student. This student must maintain a certain grade in order to graduate, right? Let us think of a medical student. This medical student needs to maintain a high grade average, but not just to graduate. The better the student, the better opportunities he or she will have for a decent job in a well-respected hospital. If this student does not meet the expectations needed to earn a degree in his or her field, they will not graduate. They will not be allowed to move into that house, the well-re- spected hospital being the house. Once they graduate with good grades, then they will be welcomed into the house. Now they are in the house and have been in the house for quite some time. They have performed many neck surgeries (I am using this because I have had two neck surgeries myself). When they have a patient come in scheduled for surgery, the hos- pital has a routine that they follow to prep the patient. Once the patient is prepped and ready for surgery, he or she is moved into the operating room. The doctor starts the procedure with a certain selection of tools. He knows where to make the proper cuts in order to get where he needs to be to per- form his or her work. They do the surgery and then the doctor may have a different team to come in and close the incisions and then a different team to clean up.

Now after reading this, we need to think about it. The patient had to be obedient to the doctor and listen and follow the instructions before the pro- cedure or the doctor could not do the procedure. The crew that prepped the patient had to be obedient to a specific set of rules for prepping the patient. If they didn't follow these rules, the doctor may not be able to do the proce- dure. The doctor had to be obedient to his or her ways of knowing what to do to perform the procedure properly or the doctor may face a malpractice lawsuit. The crew that comes in to close the incisions had to be obedient to a certain way of doing their procedure or the wound won't heal properly.

The clean-up crew had to be obedient to the rules of cleaning up properly, with the proper supplies, or the next patient needing that room might have complications.

I have just illustrated a few real-life examples of how what we do in our everyday life is exactly what the Father needs from us. It doesn't matter who you are or what you do, you live in obedience to unwritten laws. All these laws that we follow are how the world keeps moving the way it does. I am not saying, in any way, that things are the way they should be. I am just showing that we live in obedience. We do this without even thinking about it. I don't think about the laws I have to follow in order for me to keep my job. I just do them because I already know this is what I have to do. When we go to school we don't think about how we must obtain a certain grade average to advance to the next grade. We just know that we have to do well or we will not graduate. When the doctor and everybody else involved with the surgery goes into surgery, they don't think about what they have to do. They just do it because they know. It has become a routine for them. It just comes to them naturally.

To further show how everything we do is to some form of unwritten law, think about this for minute if you will. If you get up out of a chair and walk across the room and back to your chair, do you think about how much muscle it will take you to get up our of your chair? Do you think about how much muscle you need to move your legs each time you move them? Do you think about how far you will have to move each leg for each step all across the room? Do you think of where you need to aim your foot with each step? Do you think of the movements that it will take to turn around when you reach the other side of the room? Do you think about how you need to sit back in the chair you were just sitting in? No, we don't even think about any of this, we just do it naturally. We do not question it, nor do we think it should be done differently. We just do what comes natural to us.

This is what the Father needs from us. All of His laws just need to be done. We need to grow to love the Father with all of our heart, soul, and mind, so that we obey Him without even thinking about it.

Notice how it is our works that allows us to stay in each and every one of these houses. It is our works that allows us to walk across the room.

Now isn't that amazing? How much we are made in their image? We live each and every day in accordance to all these unwritten laws. We need to be in accordance to all of His laws, and they need to be obeyed without even thinking about it.

Conclusion

Now that we have a better understanding of our bibles, we all need to ask ourselves what we really want out of our lives. Do we want to continue living in confusion and blindness, or do we want to work toward a life with our Father? This is not going to be easy for any of us at any time. Even if we think we are living the way our Father wants us to, when we let Him in He is going to show us exactly how far we are away from Him and His ways. We all have blinded ourselves to His ways for so long that we do not see our own faults. We do not see our own iniquity.

Our Father has left us a letter that gives us all the instructions on how we are to become before He can allow us to come into His house. We have been looking at all of His laws as something that they did in ancient times and that they are no longer needed because Jesus died on the cross. But now that our Father is sending some clarity of the matter, we can know that these laws that our Father has put in place are actually a guideline of what we need to do to get to Him.

We hear David praying and saying that God will not hear his prayers if there is any iniquity in his heart in Psalms 66:18, "If I regard iniquity in my heart, the Lord will not hear me." We can better understand why our Father will not hear us if there is iniquity in our hearts. Our Father can't allow iniq- uity around Him. Everything has to work the way the Father has already gotten it to work. He has set His house up so that it runs perfectly at every minute, of every day, of every year. If He allows the tiniest bit of iniquity into His house, it will no longer be functioning perfectly. Remember that iniquity is breaking His laws, or His house rules.

An analogy I like to use is this: You and your spouse have just put a new white carpet in your living room. Let us imagine that I have been your friend for years. You have been having car problems and I come over to work on your car. As I am working on your car, I accidently puncture the oil pan and now have oil on me from head to toe. I am completely drenched in oil when I come to the door and ask to use the restroom. Are you going to let me walk right in and head straight for the restroom? No, you are not. You are going to make me comply with whatever house rules you have for that new carpet in your house. I, in return, am going to comply with those rules if I want to use your restroom. This is exactly what our Father is doing with us. It is our choice, but if we want in His house we will have to comply with every rule that He has.

I want to show you another spot in our bibles that our Father has let us know what will be happening.

> (Matthew 6) 9 After this manner therefore pray ye: Our Father which art in heaven, Hallowed be thy name.10 Thy kingdom come, Thy will be done in earth, as it is in heaven.11 Give us this day our daily bread.12 And forgive us our debts, as we forgive our debtors.13 And lead us not into temptation, but deliver us from evil: For thine is the kingdom, and the power, and the glory, for ever. Amen.

Now when we look at these instructions for praying, we can actually see that we are praying for the very kingdom which is coming.

I hope this message from our Father has blessed you, as it has blessed me. We all know that our Father has not withheld anything from us. We are the ones that just haven't been listening. We all have been blind to our own ways, thinking that His ways are not the best way to live. Now we can start listening to Him and open our hearts to Him. We will be amazed at how He does His work. It is a bit scary, and it sometimes can be a little aggravating because we are so used to doing things the way we have always done them. We have to keep in mind at all times that if he is chastising us, then we know that He loves us. Proverbs 3:12 shows, "For whom the Lord loveth he correcteth; even as a father the son in whom he delighteth." So at no time resist Him. Let Him in and let Him work with you because you know that you are on the right track if he is correcting you. Remember to obey every jot, every tittle, of every letter of every law of our Father's. **NOTHING LESS AND NOTHING MORE!!! AMEN!!! AMEN!!! AMEN!!!**

Works Cited

"God's Calendar and His Holy Days". Church of God, In Truth. Accessed February 10, 2015. http://www.postponements.com

Strong, James, S.T.D., L.L.D., Strong's Hebrew and Greek Dictionaries, e-sword, Ver. 10.4, Dictionary, H7723; G5011; G3958; G2647; G4137; G458; G3672; G3670; G5319; G5318; G1344; G1342; G1349; G2784; G4100; G769; H5493; G5516; H4682; H8672; H6153

www.ingramcontent.com/pod-product-compliance
Lightning Source LLC
LaVergne TN
LVHW021658060526
838200LV00050B/2412